Praise for *Accountability*

"Great leaders understand that talented people thrive in a culture where accountability is a support system for success. What makes this book different is that Greg Bustin connects the intellectual component of accountability to the heart and soul of an organization. If you're looking for new ways to drive accountability and improve individual and organizational performance, read this book."

—Daniel Pink, *New York Times* bestselling
author of *Drive* and *To Sell Is Human*

"Powerful. Greg Bustin demonstrates with example after example that a culture where accountability is embraced and not feared gives savvy leaders a secret weapon."

—Bill Cobb, President and Chief Executive Officer, H&R Block

"Greg Bustin introduces a new approach to accountability that can be a game-changer for leaders. As a CEO and a Vistage Chair, he is an authority on accountability, and his book is packed with new ideas, powerful exercises, and proven practices to improve performance."

—Leon Shapiro, Chief Executive Officer, Vistage International

"Accomplished leaders build and sustain brand loyalty by delivering on their promises. Greg Bustin's insights and examples from leaders of the world's most admired companies on the topic of accountability are a treasure trove of best practices to help you and your team consistently deliver on your brand promise."

—Ashley Sheetz, Chief Marketing Officer, GameStop

"Accountability is too often considered a bad word. Greg gets it right by focusing not on promises made or broken, but on the relationships we build to earn trust with our coworkers. This book will help you do it!"

—Paul Spiegelman, Chief Culture Officer of Stericycle, author of the *New York Times* bestselling *Patients Come Second*

"Companies everywhere are looking for ways to improve performance and their competitive position. Much of the time, this can come from simply doing the basics well. In *Accountability*, Greg Bustin defines and explains accountability in a way that is easily understood and translated into day-to-day actions. Accountability truly is the cultural infrastructure required to drive high levels of corporate performance."

—Paul Eisman, President and Chief Executive Officer, Alon USA

"Accountability is one of the most important mindsets in leadership. Greg Bustin understands it and knows how to translate his understanding into action."

—Mike Rawlings, Mayor, City of Dallas; former President of Pizza Hut

"Greg Bustin really strikes a leadership chord with *Accountability*. His thoughtful insights and real-world examples will equip leaders to achieve new levels of success. I'm a better leader for having read this book."

—Mark W. Schortman, Chairman, Coca-Cola Bottlers Sales & Services, LLC

Accountability

Also by Greg Bustin
Take Charge!
Lead the Way
That's a Great Question

Visit www.bustin.com for tools, exercises,
and to subscribe to receive free content.

Accountability

The Key to Driving a High-Performance Culture

Greg Bustin

New York   Chicago   San Francisco   Athens   London
Madrid   Mexico City   Milan   New Delhi
Singapore   Sydney   Toronto

6 7 8 9 10 11 QVS/QVS 22 21 20 19 18

ISBN   978-0-07-183137-6
MHID   0-07-183137-1

e-ISBN 978-0-07-183138-3
e-MHID 0-07-183138-X

This publication is designed to provide accurate and authoritative information in regard to the subject matter covered. It is sold with the understanding that neither the author nor the publisher is engaged in rendering legal, accounting, securities trading, or other professional services. If legal advice or other expert assistance is required, the services of a competent professional person should be sought.

—*From a Declaration of Principles Jointly Adopted by a Committee of the American Bar Association and a Committee of Publishers and Associations*

Library of Congress Cataloging-in-Publication Data
Bustin, Greg, 1955–
Accountability : the key to driving a high-performance culture / by Greg Bustin.
   pages cm
Includes bibliographical references and index.
ISBN 978-0-07-183137-6 (alk. paper) — ISBN 0-07-183137-1 (alk. paper) 1. Organizational behavior. 2. Responsibility. 3. Corporate culture. 4. Leadership. I. Title.
HD58.7.B876 2014
658.3'14—dc23

                                                                        2013046318

For Janet and Jordan

It is an immutable law in business that words are words, explanations are explanations, promises are promises but only performance is reality.
—Harold S. Geneen

CONTENTS

10 **CHANGE PRACTICES, NOT PRINCIPLES**   225

      APPENDIX   259
      NOTES   277
      INDEX   283

PREFACE

The measure of success is not whether you have a tough problem to deal with, but whether it is the same problem you had last year.
—John Foster Dulles

If accountability is so important, why do so many leaders struggle with it?

Why aren't we getting more of the results we want?

Most important, what can we do to improve?

Working with successful CEOs and leadership teams in a range of industries, I am told repeatedly that holding people accountable is easy to say but often tough to do.

I believe them. The evidence is everywhere. Politicians argue about who will be held accountable for eliminating crushing debt brought on by decades of spending more than saving. Record numbers of CEOs lose their jobs every year because they failed to hold their employees accountable to the performance expectations of boards and shareholders. And obesity continues to be a sure sign that, for many, personal accountability is nonexistent.

ACCOUNTABILITY: EXECUTIVES' BIGGEST THREAT

In a survey of senior executives by the American Management Association, only 3 percent of executives said their company is "very successful" at executing their strategic plans. Most executives (62 percent in this study) believe they are only "moderately successful" at executing their plans.[1]

In other studies examining organizational performance on a global basis, the statistics are even more troubling. A study of global companies by McKinsey & Company analyzed revenue growth and profitability over a 10-year span. The study showed that only nine of the 1,077 companies examined (less than 1 percent) achieved superior levels of performance in both revenue growth and profitability.[2]

Based on hundreds of engagements and data I have collected over a five-year period from more than 5,000 CEOs and their key executives from around the world, lack of accountability is the single greatest threat to achieving consistent levels of high performance. Year after year, accountability tops the charts of issues executives say they want to improve.

The facts are clear: Most organizations are not as effective as they could be at getting things done. And lack of accountability is a big reason why; often it's *the* reason why.

MY EXPERIENCE WITH ACCOUNTABILITY

I wrestled with accountability in the marketing firm I founded.

We worked with Fortune 500 companies (OGE Energy Corp., PepsiCo, Phillips Petroleum Co., TXU), global firms (Burger King, Ericsson, Fujitsu, NEC), large privately held companies (Avery Dennison, Mrs Baird's Bakeries, Haggar Apparel, Trammell Crow Company), and not-for-profits and industry groups (American Mensa, Boy Scouts of America, Fort Worth Zoo). Despite achieving record financial results year over year, I believe we could have accomplished more, had more fun, and suffered less drama if I knew then what I know now about accountability.

Today, I'm a chair for Vistage International, the world's largest CEO membership organization (www.vistage.com). I spend a significant portion of each month serving as a coach, consultant, and confidant to 32 CEOs and 16 key executives who are leading successful organizations in a variety of industries. Once a month, I facilitate a group of CEOs in noncompeting businesses who act as a sounding board for each other. They discuss problems and opportunities, question decisions before they're made, and then hold one another accountable to implement the decisions made in the meeting. In between the monthly meetings, I conduct private coaching sessions with these executives to ensure that accountability becomes reality. I have led more than 200 strategic planning sessions for leadership teams and conducted more than 300 workshops on accountability worldwide.

The leaders I work with—and their peers in groups that I speak to around the world—are committed to improving their businesses and their personal lives. Studies show that executives who are members of Vistage outperform their competitors by a factor of more than two to one. What's more, these organizations are outperforming themselves. They get better year after year.[3]

Yet accountability is often an obstacle in their path to achieving better results.

ACCOUNTABILITY IS A TWO-WAY STREET

Accountability stems from the Latin *accomptare* ("to account"), a prefixed form of *computare* ("to calculate"), which is derived from *putare* ("to reckon"). Although the word itself does not appear in English until its use in thirteenth-century Norman England, account-giving has roots in record-keeping activities related to governance and moneylending systems first developed in Ancient Israel, Babylon, Egypt, Greece, and, later, Rome. In this sense, accountability is concerned with the past—settling up accounts.

For me, accountability has its foundations in the past but the emphasis is on the future: *Doing what you said you would do within the time frame you agreed to do it.*

Accountability is a two-way street. As a leader, you want to know that you can count on people to do what they said they would do. Likewise, your colleagues want to know that they can count on you as the leader to do what you have promised them.

Accountability is a contract, a commitment, a personal promise. And what most people don't appreciate—and I certainly didn't when I was a young manager—is that accountability is less about carrots and sticks and more about relationships forged on purpose and trust.

Accountability is least effective when it's reduced to a single conversation.

Practiced effectively, accountability is a way of thinking and acting all the time and ultimately trumps any financial, intellectual, structural, or technological ability. The reason is simple: Accountability is not based on circumstance but rather on an attitude of accomplishing a task or achieving an objective *despite* circumstance.

Accountability is critical to anyone leading a group of people, because, after all, every business is a people business. Accountability is how people get things done—or don't get things done.

ACKNOWLEDGMENTS

Unbeknownst to me at the time, this book was conceived over a dinner in January 2009 with Greg Wells, then the top executive for North American operations for Vistage International.

I had become a Vistage speaker two years earlier, and, by the time of our dinner, had given nearly 100 workshops around the United States and Canada about the whys and hows of strategic planning as one of the first steps toward achieving high levels of performance. Greg asked me about this experience and I shared my observation that while leaders had a variety of excuses for not developing a plan with their executive team, almost every single leader among the hundreds I'd met said that their single greatest obstacle—whether operating from a written plan or not—was accountability.

Greg found this observation significant and suggested that I develop a workshop on the topic. Within weeks, Vistage invited me to host an international webinar on accountability.

In preparing for this webinar, my wife, Janet, encouraged me to interview senior leaders from high-performing companies. So in 2009, I sat down with David Alexander of Ernst & Young, Casey Shilling of The Container Store, Ray Napolitan of Nucor, and Elizabeth Bryant of Southwest Airlines. In the five-year span between those first interviews and finishing this book, each of these executives has given generously of their time and wisdom.

Stan Hart captured these initial interviews on video and Jim Curtis edited hours of footage into choice snippets for my new accountability workshop. Melanie Angermann developed the forerunner of the accountability assessment found in Chapter 3, and Michaela Mora wrote the software program for the online accountability assessment.

Fellow Vistage speaker and author Brad Hams invited me to speak at his Ownership Thinking conference, and because he thought my workshop would make a good book, referred me to his agent, Cynthia Zigmund, who agreed to represent me. She and Laurie Harper worked with me on my book's proposal, and Cindy has been there for me every step of the way.

Tom Miller at McGraw-Hill said "yes," and, along the way, his guidance throughout the process helped bring the book to life.

James Gardner and Margaret Bonner crunched the data.

Greg Carr and Jeff Travis helped me navigate legal waters. Fellow Vistage Chairs Nina Atwood connected me with Bob Hendrickson at RNDC, and Greg Behm introduced me to Bill Minnock at Marriott.

My fellow Dallas Vistage Chairs who regularly offer me their perspective include Nina Atwood, David Boyett, Ed Burke, Al Caldwell, Jim Eckelberger, Barry Goldberg, Brant Houston, Chas Humphreyson, Mike Richards, and Bob Wightman.

The men and women of my three Vistage groups—CE 3211, CE 3357, and Key 9107—allow me to work with and learn from them, as do my clients. You know who you are.

The book's stars are the leaders of high-performing organizations who spent hours with me and provided access to their teams: David Alexander, Jeff Bowling, Elizabeth Bryant, Tony Cortese, Steve Dalton, Ron Farmer, Ed Grand-Lienard, Rob Grand-Lienard, Ebby Halliday, Bob Hendrickson, Jeff Hook, Dennis Jameson, Tim Keran, Rick Kimbrell, Brian Lacey, Lorraine Luke, Fran McCann, Bill Minnock, Ray Napolitan, Casey Shilling, and Kip Tindell.

And Bill Cobb, Paul Eisman, Dan Pink, Mike Rawlings, Ashley Sheetz, Mark Schortman, Leon Shapiro, and Paul Spiegelman took time from their insanely busy schedules to read the manuscript and allow their names to be associated with this work.

My wife, Janet, and our daughter, Jordan, answered hundreds of questions, read countless drafts, and spoke the truth in love.

Thank you all.

INTRODUCTION

Every big problem was at one time a wee disturbance.
—Scottish proverb

I had never fired a partner. Until today. The time for talking, threatening, pleading, and procrastinating was past.

Today I would fire not just my partner, but my mentor.

It was natural for my partner to believe the conversation we were about to have would never come. After all, he had been a senior executive when we worked in separate divisions of a different firm, and he had thrown his considerable support behind me as I worked my way up the corporate ladder. Fast forward 10 years and my mentor had joined my firm believing this would be his last hurrah, and that we would accomplish great things together. Then his performance lapsed, and, because of our history, I gave him first one pass and then another.

Even after six months of his erratic behavior, it was difficult for me to talk to him about his poor performance. He was a member of Mensa, the IQ society for persons in the top 2 percent of intelligence. Surely he knew he was not measuring up. Why did I have to point it out? When I finally summoned my nerve to discuss his performance, I indicated to him that, without change on his part, something vaguely unpleasant lay ahead. Yet he sensed, and rightly so, that my words were empty threats. When it came to holding people accountable, history showed that my bark was worse than my bite. In my 15 years as a manager, working with nearly 200 colleagues, I had fired just three people.

As my partner's excuses kept piling up, I suspected that everyone in my firm believed one of three things: that I didn't care, that

I was clueless about this performance, or that I was scared to take the necessary action.

I eventually concluded that if I failed to fire my partner, the other 50 people in my firm would be right in thinking that they could not count on me. My failure to hold my partner accountable along the way had cost me time and money, and now it was costing me credibility with my colleagues.

My failure to confront these issues had inadvertently changed our high-performing culture to one where excuses, double standards, and an attitude of "that's close enough" were the norm.

So the day came when I would tell my partner he must leave the firm because we could no longer count on him to keep his commitments. What began as a "wee disturbance" had become a big problem.

I called the meeting with my former mentor, and I delivered the news that, as of today, we were finished as partners.

It didn't need to end this way.

WE ARE OUR WORST ENEMY

As leaders, we get the behavior we tolerate.

When it comes to holding people accountable, we are often our own worst enemy. We accept excuses that sound logical even when we know better. We allow emotions to cloud our decision making. We delay having a conversation with an underperformer because it's easier to avoid a difficult conversation than having one. Instead of practicing accountability, we practice avoidance.

That was certainly the case with me. By the time I asked my partner to leave, I had learned three valuable lessons:

1. **Clear expectations must be established.** I assumed my partner and I both had the same definition of success. We didn't. My failure to set clear expectations meant that evaluating his performance was subjective. When your purpose, expectations, and rewards are crystal clear, your employees will

embrace accountability as a way to become even more successful. The opposite is also true: If you are not clear about everything—vision, values, objectives, strategy, rewards, and, yes, penalties—the likelihood of achieving your vision is slim.

2. **Bad news does not improve with age.** I avoided discussing my partner's performance issues for too long because I assumed his performance would improve. Now I know that as soon as you see a problem, it's best to address it immediately. Failure to speak frankly with the person about his or her performance means nothing will change.

3. **It's not personal.** Yes, you're talking with a person, but leave emotions and opinions behind. Stick to the facts, set a plan to get performance back on track, and communicate specific consequences for underperformance. If underperformers require termination, do it professionally and allow them their dignity.

The day after we separated, my partner called to say he appreciated the straightforward, professional, and respectful manner in which I had handled our final meeting. Even though these comments reflected well on his gracious acceptance of tough news, they reminded me that everyone feels better when accountability issues are addressed.

I figured there's got to be a better way to build and sustain a culture where accountability is part of the DNA of high-performing organizations.

ACCOUNTABILITY TRANSCENDS BORDERS AND INDUSTRIES

To discover that better way, I asked leaders at widely admired companies in completely different industries to share the steps they have taken to create, nurture, and sustain a high-performing culture.

I spoke to senior executives at The Container Store, Ernst & Young, Herman Miller, Marriott, Nucor, Sony, and Southwest Airlines. I also spoke to CEOs of successful small and midsize companies. In each case, accountability at these organizations is more than a conversation. It's an attitude and set of expectations that show up in every aspect of their firm's operations: how they hire, communicate, develop people, and make decisions. The beliefs, insights, and practices are examined in this book and supported by data collected from more than 5,000 executives from around the world.

What I learned is that organizations wrestle with accountability in similar ways, and exceptional organizations succeed by following principles and practices that are similar regardless of:

- Age of the organization
- Geography (where the organization operates)
- Industry
- Size

In this book you will find powerful concepts and practical examples you can apply in your organization, plus exercises, provocative questions, and an assessment to help you create and sustain a high-performance culture in your organization—one that is based on purpose, trust, and accountability.

You will be pleasantly surprised by how straightforward and effective these practices will be in helping you use the keys of accountability to drive a high-performance culture and improve your organization's effectiveness.

ACCOUNTABILITY STARTS WITH PURPOSE

He who has a why to live for can
bear almost any how.
—Friedrich Nietzsche

Any examination of accountability should start at the beginning, that is, in the Garden of Eden.

Accountability issues have been around since Adam and Eve ate the apple in the Garden of Eden. Adam blamed Eve. Eve blamed the snake.

Blaming others rarely works as a long-term solution. The snake's reward for his behavior was a lifetime of crawling. Eve's reward was painful childbirth. Adam's reward was a lifetime of toil.

"Hold on," you're thinking, *"you just said, in the Preface, that 'accountability is less about sticks and carrots and more about purpose and trust,' yet this Old Testament story clearly describes the wielding of a cosmic stick."*

True, but perhaps you missed the words *purpose* and *trust*.

My use of the word *reward* is deliberate. The characters in the Book of Genesis each made a choice to test the limits of the trust they had been given. They were told, "You may freely eat of every tree of the garden, but of the tree of knowledge of good and evil you shall not eat." Despite this covenant, or contract, Adam and Eve made a decision to eat the forbidden fruit, and their individual choices set off a chain reaction of events for which they were rewarded. Some may view the reward as "punishment." Others may see the result as the logical outcome of a poor choice made despite a clear set of expectations.

We have been struggling with accountability ever since.

IT ALL STARTS WITH YOU

Before you can hold others accountable, you first must hold yourself accountable.

And before you can hold yourself accountable, you first must know what matters most to you.

In my work with leaders, I have found that two of the hardest questions any of us will ever answer are "Who am I?" and "What do I want?"

It is pretty easy for most of us to describe to others *what* we do. We have labels that provide verbal shorthand: CEO. CFO. GM. HR exec. PR exec. Engineer. Scientist. Consultant.

This is the *doing* part of our life.

What about the *being* part? After all, we're human beings, not human doings.

Who do you want to *be* that causes you to do what you *do*? Do you do what you do only for the money, the cash, the moolah? Or for something else?

Sure, money's important. But what drives you? What fulfills you? What causes you to make the sacrifices you make?

Ever wonder what drives your colleagues?

DO WHAT YOU LOVE

Shortly after resigning from running the Dallas office of an international firm to start my own business, my father and I were chatting over a beer when he gave me the best advice I've ever gotten.

John Bustin was a highly regarded entertainment critic and had opportunities to move to Houston, Dallas, Chicago, Los Angeles, and New York. Each time an offer materialized, my father would thank the suitors for the opportunity, and each time he would turn them down.

As my father and I talked, our conversation turned to my business. He listened attentively, asked questions as I shared my worries as a new owner already wrestling with internal conflict, then said: "Do what you love doing with people you really care about at a place you really care about."

"What about the money?" I asked. I was making four times more money than my father, so why wasn't I as happy?

His advice should have been a clue to why he declined those other opportunities. "If you take care of those first three things," he told me, "the money will come."

My father's advice didn't sound right for me. It sounded naïve. Had I taken his advice sooner, my struggles with purpose, trust, and accountability might have been avoided. Predictably, however, I ignored it.

PAIN DRIVES CHANGE

Months later on a particularly difficult day, I thought back to my father's words and figured it was time to heed them.

Most of us are motivated to change when the pain of doing the same thing becomes unbearable. For most of us, pain is a more powerful motivator than opportunity.

Even then, changing our behavior is hard. Almost as soon as I began acting on my father's advice things got worse, which is usually how change works. When "worse" happens, the challenge is to press forward and not revert to your old ways. As I began to change, my firm continued to lose clients, colleagues, and lots of money. These results were my reward for not being clear on my purpose, not holding myself and others accountable, and failing to act decisively.

But I persevered, and soon a few lightbulbs turned on in my head. I was able to discern the things I didn't like doing, and so I stopped doing them. I became acutely aware of the things I liked to do, and they happened to be things I was good at doing. One thing led to another, and within a year of making one of the hardest decisions of my life, I found myself in a new, more fulfilling career—not as a consultant, but as a confidante to successful executives who wanted to learn from my successes . . . and my failures.

I would love to tell you that I discovered my purpose, but I believe my purpose actually discovered me. All I knew at the time was that I was not fulfilled by the work I was doing, and it took a lot of pain to make me change. Once I was clear about what really mattered, the initial sacrifices seemed less arduous and my work was more rewarding. And as it turns out, my father was right about the money, too.

Discovering what matters and doing what you love can be achieved without experiencing hardship, and in this chapter I will refer you to two exercises found in the Appendix to help you think clearly about what matters to you.

Changing our own behavior in order to live a more fulfilling life can be difficult. But if we don't change our behavior, how can we expect to change the behavior of others?

When my father died, the church was packed with hundreds of people for his service. At the reception afterward, I heard stories of what a great guy my father had been. What really impressed them, I think, was that my father lived life on his terms, which is why he never moved to bigger cities. He was happy doing what he was doing in Austin. He may not have made tons of money, but like George Bailey in *It's a Wonderful Life*, my father was the richest man in town.

HUMAN BEINGS, NOT HUMAN DOINGS

Most business leaders aspire to their positions because they are skilled and hard-working, and they envision a better life for themselves. More freedom. More personal satisfaction. More of the good life. Their natural abilities and persistence to succeed help make them winners on a certain scale.

As their responsibility grows, some leaders gradually discover they are working harder than ever. They may have some nice grown-up toys and are still in charge, but they often find they spend more time away from their personal pursuits of happiness than they would like. Or that the work they are doing is no longer fulfilling. Unexpected personal challenges may surface. Work-life balance is a joke. The idea of a "better life" is an elusive goal. They have changed from *human beings* into *human doings*. Does this description resonate with you? Could it be you in a few more years?

If so, try answering these two fundamental questions:

What do I want out of life?

Is my business helping me get it or keeping me from it?

These two simple but powerful questions help leaders discover what really matters. Along the way, some leaders realize they are so busy doing what they are doing that they might be enjoying less of who they are being.

YOU ARE THE CAPTAIN OF YOUR SOUL

In England in 1875, William Ernest Henley published a four-stanza untitled poem he wrote in response to the amputation of his leg just below his knee. The title "Invictus," which is Latin for "unconquered," was added by editor Arthur Quiller-Couch when the poem was included in *The Oxford Book of English Verses*.

The poem's final two lines are "I am the master of my fate: I am the captain of my soul."

Ray Napolitan is an executive vice president of Nucor and president of Nucor's Vulcraft/Verco Group, the foundation upon which Nucor was built. Vulcraft/Verco is the largest producer of steel joists and steel deck in the United States and a division of Nucor, the largest producer of steel in North America, with a capacity of 27 million tons, and one of the world's largest recyclers. Nucor has earned *Fortune* magazine's "Most Admired Companies" distinction for nearly a decade and has been named one of the "100 Best Corporate Citizens" by *Business Ethics* magazine.

Ray's father, a carpenter and floor layer, provided a strong influence, and Ray's early fascination with bridges and structures led to a degree in structural engineering. Ray took finance and accounting classes as his undergraduate engineering electives, and then attended school at night to earn his master's degree in structural engineering as well as an MBA. His hunger to learn and desire to contribute grew, so he volunteered for assignments outside his comfort level. "These turned out to be some of my best growth opportunities," he told me.

"I've always believed that no one else is responsible for me other than me," he continues. "It's up to me to be proactive, whether it's learning new skills, contributing to new ideas, or helping others achieve things they never thought possible or probable in both their work and home lives. Of course, this is a two-way street. We cannot change others. We can only help others change themselves."

When Napolitan talks with people who are interested in advancing their careers, he asks, "What have you done to prepare for this opportunity?"

"In many cases," he says, "the person says something like, 'If I get this position I will change.' In my opinion, that's too little, too late."

In my work with executives, it's not unusual for leaders to find themselves in a position where their business life and personal life are not aligned.

Because you are the captain of your soul, only you can command it. I have used an exercise called "Heaven & Hell" for years to help leaders gain insight into one of the thorniest problems they will ever untangle: figuring out who they are.

Coming to grips with this question is the natural first step in the accountability process. You must know who you are, what you want and what you don't want before you and your organization can codify and live out the core values you will use as guidelines for holding everyone in your enterprise accountable.

Your responses to the "Heaven & Hell" exercise in the Appendix will serve as the foundation for everything else that follows in this book. We will revisit this exercise in Chapter 4 when we codify your organization's character.

HOW CLEAR IS YOUR PICTURE?

In his 1959 groundbreaking book *Man's Search for Meaning,* Holocaust survivor Viktor Frankl says that, "It is a peculiarity of man that he can only live by looking to the future . . . and this is his salvation in the most difficult moments of his existence."[1]

Frankl echoes Nietzsche's idea of "why" and "how" in describing his own methodology for surviving the daily inhuman suffering of Auschwitz. "I forced my thoughts to turn to another subject,"

Frankl says. "Suddenly, I saw myself standing on the platform of a well-lit, warm and pleasant lecture room. I was giving a lecture on the psychology of the concentration camp!"[2] Getting through the grind of today requires a clear picture in our minds of our desired future state.

Athletes excel at this exercise.

Jerry Rice is considered the greatest wide receiver in NFL history, leading in virtually every significant receiving statistic. When Rice was inducted into the Pro Football Hall of Fame, he reflected on his career and said, "There was no way I was going to be denied. I kept working hard, and my dream came true. I tell kids, 'Do not let obstacles stand in your way. If you want to achieve something, go for it.' I'm living proof."[3]

Emmitt Smith holds the record as pro football's all-time leading rusher. Smith's Cowboys played against Rice and the 49ers—many times in championship games. When Smith was inducted into the Pro Football Hall of Fame, the story was told how, 20 years earlier, Smith walked into the office of Cowboys owner Jerry Jones and handed him a piece of paper listing his goals: Win the Super Bowl more than once; lead the league in rushing; lead the league in touchdowns; become the NFL's all-time leading rusher; play for 13 seasons like his idol Walter Payton. "At the age of 21," said Smith, "I knew what I needed to do to make my mark on history."[4]

Not every kid's dream of playing professional sports comes true, but for high-performing executives, the desire to compete and win while doing something they love burns brightly.

Steve Dalton is managing director of Sony's UK manufacturing operation, serves on Sony's UK Ltd. board of directors, and holds the prestigious Order of the British Empire (OBE) awarded by Queen Elizabeth for his service to Wales and the industry.

Dalton wanted to become a professional soccer player and played organized sports, honing his competitive edge and experiencing the power of a team driving toward a common goal. For his tenth Christmas he had received an electronics set. "I was thrilled when I managed to get a small lightbulb to illuminate," he told me. So when the dream of playing soccer professionally faded, becoming an electronics engineer was Dalton's new dream.

Dalton joined Sony in 1983 as an engineer testing TVs and within two years he was managing production engineering, new model production, and new product introduction. Over the next seven years, Dalton was placed in roles with more responsibility in virtually every part of Sony's UK manufacturing operation. Dalton supported the start-up of a new TV manufacturing facility in Wales, and then led the introduction of broadcast and professional camera manufacturing for worldwide distribution.

"I've always had the sense from very early days," he says, "that whatever I did I wanted to enjoy coming to work with a willingness to learn and improve. It may seem strange but I honestly never had a personal dream or mission that I would be heading the organization and leading so many people—which is different from what I tell people they should do."

When asked to lead Sony's UK manufacturing operation in 2006, Dalton accepted, admitting he was "nervous that my responsibility suddenly expanded to a large number of people who were relying on me." It was, he says, "just another challenge in life."

We will see in Chapter 10 that Dalton was up to the challenge. Looking back, he says he was "really fulfilled seeing a team effort produce successes, particularly when some didn't think success was possible."

Dalton coached his colleagues to victory.

What legacy are you leaving?

WHAT DO YOU WANT?

A second exercise that I developed, "The 7 Fs," reminds busy leaders that a business goal is simply one of several goals comprising a fulfilling life (see Appendix, page 261).

The exercise prompts you to consider what these seven significant life categories will look like in a given time period and is another early step in holding yourself accountable.

Executives tell me that thinking through what is significant in their life, articulating those thoughts as a set of measurable goals, and then writing them down is a powerful process that drives personal accountability. Story after story from executives tell examples of them writing down goals, tucking them away, and not looking at them for several months, only to pull out their list later to see that they had accomplished many of their stated objectives. Written goals are even more powerful when you look at them every day.

Once you complete your list, compare your personal goals with the goals you established for your career. How do these two sets of goals complement each other? Where are they out of alignment?

Will your career—on its current trajectory—help you achieve your personal goals? If so, congratulations. Stay the course. If not, ask yourself what changes must occur in order to help you achieve whatever it is that you want to have, do, or be.

What part of your soul is not satisfied?

What must you do to move from success to significance?

FIND YOUR SWEET SPOT

To achieve extraordinary results, do what you love with people you care about in a place you care about.

Your sweet spot is where your personal core values (what you're *willing* to do) intersect with your experience (what you *can* do) and your interests (what you *want* to do).

Finding your sweet spot is one of the most gratifying accomplishments you can experience. It's also a key to driving accountability.

The concept is worth repeating: Before you can hold others accountable, you first must hold yourself accountable.

And before you can hold yourself accountable, you first must know what matters most to you.

We all have dreams. Some of us dream bigger and are more focused about turning those dreams into reality.

When you were a little kid, what did you want to be when you grew up?

There is still time.

LEARNING FROM
WINNERS

A single conversation with a wise man is
better than ten years of study.
—Chinese proverb

Every leader is tasked with getting from Point A to Point B.

The leaders I work with tell me it's their most significant objective and the hardest to achieve, and accountability is the single greatest threat to reaching Point B.

In the previous chapter, you were prompted to consider your personal Point B.

In this chapter, we consider Point B from the perspective of the enterprise you are leading.

Whether you are in charge of a corporation, a partnership, a business unit, a department, a single project, or a not-for-profit organization, you must marshal the resources of your team to move from Point A (your current situation) to Point B (your objective).

Accountability is an obstacle in your path. More times than not, it's *the* obstacle in your path.

My interviews with senior leaders at high-performing companies and my 30 years of working with leadership teams in dozens of industries indicate that all organizations wrestle with accountability in much the same way. Data I have collected from executives worldwide over a five-year period support my observations.

What separates high-performing organizations from average ones? What factors propel some firms to winning heights?

As discussed in the previous chapter, accountability starts with knowing who you are, what you want, and what you don't want.

In this chapter, we begin our examination of how leaders at high-performing companies transfer their personal accountability to their entire organization to achieve exceptional results.

A CULTURE,
NOT A TECHNIQUE

Even though you will not find a silver bullet to achieve high levels of accountability, high-performing organizations have in common a way of doing things that distinguishes their culture.

We will examine how high-performing organizations create and sustain a culture of purpose, accountability, and fulfillment, and equip you with a set of principles and practices to help you drive accountability in your organization.

If you are expecting tips and techniques for having a tough conversation about accountability, you will miss the bigger point. Yes, we examine a model for a conversation with an underperformer in Chapter 9, but long before that conversation occurs dozens of other practices must be in place if you expect to drive accountability throughout your organization to create and sustain a high-performance culture.

You will meet leaders at these high-performing companies who, in describing their approach to accountability and performance, use phrases such as "It's not rocket science," "It's really pretty simple," and "You've heard this before." The key to accountability is bringing together these principles and then acting on them with consistency and urgency.

Let's look first at why accountability continues to be a problem for so many leaders.

ACCOUNTABILITY'S CHOKEPOINT

All organizations wrestle with accountability in much the same way. Although the scope and complexity may differ from organization to organization, the problems leaders encounter on their journey from Point A to Point B are similar.

Every organization deploys three fundamental resources: time, people, and money. (You may be tempted to include equipment, inventory, or real estate holdings, but these inanimate items are purchased. And while you also may be tempted to argue that people are purchased because you pay them a salary, you don't own them and they are free to leave anytime they wish.)

Think of your organization as a funnel into which time, talent (people), and treasure (money) are poured.

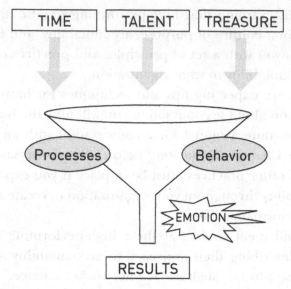

Figure 2.1 Performance Funnel

Emerging from the funnel's spout is the result of your investment in those three commodities. The result may be satisfactory or unsatisfactory. As time, talent, and treasure move through your funnel toward a result, their original state is altered as they come into contact with one another. This contact is shaped by two key contributing factors: the processes inside your organization (your belief systems, policies, operating procedures, and technical support systems that form the infrastructure of your organization), and the behavior of people comprising teams, departments, remote locations, business units, and outside suppliers (it's the rare individual who works in solitary confinement). The sum of this behavior is your organization's culture.

For many leaders and their organizations, the narrowest point of the funnel is a chokepoint because it's a place where emotions can enter into decision making and influence the results. Emotions can prevent successful leaders from holding themselves, their peers, and those who report to them accountable. And when that happens, the results can be less than satisfactory.

Part of what makes accountability difficult is that when you are working with smart people and things don't get done well or on time, you are often handed excuses. Here's what lack of accountability sounds like:

Time

I rush from one fire to the next, so there's no time to work on my project.

Our deadlines are unrealistic.

The deadline was unclear.

I spend my time doing my boss's work.

I spend my time doing work my staff should be doing.

I have to spend my time on tactical—not strategic—work.

We're always in a hurry, but when we hurry we make mistakes and have to do the work again.

There's no sense of urgency around here.

I ran out of time.

His performance will improve with time.

Talent

We don't have the right people.

We don't have enough people.

We don't have enough of the right people.

The people on our team can't think for themselves.

He let me down.

These people don't report to me, so I have no control on work product.

I didn't know I was allowed to make that decision.

I didn't understand the assignment.

It wasn't my job.

The changes we made are preventing me from getting things done.

My team won't like me if I confront their performance issues.

The people here are not team players.

That person is a family member and the rules don't apply to her.

We can't seem to keep our best people so we are not very effective.

Treasure

We underprice projects (or products) so we can't staff properly
for the work (or products) we have agreed to deliver.

We can't agree on priorities so our budgets are spread too thin.

Our customers beat us up on price so we can't possibly charge
more.

We are constantly being asked to do more with less, including
more work for the same salary.

Money is tight so we can't hire the people we need.

It is a vicious circle, and the excuses are infinite. Talk is cheap
so we often buy it.

When we do, accountability suffers. And even though accountability is a significant component of any leader's success, it is not
even your biggest problem. Your biggest problem is reaching
Point B.

THE LEADER'S BIGGEST PROBLEM

If you have visited Provence, you may have taken the opportunity to view one of the most picturesque sites in all of France:
the Gorges du Verdon, the "Grand Canyon of France," a 13-mile
(21-kilometer) scenic stretch of rock and water considered to be
one of the world's natural masterpieces.

On our trip, my wife, Janet, noted two routes we could take
to reach our next destination—one route took us *around* the canyon, the other *across*. Janet and our daughter, Jordan, were excited
about what lay ahead. I am petrified by heights and asked if our
route would be taking us across the abyss. Knowing my fear, Janet
replied that she wasn't sure which route would get us to our destination, which I immediately should have taken as code for "Yes,
we're going to cross the canyon!" and handed her the car keys.
Instead, I remained at the wheel while Janet consulted the map
and provided driving directions.

Rounding a turn, there it was: Europe's greatest canyon. We have visited the Grand Canyon in Arizona, but this view literally took my breath away—partly because of its awesome beauty, and partly because I now knew for certain we were about to drive across Europe's deepest canyon to reach our destination.

To give you some idea of what we were facing, the gorges drop 2,200 feet (670 meters) to the Verdon River at their deepest points, and at their widest points, the walls of the canyon are 4,700 feet (1,433 meters) apart. This height is roughly equivalent to the Empire State Building and Chrysler Building stacked one on top of the other.

Guidebooks call the route along the canyon *corniche sublime* (literally, "heavenly ledge"), but I call it *corniche de la terreur* ("ledge of terror"). The bridge we were to cross, the Pont d'Artuby, spans a place in the canyon where the walls are only 350 feet (197 meters) apart, but to me it looked like a mile. The bridge itself is an engineering marvel constructed of reinforced concrete and was completed in 1940. I like bridges close to the ground and supported by pillars to assure me they won't collapse as I cross, but this bridge consists of a single arch. To my nonengineering mind, the bridge seemed to have little visible support as it rose 410 feet (125 meters) above the canyon floor, the equivalent of a 27-story building.[1] Not exactly a high-rise, but plenty tall for a guy scared of heights. I was paralyzed with fear.

So at a pullout near the bridge, Janet took the wheel, Jordan hopped in the passenger side, and I cowered in the backseat. As we were about to cross the abyss, Jordan said, "Close your eyes, Daddy, and don't worry—it will all be over in 12 seconds."

"I know," I replied, "that's what I'm worried about."

CROSSING THE ABYSS

It is obvious that we made it across the abyss, over the bridge, and onto our next destination, but my experience illustrates the biggest problem every leader faces: Starting at Point A and then crossing the abyss to reach Point B. As a leader, your vision is an exciting journey filled with wonderful experiences, a setback or two along the way, some exhilarating moments, but overall a great adventure capped by the emotional and financial rewards that come with fulfilling a dream. To others, your vision is downright scary.

To cross the abyss, your first challenge is to help those on your team see that it is both necessary and possible to get to the other side. They not only need to share your vision, they need to *believe* it. Doing so can be a challenge, though the idea of a better future is usually greeted with approval. In my case, I wanted to reach our next destination, but the journey across the bridge was terrifying.

Many people will share your enthusiasm for the journey ahead and can't wait to get going. Just as players of Texas Hold 'em respond to a great poker hand by betting all their chips, going "all in," so, too, do the leaders on a winning team respond to a clear vision they believe in with their full commitment. Unfortunately, those who share your enthusiasm are usually outnumbered by those who do not.

It is likely that some on your team listening to you describe Point B are thinking, "*Wow, that's really going to take some work to get from Point A to Point B. I'm not sure if we can do it.*" They will be taking a wait-and-see approach to determine your conviction. Others may think, "*I can do this, but I'm not sure I trust everyone on this team to help us achieve this vision.*" And just as I asked at Pont d'Artuby, some may wonder, "*Why do we need to go this way?*" Finally, others may resent this change and ask, "*Why do we need to go at all? I'm comfortable where I am.*" Those in this group may even try to undermine efforts to move to Point B.

You will need everyone's help achieving the organization's vision, not just a select few. So your second job as the leader is to bring everyone along so that they, too, believe in the vision and commit to achieving it. People are more likely to support a plan they helped develop, so guide your team through the development of a plan that shows how you will cross the abyss and get from Point A to Point B. Your plan should include objectives, strategies, budgets, responsibilities, and schedules. Be honest about the problems you foresee and make specific plans ahead of time for how those obstacles will be addressed. Sugarcoating difficulties does not build trust.

Your plan is your road map. It's also your contract with each other.

Without a plan, expectations are not clear. And without clear expectations, accountability is not possible.

PLANNING IS TRUST-BUILDING

When I lead strategic planning sessions with leadership teams, philosophical differences frequently expose themselves. These differences can include lack of alignment on these significant issues:

- Company direction
- Financial objectives
- Organizational structure
- Talent development
- Growth strategies
- Rewards and penalties

Differences may show up in other ways. Some people may not trust the CEO to carry out tough decisions, including addressing underperformance. Some may question whether the CEO will follow through with promised rewards (i.e., money, increased responsibility, approval to hire a star, etc.) commensurate with the emotional investment, hard work, sacrifice, and discipline required to accomplish stated objectives. Others may not trust peers to behave in a manner consistent with the organization's values. Still others may doubt the ability of a peer to perform at the higher level now required by the firm's trajectory.

These issues are all rooted in trust, which is why I believe the process of planning for the future is less about list-building and budget-building and more about trust-building. To achieve the objectives you and your team say you want, you must trust one another's character and competency.

Alignment does not mean absence of conflict. Just the opposite. Authentic alignment is achieved only when conflict is encouraged, options for resolving the conflict are weighed, and a solution is reached that all leaders support. Debate is healthy. Argument is not.

For healthy conflict to occur, leaders must trust each other. Think about it: You don't talk openly and candidly about problems, fears, and controversy with people you don't trust and care about.

If you are not talking about real issues, your planning process is going to be a waste of time and you might as well give up on the idea of holding people accountable.

Trust and purpose are the cornerstones on which you will build your team, your organization, and a future of high performance.

ACCOUNTABILITY'S OTHER SIDE

Ron Farmer founded US Signs in 1980 and led his company through nine tough months the company's first year as well as through three recessions before selling his company in 2011 for full value. Growing more than 1,000 percent in the first 5 years landed US Signs on the Inc. 500 list at #196. Farmer started a second company, US LED, in 2001, and he and his team achieved average annual growth rate of 73 percent over the first 10 years. In 2012, he was an Ernst & Young Entrepreneur of the Year finalist.

Like many of the leaders I interviewed, Farmer believes accountability has two sides: a positive side and a negative side.

Accountability gets a bad rap. Just saying the word conjures all sorts of negative images: micromanagement; an emotional, mean-spirited conversation; punishment. It can be all of those things, but it doesn't have to be any of them.

"People do their best work," Farmer told me, "when they know they're going to be given credit for their contribution. So there has to be a certain amount of autonomy in people's work so they can contribute without reservation. There's accountability at work in this type of approach, but I view accountability not from the side that says, 'This is what happens if you don't do something,' but rather, 'See what's possible if you do your best.' It's the other side of the same coin."

To Farmer, accountability with autonomy can be exciting to people.

"If people don't have a sense of accountability—to themselves and to each other—they don't warrant having autonomy," he says. "And when creative, self-referenced people do have autonomy, they have the incentive, the energy, and the enthusiasm to do their best. They're proud of their accomplishments and love being given credit for their contributions.

"Teamwork is great," says Farmer, "but even within the team you need to have enough of an understanding of human beings' need for individual contribution and recognition because people—most people, the kind of people we hire—crave challenging work so they can develop a mastery of something that counts . . . something they can point to with colleagues, spouses, and friends. These people have a sense of ownership, a sense of pride. And so on the one hand, you're holding them accountable; on the other hand, you're rewarding them with the freedom to be their best. So the accountability structure is really a recognition structure. I would rather talk to my employees about a recognition program than about an accountability structure with negative implications."

It is the leader's job to make accountability a support structure, not a blame structure.

GETTING COMFORTABLE WITH CHANGE

If you don't plan to change, don't bother to plan.

Planning, by definition, means doing more of what's working and less of what isn't.

So the planning process should be expected to identify people, processes, and programs that are delivering high levels of performance, as well as those that no longer serve the enterprise or are inefficient.

Tackle change head-on and expose difficult issues that must be addressed if the company expects to improve its financial and operational performance. Leaders in these sessions talk openly, perhaps hesitantly at first, but then more confidently as the session continues, about fixing problems, replicating successes, and carving up sacred cows.

At the conclusion of these debates, a choice must be made. Those who agree with the decision are prepared to be held accountable by colleagues and likewise are prepared to hold colleagues accountable for implementing the plan.

Southwest Airlines has built a reputation as a great place to work and a great airline for travelers because of its emphasis on doing things differently, caring about people, and having fun. But the company is completely serious when it comes to saying what you mean and meaning what you say.

"We care enough about each other to tell the truth," says Elizabeth Bryant of Southwest Airlines, who, as vice president of the company's training initiatives, is responsible for nurturing the culture among Southwest's nearly 46,000 employees. "So if we really care about each other," she told me, "we must have the courage to be honest with each other. Because if we only focus on having a conversation when things are going well, then we're not sharing the whole picture."

When differences are not resolved, any person who disagrees with the situation—whether the disagreement is philosophical, financial, strategic, or cultural—is out of alignment with the top decision makers' view of the situation. It is difficult to be committed to something you don't believe in.

"As a rule, people don't leave Herman Miller because of poor skills as much as they do because of poor behavior," says Tony Cortese, who, as the organization's senior vice president of human resources, guides employee-related strategies for the $1.6 billion company whose furniture is sold in 100 countries.

"Behavior and cultural issues probably account for the majority of terminations at Herman Miller," Cortese told me. "It's not often that it's a skill- or competency-based issue. I've seen some very competent people who just didn't navigate our culture well."

The company's structure is characterized by a certain amount of ambiguity because of its ad hoc teams and a "distributed leadership model," and Herman Miller recognizes that some people are more comfortable in highly defined structures and can't handle ambiguity. "When you get into those situations," says Cortese, "the people involved are professional and they will start to feel, 'Maybe this isn't the right fit.' We may have that same impression, and that will begin to lead to a mutual understanding and parting of our ways."

ALL IN OR PLAYING ALONG?

In good times with plenty of good jobs available, a worker—whether it's a top executive or a member of the rank-and-file—will simply say, *"I don't agree with the decisions that have been made and I've found another company that suits me better. I'm outta here!"*

When people leave because they no longer agree with where things are going or how things are done, their departure should be viewed as a happy event for all.

Trouble occurs when disillusioned and unproductive employees don't leave.

When the market is down, plenty of unhappy, disengaged workers go through the motions in their jobs. These people are technically okay at what they do but are not as committed to an organization's mission and their colleagues' success as they are to their own preservation. These employees have been waiting for the market to improve so they can move on. Or, worse, they have quit their job but are still collecting a paycheck while they work against your improvement initiatives.

For whatever reason, these employees no longer agree with nor are they passionate about the mission, vision, values, or strategy of their current organization. They are playing along.

No one wants a disgruntled person on their team. People who are unhappy *should* go for their sake as well as for everyone else's.

Let's face it. If your biggest problem is getting from Point A to Point B, you want people on your team you can count on. Performing at high levels has never been tougher. You need full commitment, not halfhearted effort.

As you and your team start to execute your plan, plenty of external forces will be standing in your way. If you imagine your destination as a place on the opposite side of a deep abyss, why in the world would you want someone in your organization who has little interest in helping you make it across safely?

Jeff Bowling is the CEO of The Delta Companies. Bowling started in a 10×10-foot office in 1997 with a passion for finding a better way to provide healthcare staffing and treating employees better in the process. He now has a team of more than 200 engaged colleagues who help make The Delta Companies an industry top performer and one of the best places to work in Texas.

The Delta Companies operated under a parent company owned by an angel investor, and after six years the investor was ready to close the company and split the assets. Bowling proposed buying the company, and the investor—hardly an angel—gave Bowling just two weeks to secure funding.

Bowling asked friends and family to commit the money, including 10 of his colleagues who borrowed against their credit cards, took out loans, and agreed to work without pay. Looking back, Bowling says the commitment to one another was so high, "we never considered it a risk."

But it was a sobering moment. "In that nanosecond," Bowling told me, "I understood the new level of responsibility I was assuming because it wasn't only me taking the risk. Others were also at risk. They were providing me a level of trust and they believed. I couldn't let them down. It got real in a hurry."

You and those on your team must be able to "get real" and count on one another. It is in such situations where the importance of accountability—or lack of it—brings your own workplace culture into sharp focus.

CULTURE TRUMPS STRATEGY

How your plan is executed reveals your organization's culture.

"Culture eats strategy for breakfast," said management guru Peter Drucker. Your culture—the sum of your behaviors—is what drives the satisfactory or unsatisfactory results you are getting.

For The Container Store, getting culture right was important from the beginning. "When The Container Store first opened its doors, it had the same culture then as we do now. Actually, the culture is stronger now," said Casey Shilling, vice president of public relations and marketing communications who works directly with Tindell and who joined the company in 1997. With an investment of $35,000, Tindell (chairman and CEO), Boone (chairman emeritus), and architect John Mullen originated a new retailing concept: a store devoted exclusively to storage and organization. The first store opened on July 1, 1978, in a 1,600-square-foot retail space in Dallas and was filled with products such as commercial parts bins, mailboxes, popcorn tins, burger baskets, milk crates, and wire leaf burners that consumers couldn't find in any other retail environment. When used in a home or office, the solutions saved customers space and, ultimately, time.

Many doubted the concept would work, but the home-organization pioneer has enjoyed growth at an average rate of 20 percent annually every year of its operation. Today it operates 61 stores in 20 states with a workforce of more than 6,000. In 1999, The Container Store bought elfa International, a Swedish company that was a significant supplier of shelving and storage units. In 2013, the company went public. Its commitment to culture has earned The Container Store a spot on *Fortune* magazine's 100 Best Places to Work list every year since 1999.

"We do invest a lot in our people," Shilling told me. "Our SG&A costs are in the mid-40% of sales. But our employee-first culture—having conversations, thoughtful performance reviews, caring about people, making good hiring decisions, having fun—doesn't cost a lot of money. So I would say to organizations of all types, ages, and sizes that you *can* create a culture where account-ability matters. You have to take the time to put things down on paper about what your goals are and what you want your culture to look like, and then make sure you execute with excellence. And if you are the CEO, have a face. Have presence as a conscious leader. Make sure that people know who you are and what you stand for and your employees will feel ownership. They will feel part of something exciting, and they will do good work for you."

A similar commitment to finding a better way took shape one evening in 1966 when Rollin King sat with his lawyer Herb Kelleher in San Antonio's St. Anthony Club to sketch out on a napkin a plan that would change air travel forever. Following five years of lawsuits by competitors that sought to keep Southwest Airlines grounded, the scrappy airline thwarted its competition by flying three Boe-ing 737s between Dallas, Houston, and San Antonio. Today, while every other major airline has declared bankruptcy over the past 30 years, Southwest Airlines has become the largest domestic car-rier with the highest customer satisfaction rating and best on-time performance—all while turning a profit. It's a $17 billion success story, and culture has played a big part in that success.

"Southwest Airlines has had a unique culture from the very beginning," Elizabeth Bryant told me.

For Southwest, culture is not considered a training program, a technique, or strategy du jour, and that surprises even seasoned executives who join the airline. "I've heard a senior leader at Southwest Airlines say after joining us that she had to go through corporate detox," says Bryant, because "to truly experience our culture feels a little bit different. Culture isn't something that we have to make our employees do, culture is who we are. And whatever role employees are in, they take great pride in the fact that we're connecting people to the important moments in their lives through friendly, reliable, and low-cost air travel."

Bryant says this culture "is fully embedded into the DNA of Southwest Airlines." Employees are involved in decision making. "When you have that type of trusting environment where we can have open dialogue that leads to a decision, by having the ability to weigh in on that decision, as an employee I am more committed to that decision and therefore I'm going to hold people accountable to it. So it's less about a leader holding an employee accountable and more about as employees of Southwest Airlines we hold one another accountable."

The Southwest Airlines culture reflects its underdog beginnings. "Think small and act small, and we'll get bigger," preached founder Kelleher. "Think big and act big, and we'll get smaller." Other airlines scoffed at that thinking.

They shouldn't have. Today, one out of every four Americans has flown Southwest, and now the company is setting its sights on service beyond the 48 contiguous states.[2]

"Our approach is so simple," says Southwest's Elizabeth Bryant, "it's hard for people to understand. There are many smart organizations with people who are able to make smart decisions, but without a culture of trust and honesty and accountability then those great ideas are going to stay on the table and not get executed."

Southwest trusts its employees to make good decisions based on the company's vision—"to become the world's most loved, most flown, most profitable airline"—and values. "We have a laser focus on our values," Bryant says, "and that means holding people accountable to the company's values and mission and vision. Our employees know this. People typically don't come to work at Southwest Airlines just because it's an available job. When they understand who we are, they connect with the cause of Southwest and they strive to achieve this vision every day."

Over the years, Southwest heard critics say that the company's great culture was easy to achieve because the airline was so small. *Wait until they grow. They'll focus on just being smart and not all of that people stuff.* Yet Southwest has stayed true to its roots, and doing so has proven successful.

"We have always understood and valued that it's the people that make the difference for an organization," says Bryant, "and that has been the differentiator between us and other companies."

Big, small, or in between, success is not predicated on size.

"A lot of what we do here you wouldn't expect to find in a large corporation," says Tony Cortese of Herman Miller. Look on any list—Most Admired, Best Places to Work, Most Innovative—and you'll find this pioneering company.

"What works so well for us here at Herman Miller," Cortese told me, "is the stuff that small companies would, could, and should do: look for talented people who are energized about what you're doing, give them latitude to express themselves and explore opportunities, be very open in your communication, establish high expectations and put systems in place to measure those expectations, talk to them frequently about performance, and then get out of the way and give them the opportunity to excel."

That sounds like common sense, and yet those principles are not common practice in most organizations.

COMMONSENSE APPROACH

Ray Napolitan has followed a similar commonsense approach in leading three different organizations to success for Nucor: a start-up, an acquisition, and an established business.

Napolitan earned his start-up spurs when he spearheaded Nucor's expansion into Texas with the Nucor Building Systems Division he helped start from scratch in Terrell, Texas. After eight years in Texas, Napolitan was next asked to integrate Nucor's 2007 acquisition of American Buildings Co. into the Nucor culture. For three years, he led a team of 1,000 employees in seven locations where he helped establish the company's safety-training culture, its pay-for-performance incentive system, and business and leadership training at all levels within the company. In 2010 he was promoted to president of the Vulcraft/Verco Group, and subsequently to his current position.

Napolitan has been part of creating cultures from the ground up and changing existing ones. Was it easier or more difficult to change a culture or create one?

"With a start-up and with an acquisition," he told me, "we had to build a culture of accountability. We had to build trust. And we had to create vision and alignment. With a start-up, people didn't know any differently so there were no ill feelings. We had to teach not only culture but product and technical training. We started with great folks, but there was more training involved.

"With the acquisition, we had great people but there was a big mistrust of management—and I'm using the word *management* and not *leadership* on purpose. So building trust was key."

With the acquisition, Napolitan started with two advantages. First, despite the mistrust of management, he inherited a great team who, for the most part, fit the Nucor culture but who had never been exposed to the Nucor thought processes. Second, these people knew the metal-building industry. "There was a strategic fit to our acquisition," says Napolitan, "and, just as important, there was cultural fit that matched our core values."

Napolitan is playing change agent within the Vulcraft/Verco Group as well. The organization he's leading was the first Nucor division that goes back to the 1940s, and originally was called the Nuclear Corporation of America.

"For many years in the Vulcraft division," says Napolitan, "we really didn't need to be very strategic. If the order book got too heavy, we turned the margin dial up. If we needed some work, we turned the margin dial down. We were—and still are—the most operationally effective company in the industry, and we had such a cost advantage over our competition."

The Great Recession changed that approach.

"That recession," says Napolitan, "prompted us to develop a vision that could answer the question, 'What are we really doing here?' We realized we had to change our culture from one that was used to 'catching' to a culture of 'pitching.' Fortunately, we have many great teammates to help us think differently and execute our strategies." Napolitan says that start-ups, acquisitions, and established businesses each have their challenges. "I would not say that one is easier or more difficult than the other," he says, "and each has different challenges. In each case, the key to building and maintaining a culture of accountability is great people."

HIGH-PERFORMANCE CHARACTERISTICS

Whether you are starting a company, blending two organizations as part of a merger or acquisition, joining an existing company in a leadership position, or getting ready to amp up your organization's performance, you'll discover similarities that are transferrable to your organization:

1. Beliefs that form the bedrock of trust
2. A mindset and discipline to achieve excellence
3. A commonsense approach to getting things done

It became clear from my interviews with the leaders you will meet in this book that high-performing organizations share seven distinct characteristics that I call the Seven Pillars of Accountability.

- **Character.** An organization's character is shaped by its values, and these values are clearly defined and communicated. The organization does what is right for its customers, employees, suppliers, and investors, even when it's difficult to do so.

- **Unity.** Every employee understands and supports the organization's mission, vision, values, and strategy, and knows his or her role in helping to achieve them.
- **Learning.** The organization is committed to continuous learning and invests in ongoing training and development.
- **Tracking.** The organization has reliable, established systems to measure the things that are most important.
- **Urgency.** The organization makes decisions and acts on them with a sense of purpose, commitment, and immediacy.
- **Reputation.** The organization rewards achievement and addresses underperformance, earning the organization and its leaders a reputation, both internally and externally, as a place where behavior matches values.
- **Evolving.** The organization continuously adapts and changes the organization's practices to grow its marketplace leadership position.

You probably noticed an acronym: C.U.L.T.U.R.E. It's deliberate and will help you remember the seven pillars.

This acronym also will help you remember that your culture is a significant predictor of your future performance.

As I thought about the challenge of getting from Point A to Point B, I recalled my experience in Provence and imagined a bridge spanning an abyss supported not by a single arch like the one at Pont d'Artuby but instead by seven pillars, each

The Seven Pillars of Accountability

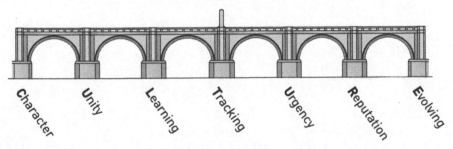

Character Unity Learning Tracking Urgency Reputation Evolving

representing one of the seven characteristics that are essential in high-performing cultures:

Crossing the abyss—moving your organization from Point A to Point B—requires the commitment of you and your team.

Many of your teammates are ready for the journey. Others are not: They may be unsure of the destination, they may believe there's a better way to make the journey, or they may be scared of where you're asking them to go.

The leaders you will meet and the lessons you will learn will help you create a culture where accountability drives performance and helps you cross the abyss and reach your destination.

3

THE SEVEN PILLARS
OF ACCOUNTABILITY

Corporation: An ingenious device
for obtaining individual profit without
individual responsibility.
—Ambrose Bierce
from *The Devil's Dictionary*

For centuries, bridges have been built to connect two points of land separated by valleys and bodies of water.

The ancient Greeks are credited with constructing the world's first arch bridge during the Bronze Age around 1300 B.C.E. near the modern road from Tiryns to Epidaurus, but it was Roman engineers who first fully realized and exploited the potential of arches for construction.[1]

Despite other types of bridges (beam, cable-stayed, cantilever, suspension, truss), the arch bridge is a metaphor for the four significant attributes to building and sustaining a culture where accountability is the essential factor in high-performing organizations:

1. Interdependence. Each piece of stone in an arch is vital. If just one stone from the arch fails, the entire arch fails and the bridge collapses. The arches create the span between pillars, giving the bridge its strength while the pillars anchor the arches, giving the bridge its stability. As we examine the Seven Pillars of Accountability, we'll see again and again that all seven pillars must be in place for an organization to be considered a high-performing enterprise. Consistent performance across all seven pillars is where organizations struggle.

2. Endurance. The Romans built their bridges to last. Most were constructed more than 2,000 years ago, and except for those destroyed during war, virtually all of them are in use today. One of the most famous and beautiful Roman arch bridges is the Alcántara Bridge (also known as Puente Trajan at Alcántara) built over the Tagus River at Alcántara, Spain. This bridge was built between 104 and 106 C.E. by order of Roman Emperor Trajan, and bears the inscription PONTEM PERPETUI MANSURUM IN SAECULA (I HAVE BUILT A BRIDGE WHICH WILL LAST FOREVER).[2] Like these Roman bridges, successful organizations endure.

3. Adaptive. The Romans didn't invent the arch bridge, but they perfected it. The Etruscans were building arch bridges but struggled with creating a structure strong enough to span great distances while being able to bear heavy loads without collapsing under the bridge's own weight. Roman engineers solved this problem by developing the voussoir keystone arch. This adaptation of an existing technology enabled the Romans to build highly effective aqueducts and bridges throughout their vast empire, including the Puente Romano over the Guadiana River at Mérida, Spain, which for 1,000 years was the longest arch bridge in the world. The principles, approaches, and tools in this book work for any organization, transcending age, geography, industry, and size. Enduring organizations aren't afraid to adapt.

4. Responsibility. According to legend, Roman engineers in charge of designing and directing bridge construction were expected to stand directly beneath the center of the arch as the capstone was placed in position. Smart design, flawless execution, and trust were no longer abstract ideas. The ultimate test of responsibility occurred when the final stone holding the entire arch in place was inserted and the engineer's life literally was at stake. Accountability in the workplace is most noticeable at the end of projects, but we will learn—as the ancient Romans learned—that failure to pay attention to accountability along the way can be deadly. Are you and your colleagues willing to stand under the weight of your decisions?

Because accountability is a collection of beliefs and steps applied on a consistent basis, I would like you to invest a few minutes to take this assessment. The assessment is based on the principles, beliefs, and activities of some of the world's most admired companies and is designed to help you get a sense of your own organization's effectiveness.

Let's face it: You can't improve if you don't know what's working and what's not.

Respond to each of the following statements by choosing a number:

5 our organization consistently conforms to this statement
4 our organization usually conforms
3 our organization conforms or doesn't conform about equally
2 our organization occasionally conforms
1 our organization rarely or never conforms

This assessment is for your benefit. If you are not brutally honest with yourself, your score will be meaningless and fail to indicate opportunities for improvement. Respond to each statement as things are now, rather than as you wish they were.

You will tally your scores at the end of this chapter.

SECTION A—CHARACTER

5 4 3 2 1   Our values are clearly defined and consistently communicated.

5 4 3 2 1   Our values are easy to understand and simple to remember.

5 4 3 2 1   Our values reflect our distinctive personality (e.g., you won't find our values on other organizations' walls).

5 4 3 2 1   We live our values every day (e.g., we regularly refer to them and they serve as guidelines for our behavior).

5 4 3 2 1   We do what's right for our customers, employees, suppliers, and owners, even when it hurts.

5 4 3 2 1   We are accountable for our performance and accept responsibility for our mistakes.

5 4 3 2 1   We trust each other to make good choices and do our best.

5 4 3 2 1   We seek first to understand others' points of view before seeking to persuade them to ours.

Subtotal _____ **of 40**

SECTION B—UNITY

5 4 3 2 1   Our organization's vision and mission are clearly defined and articulated.

5 4 3 2 1   Our organization's direction generates excitement and enthusiasm among everyone.

5 4 3 2 1   Everyone knows the organization's top objectives.

5 4 3 2 1   Every role in our organization is clearly defined and communicated.

5 4 3 2 1   Everyone knows what's expected of them.

5 4 3 2 1   Accountability isn't just top-down; everyone knows they are accountable to each other.

5 4 3 2 1   Rewards and penalties related to performance are clearly defined and communicated.

5 4 3 2 1   Our leaders agree with where we are and where we're going before we implement any initiative.

5 4 3 2 1   Our top leaders communicate at least once a month with their teams.

5 4 3 2 1   We use multiple vehicles (e.g., social media, email, one-to-ones, all-employee meetings, small team meetings, newsletters, etc.) to communicate with our colleagues.

5 4 3 2 1   We put our plans, procedures, and policies in writing and make them accessible.

5 4 3 2 1   It's the leader's job to forge relationships with employees.

Subtotal _____ **of 60**

SECTION C—LEARNING

5 4 3 2 1   We view ongoing training and development as an investment, not an expense.

5 4 3 2 1   We are committed to providing training in good times and bad times.

5 4 3 2 1   We conduct face-to-face training to get to know our employees better.

5 4 3 2 1   We provide training for all employees, including all employees who work outside of headquarters.

5 4 3 2 1   We follow up to ensure employees "get it" and we review regularly.

5 4 3 2 1   Our organization develops our employees' technical skills.

5 4 3 2 1   Our organization develops leadership skills (e.g., strategic thinking, problem solving, interpersonal communication, executive presence, etc.) among our leaders and emerging leaders.

5 4 3 2 1   We have a formalized program or approach for mentoring.

5 4 3 2 1   We communicate that employees must "own" their career.

5 4 3 2 1   We learn from our successes so that we can replicate what works best and improve our performance.

Subtotal _____ of 50

SECTION D—TRACKING

5 4 3 2 1   We have systems to measure the things that are important to us.

5 4 3 2 1   We monitor and address "soft" indicators (e.g., morale, opportunity for advancement, speed of decision making, etc.).

5 4 3 2 1   We measure everything that matters by relevant categories (e.g., overall company, location, functional area, individual, industry, etc.).

5 4 3 2 1   We have a system in place for gathering employee feedback.

5 4 3 2 1   We have a system in place for gathering customer feedback.

5 4 3 2 1   We share progress against key performance indicators (KPIs) with all employees at least quarterly.

5 4 3 2 1   We review individual performance with every employee in writing at least two times per year.

5 4 3 2 1   We align individual objectives with company objectives.

5 4 3 2 1   People know where they stand when they are underperforming.

5 4 3 2 1   We base decisions on logical, factual information, and not on emotions.

5 4 3 2 1   We differentiate between occasional mistakes and long-term underperformance.

Subtotal _____ **of 55**

SECTION E—URGENCY

5 4 3 2 1   We drive to the highest levels of excellence in all that we undertake.

5 4 3 2 1   We have a laser-like focus on improving our performance against our key performance indicators (KPIs).

5 4 3 2 1   We are willing to make decisions with less than 100 percent of the data.

5 4 3 2 1   Our organization moves forward with sound ideas, even if those ideas are unpopular.

5 4 3 2 1   We encourage, empower, and reward decision making at every level of our organization.

5 4 3 2 1   When we make a decision, we move forward to implement it in a timely manner.

5 4 3 2 1   We take action to solve problems immediately.

5 4 3 2 1   We recognize our mistakes and move quickly to address problems.

5 4 3 2 1   We minimize "red tape" to speed decision making.

5 4 3 2 1   Our processes drive efficiency and productivity without encumbering our people.

Subtotal _____ **of 50**

SECTION F—REPUTATION

5 4 3 2 1   We know that a favorable reputation is dependent on our behavior matching our values.

5 4 3 2 1   We will terminate a high-performing employee who does not share our values.

5 4 3 2 1   We reward results, not activities.

5 4 3 2 1   We recognize that failure to address underperformance costs us personal and institutional credibility that damages our reputation.

5 4 3 2 1   Our employees know that we are consistent in addressing underperformance.

5 4 3 2 1   We know that people are motivated by different things, so our recognition programs and actions are tailored accordingly.

5 4 3 2 1   Our employees will tell us the news and information we need to hear.

5 4 3 2 1   Employees who are underperforming are not surprised when we penalize or terminate them.

5 4 3 2 1   We are not afraid of respectful conflict so we will initiate tough conversations.

Subtotal _____ **of 45**

SECTION G—EVOLVING

5 4 3 2 1   We change things that aren't delivering the results we expect.

5 4 3 2 1   We look regularly at changing what we are doing, even in areas where we have been successful consistently.

5 4 3 2 1   We value the benefits of planning so we take time to plan.

5 4 3 2 1   In the past 24 months, we have developed and introduced a new product or service based on customer feedback.

5 4 3 2 1   When planning, we think big, view old problems in new ways, and encourage radical ideas.

5 4 3 2 1   New approaches and initiatives are received enthusiastically versus being resisted.

5 4 3 2 1   We regularly ask, "Is there a better way?"

5 4 3 2 1   We regularly exercise applied and practical creativity enterprise-wide (e.g., problem solving is not limited to a few people).

5 4 3 2 1   We won't compromise our values, but we appreciate that mistakes can lead to breakthroughs.

5 4 3 2 1   We look outside our industry for practices we can adapt to our business.

Subtotal _____ **of 50**

Total Score: _____ **of 350**

This assessment will benchmark you and your organization against some of the most exceptional companies in the world.

COMPARE YOUR SCORE

To receive even greater benefit from this assessment, ask your direct reports to take the assessment.

When you provide the assessment to your colleagues it would be ideal if you eliminate the headings on the assessment and rearrange randomly the prompts to ensure a more truthful response.

Over a 24-month period, 1,042 executives from 150 leadership teams in the United States, Canada, Australia, and New Zealand completed the accountability assessment. In 79 percent of the cases, the overall score of the 150 CEOs taking the assessment was the highest or second-highest score on the leadership team (shown in the graph). Although no additional analysis was conducted to explain the gap, the fact that 79 percent of these CEOs viewed their organization's performance against key accountability drivers as markedly better than their direct reports is a gap that likely will occur when you and your leaders complete the assessment.

Your position in the organization will give you a biased view of performance. Leaders usually are more optimistic than their colleagues.

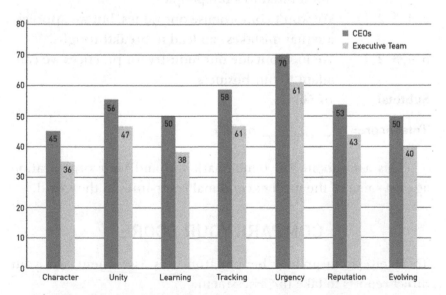

Figure 3.1   CEO vs. Executive Team

When all of your leaders have completed the assessment, ask them to bring their individual assessments to a meeting to discuss their results. The scores will tell you one thing, but it's the conversation your team has about the assessment that has the potential to make the most impact on your organization's performance. Discuss as a team the learning that occurred from the assessment. Seek to understand differences of opinion about how and why people responded to certain statements the way they did. Pinpoint areas with opportunity for improvement and agree to take action.

If approached with candor and the willingness to understand points of view that differ from your own, this conversation can be a game-changer. The trust you build and the action you agree to take are essential steps toward becoming an exceptional organization.

WHAT THE SCORES MEAN

70–244   Systemic issues across all areas of your organization are hindering performance. You are succeeding in spite of yourself.

245–279   You are in a category with organizations where accountability—and, therefore, performance—is an uphill battle for you and your team. This battle negatively affects your performance as well as your organization's performance.

280–314   This score shows solid performance, and you are well above average. This book will help you and your organization improve in the areas indicated by the assessment.

315–350   Congratulations. You and your organization are exceptional. Even so, read on and learn how other exceptional companies got there. After all, exceptional leaders and organizations are always looking for ways to improve.

Beginning with the next chapter, we examine in detail how exceptional companies nurture and sustain a culture of purpose, accountability, and fulfillment by building a bridge to help them get from Point A to Point B. This bridge is supported by the Seven Pillars of Accountability.

4

CHARACTER COUNTS

Character

Our values are clearly defined and communicated. Values shape
our character: we do what's right for our customers, employees,
suppliers, and investors . . . even when it's difficult.

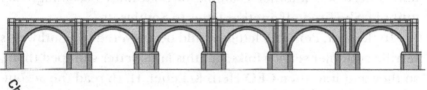

Character

Nearly all men can stand adversity,
but if you want to test a man's
character, give him power.
—Abraham Lincoln

"In the unlikely event of a water evacuation," the Southwest Airlines flight attendant announced to a plane filled with paying customers, "we'll be handing out towels and drinks."

The response by passengers to the flight attendant's funny reading of dry federal aviation regulations was predictable: everyone laughed, chuckled, or smiled.

Well, almost everyone.

One passenger on board was in the habit of finding fault with everything the airline and its personnel did. She had become known as the Pen Pal at Southwest Airlines' headquarters because she wrote the company on a regular basis.

Pen Pal didn't like Southwest's boarding procedure, not to mention the lack of a first-class section. She didn't like the absence of meals on flights. And she certainly didn't like humor related to the serious business of flying. To her, this crack about "drinks and towels" was another example of Southwest's seemingly lax attitude. She fired off another letter to Southwest.

In the past, Pen Pal's letters would be answered by Southwest's terrific customer service folks, but this latest letter stumped them, so they sent it to then-CEO Herb Kelleher. Herb read the accompanying note the customer service folks had attached to the complaint and in less than a minute made up his mind and wrote this response: *Dear Mrs. [name], We will miss you. Love, Herb.*

Herb's decision—while quick—was not made lightly. His decision was entirely consistent with the airline's character. Herb was simply acting on Southwest Airlines' principles that were galvanized in the early days of the company's struggle against bigger competitors. These principles are codified in the mission of Southwest Airlines: "Dedication to the highest quality of customer service delivered with a sense of warmth, friendliness, individual pride and company spirit." This mission is lived out every day by the 46,000 employees in the Southwest Airlines system, and it is part of what gives the airline its unique character. Working hard, having fun, and treating everyone with respect are what the airline calls "The Southwest Way."

Most mission statements are a dime a dozen. We've all seen these impressive declarations that sound good but that are rarely lived out in the behavior of the people in the organization. It's one thing to say you are committed to a particular belief or behavior; it's another thing to believe it and live it. Your character, whether organizational or individual, is not what you *say* you are; it's *how you behave* all the time. Words are cheap. Deeds matter. Especially, as Lincoln reminds us, when the stakes are high and your response reveals your character.

The behavior of the flight attendant who made the "drinks and towels" comment was in complete alignment with Southwest's character that pledges a unique combination of "the highest quality of customer service" delivered with "company spirit." Southwest Airlines employs a multistep employee screening process that probes to learn as much about a person's character as it does their technical proficiency. So Herb could trust that the flight attendant and the customer service people had behaved in a manner consistent with the airline's character. He also knew that his company could likely never do anything to please this customer, therefore he was willing to support his employees and focus his attention on those who flew Southwest precisely because of its spirit.

For a quick glimpse at other ways Southwest's spirit shows up on a flight, check out this collection of flight attendant announcements I've collected as a passenger aboard their flights.

SERVING UP SOUTHWEST AIRLINES' CHARACTERISTIC BRAND OF HUMOR

Announcement as airplane is pushing back from the gate: "Hello ladies and gentlemen and welcome aboard. This is Southwest flight ABC with nonstop service to Dallas Love Field. So if Dallas is not on your itinerary today, it is now!"

"This will be a completely full flight. You're not picking out living room furniture, so get a move on. If you see an empty seat, take it, it's yours."

"In the unlikely event that this flight turns into a cruise, your seat may be used as a flotation device, which you can take with our compliments."

"You paid for these corny jokes, so you're going to get 'em!"

"There may be 50 ways to leave your lover, but there are only 6 ways out of this airplane."

"If you don't like our service or the flight gets too long, we have 6 emergency exits."

"Welcome aboard. To operate your seat belt, insert the metal tab into the buckle, and pull tight. It works just like every other seat belt and if you don't know how to operate one, you probably shouldn't be out in public unsupervised. In the event of a sudden loss of cabin pressure, oxygen masks will descend from the ceiling. Stop screaming, grab the mask, pull it over your face, and try to breathe. If you have a small child traveling with you, secure your mask before assisting with theirs. If you are traveling with two small children, decide now which one you love more."

"In the event of a sudden loss of cabin pressure, oxygen masks will descend from the ceiling. To activate, please deposit your quarter."

"Ladies and gentlemen, please fasten your seat belts. The captain would like to try something new today."

"We'll be cruising at an altitude of 35 feet [pause as passengers look around questioningly]. Just kidding to see if you were listening. That's 35,000 feet."

"Flight attendants will be coming through the cabin to make sure your seat belt is fastened and that it matches your outfit."

"Please make sure that your seat backs and tray tables are raised to their full, upright, and most uncomfortable position."

"Contrary to popular belief, the seat-back pocket is not a trash can, so please give your trash to a flight attendant."

"Please make sure that your carry-on bags are kicked, pushed, shoved, or crammed underneath the seat in front of you."

"Take out and review the safety information card in the seat-back pocket in front of you . . . or to learn a little Spanish on our way to Ft. Lauderdale."

"For those of you who paid attention, thank you. For those of you who didn't, good luck."

"We're beginning our descent. We know that many of you just got your drinks and are still enjoying them. You'll need to stop enjoying them and start drinking them because flight attendants are coming through the cabin to pick up any remaining cups, cans, and glasses."

"If you plan to leave something behind, please make sure it's something we want."

As the airplane pulls into the gate: "Those of you standing have an excellent view of the 'Fasten Seat Belts' sign. So please remain seated until we've come to a stop at the gate."

"This is the captain speaking: We're waiting for another aircraft to push from the gate. When that happens, we'll proceed to the gate. When we've come to a stop, I'll turn off the fasten seat belt sign, and you will then be able to stand up, grab your bags, and not go anywhere."

"We'd like to thank you for flying Southwest Airlines. On behalf of the flight deck we'd also like to extend a very special and very happy 101st birthday to a gentleman seated near the front of the aircraft [scattered applause]. So, if you happen to see the captain on the way out, mind his walker, shake his hand, and wish him well with another 100 years working here at Southwest Airlines."

Sung to the tune of "Auld Lang Syne": "May other airlines be forgot/ And never brought to mind/'Cause Southwest gotcha here tonight/ And we gotcha here on time."

Although many myths, legends, and fables illustrate Southwest Airlines' one-of-a-kind culture, the Pen Pal story you just read is true. Even if this story was just another tall Texas tale about a maverick airline, you would likely believe the events occurred simply because the conduct of flight attendants, gate agents, and baggage handlers, all the way up to the street-smart founder, is consistent with the behavior Southwest Airlines says it values, encourages, and rewards.

The bigger question is not whether this incident really happened, it is *How is your organization's character revealed when a valued employee disappoints a paying customer?*

THE GREAT PARADOX

The Dutch theologian and teacher Desiderius Erasmus wrote in the late 1400s that, "We sow our thoughts, and we reap our actions; we sow our actions, and we reap our habits; we sow our habits, and we reap our characters; we sow our characters, and we reap our destiny."

When I visited the Nucor plant in Eufaula, Alabama, to meet with Ray Napolitan for the first of my interviews with him, I found a version of Erasmus's quote on the wall of Ray's office.

Spend a few minutes with Ray Napolitan and you hear all the right words. Talk to his employees and look at the terrific results that teams led by Ray have produced over the years in four different locations across the United States, and you know that his actions match his words.

Yet that's not the case in most organizations.

Character counts. Or, rather, we say it does.

In my survey of leaders, when asked, 80 percent of the executives said "we do what's right for our customers, employees, suppliers, and owners, even when it hurts." And 76 percent said "we are accountable for our performance and accept responsibility for our mistakes." Commendable.

But when executives were asked specific questions from the accountability assessment found in the preceding chapter, the good intentions they said existed inside their organizations were practiced with less consistency. For example, the numbers drop to 66 percent who "strongly agree" or "agree" that "our values are easy to understand and simple to remember;" the implication of this statistic is that one person in three—even among an organization's top leaders—doesn't fully understand the principles used as a basis for making decisions and driving individual and organizational behavior. The numbers drop further to 58 percent who "strongly agree" or "agree" that "accountability isn't just top-down; everyone knows they are accountable to one another." The implication of this statistic is that 4 of every 10 employees view holding people accountable as the responsibility of the supervisor—not the peer. When employees operate in their own world with little sense of shared responsibility with their coworkers for making sure things are done right, on time, and on budget the performance of the organization suffers. Imagine the new levels of performance that can be attained when everyone in the organization—not just management, midlevel executives and supervisors—views holding one another accountable as an essential part of their daily duties.

The paradox of saying one thing and doing another are prevalent in most organizations: the things we *say* we value— treating others how we want to be treated, quality, innovation, and even accountability—we don't *treat* as valuable. We say one thing and do another. Our actions are the outward expression of our character.

In a workshop I was conducting for a successful manufacturing company, I began by asking the participants if they could tell me their corporate values. "Yes," they answered enthusiastically, "we recently updated them because people couldn't remember all eight values. We reduced our values to four words so everyone could remember them."

One of the four values was "integrity" ("integrity," "respect," and "honesty" are the trifecta of values because they appear regularly in values statements, so the universal use of these words tends to dilute their impact; even so, if that's your value, let's see how it shows up).

"What time was this meeting supposed to start?" I asked the workshop participants. "Nine o'clock," was the collective response. "What time did we start?" I asked. "Nine fifteen." "How is that acting with integrity?" "It's not," they admitted. So is "integrity" really how things are done at this company, or is it just a word that sounds good?

Starting a meeting late is a small thing, a "wee problem," but small things become big things and big things can turn into big problems.

The behavior you see is the default culture of your organization. Your culture mirrors your character. Leaders who commit what my friend Mardy Grothe calls "little murders," such as starting a meeting late, are contributing to a culture that eventually makes accountability all but impossible. We say one thing and do another, showing our organization's true character is out of alignment with the words we say matter.

What would an impartial visitor to your organization see, hear, and experience? How would the observed behavior align with the behavior you say you want? Is yours a culture that is created and nurtured intentionally, or is yours a culture that occurs by happenstance? Just as you cultivate a garden, you must cultivate a workplace environment where high performance is the expectation.

DO OUR WORDS REFLECT OUR CHARACTER?

"A culture of accountability in any organization starts with its shared values," says David Alexander, former vice-chair at Ernst & Young and, at the time of our first interview, one of six regional managing partners in the United States. The Ernst & Young global workforce consists of 175,000 men and women, and the "Big Four" firm has enjoyed a reputation as one of the best places to work year after year. As a professional services firm, EY relies on having great people to deliver to its clients the timely, quality work that's been promised, so you would expect the firm to use a proven system to hire what Alexander calls the "best and brightest" people. "We use our values as a guideline for hiring and for making other decisions," Alexander told me. EY recruits people who demonstrate integrity, respect, and teaming—the first of the firm's three values. "We're very team-oriented, and we want people who can work in a team environment. In order to have effective teaming, you've got to have individual integrity and respect for opinion and thoughts." Second, EY looks for people with a winning attitude. "We characterize our culture as one that's comprised of people who have the energy, the enthusiasm, and the courage to lead," says Alexander. "We try to assess people's leadership attributes early on when we recruit them, and then develop that throughout the course of their career." We will examine EY's approach to talent development in Chapter 6.

Courageous leadership and a willingness to make decisions are characteristics that are valued at Nucor. Says Nucor's Ray Napolitan: "One core Nucor philosophy that was started by Ken Iverson—who laid the foundation for this culture, set the culture, and set the stage for the great profitable growth we've had—is, 'We allow, no we expect, our employees to make decisions. We also know that our employees will make the correct decision about 60 percent of the time. However, we expect you to learn from your mistakes and don't make the same big mistake twice.' And while that 40 percent number may seem high, what it means is that if you're not making mistakes, you're not running your part of the business like an entrepreneur, like it's yours. It's similar to the Vince Lombardi quote that says, 'If you're not making mistakes, you're not trying hard enough.' Now we definitely expect our people to learn from their mistakes, but because we have hired great people who we trust, our culture is one of empowering our people and encouraging them to think for themselves."

Trusting, empowering, and encouraging employees are behaviors most bosses claim to support. But when asked directly, only about half of the executives I surveyed (54 percent) agreed with the statement that "we encourage, empower, and reward decision making at every level of our organization."

Sooner or later, encouraging certain behavior or ignoring other behavior will result in that behavior becoming your organization's default culture.

So you can say that you "encourage decision making at every level of our organization," but if what your employees observe is a command-and-control approach to getting things done, after a while they will stop bringing leaders ideas that are never explored (much less implemented), they will stop thinking for themselves, and they will decide that trying to take the initiative is a waste of their time.

Such behavior is entirely predictable—and preventable. In Chapter 8, we examine how one CEO "let go of the reins" and watched his employees become more accountable to one another and, in the process, save their midsize company hundreds of thousands of dollars year after year.

HIRE PEOPLE WHO SHARE YOUR VALUES

Every company and every person will make a mistake. Leaders at the exceptional companies I spoke with minimize those mistakes by hiring people who share their values. This practice is critical for any organization, whether you are a professional services firm, a manufacturer, a retailer, or in distribution-related industries like Southwest Airlines, which moves a lot of planes, luggage, and people on more than 32,000 flights, every day of the year.

"At Southwest we firmly believe in the importance of hiring the right person," says Elizabeth Bryant. "You cannot train somebody to care about other people or to smile when they see a customer. That's something you either have or you don't have. So we first find the people who embody the values that we have at Southwest Airlines. From there we can cultivate them and grow them and train them in the technical skills."

The values of Southwest Airlines are as simple to remember as they are compelling because they reflect the distinct personality of the airline. It's unlikely you'll find these words on the walls or websites of any other company:

- Warrior Spirit
- Servant's Heart
- Fun-LUVing Attitude

Bryant describes the warrior spirit as "that ability to work hard and persevere and—no matter what the situation—to see it through." The servant's heart, she says, is putting other people before yourself and serving them.

And last, but not least, having fun. Because so much of our time is spent at work, we would all enjoy it more, work harder, and work smarter if we were around people we like and respect. "We're going to have more colorful debate and dialogue and tackle problems with some energy and some enthusiasm," says Bryant, "and that's going to lead to better decision making, which will lead to more commitment to that decision, which will lead to more accountability to that commitment."

How do you find a fun-loving person with a warrior spirit and a servant's heart? It takes a lot of work. In 2012, Southwest Airlines received nearly 115,000 résumés and hired only the best 2,500 people. To join this frequent flyer club, you've got to be special.

ONE GREAT PERSON

When it comes to people, The Container Store has also done the math.

"One of our Foundation Principles," founder and CEO Kip Tindell told me, "is 'one great person equals three good people.' And if one great person equals three good people, and one good person equals three average people, and one average person equals three lousy people, then one great person equals 27 lousy people. And we're talking in terms of business productivity. We have chosen to hire great people."

Great people attract other great people: 36 percent of The Container Store's 6,000 employees have joined the company through a referral from an existing employee.

At The Container Store, the employee comes first.

"We're creating a place where people want to get out of bed and come to work in the morning," says Casey Shilling. "And so the employee comes first. The customer comes second. You don't hear a lot of retailers say that. You always hear, 'the customer is always right' and 'the customer comes first.' But we believe that if we take care of our employees and create a workplace that is delightful, then the customer will be taken care of and then the shareholder will benefit."

To find that great employee, the interviewing process is quite thorough. "We train on interviewing for great employees," says Shilling. "Asking questions about a candidate's life experience, asking a candidate to describe a recent experience where they had good service, and asking, 'What does good service mean to you?' And once we hire those great employees, accountability is key. During performance reviews, we discuss contributions and opportunities for growth, our Foundation Principles and the employees' practice of them in their role, and we define SMART goals and an action plan for each employee for the coming year."

An organization's foundation is great people who share the values of learning, supporting others, and excelling. "We want the best of the best, so we hire about 3 percent of those who apply with us," says Shilling. "Our great people tend to weed out the people who are not pulling their weight."

In an industry where the average annual turnover is greater than 100 percent—imagine replacing your entire workforce year after year—The Container Store's turnover averages less than 6 percent annually.

Like other exceptional organizations, The Container Store is clear about its purpose and the type of people they want on their team. They look for, hire, and retain people who have a bias for making good things happen.

CODIFY YOUR CHARACTER

The strategy is simple but powerful: Hire the best candidates who align with your values and then pay them accordingly.

Whether you call them values, beliefs, or principles, you can use them every day as a filter for making decisions, including who you hire.

Remember the "Heaven & Hell" exercise from Chapter 1? I've made a few changes to enable you to use it with your leadership team to codify the character of your organization (see Appendix).

If one of your values is having fun, ask the person you are interviewing to tell you a joke or funny story. If you place a premium on innovation, search for an understanding of a person's problem-solving capability. If achieving results matters, explore a time when the person overcame an obstacle.

Use the "Heaven & Hell" exercise to ask interviewees about their character-building experiences. They will be surprised by your approach. And they can't fake the answers.

When you hire for character as much as skill, you improve accountability because you are in alignment on big things like mission, vision, and values. Your debates and decision making will be centered on practices not principles. And you'll be rewarded with less turnover, lower recruiting costs, and a higher-than-industry-average productivity rate.

WHO ARE WE?

You've got to know yourself before you can be yourself.

Knowing who you are and your character sets the foundation for your future performance. Your company will evolve as the world around you changes, but what you stand for shouldn't. When I work with companies to help them improve their performance, one of the first exercises involves completing the model, the Identity Pyramid™, on the following page.

We start at the bottom of the pyramid, the organization's foundation, and work our way to the top.

You probably have a clear idea about how you would complete each section. What may surprise you as you move forward with this exercise are the differences of opinion that emerge from your team.

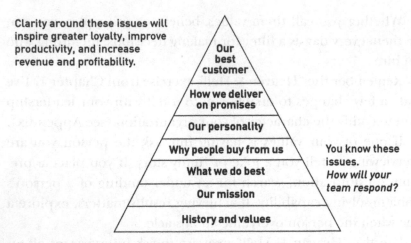

Clarity around these issues will inspire greater loyalty, improve productivity, and increase revenue and profitability.

Our best customer

How we deliver on promises

Our personality

Why people buy from us

What we do best

Our mission

History and values

You know these issues. *How will your team respond?*

Figure 4.1 Who Are We? The Identity Pyramid

A *Harvard Business Review* article notes that the "dirty little secret" in companies is that "most executives cannot articulate the objective, scope, and advantage of their business in a simple statement. If they can't, neither can anyone else."[1]

I find the same is true of values, which is why I recommend you limit your values to three, four, or five words rather than phrases or sentences that few people can remember. Your values codify your character.

The leadership team of a successful technology company was working through the Identity Pyramid exercise and it came time to review the company's values. I wanted to hear from the CEO and his leaders to ensure I understood the beliefs we would be using for guidance as we fine-tuned the company's strategy and operating plan. The company leaders could recall only four of the company's seven values, so one of the executives pulled up the company website on her tablet and retrieved the other three forgotten values.

These so-called values presented three problems:

1. **Phrases fail the test.** I've seen core values statements that look like the Ten Commandments. Perfectly crafted phrases

may look good on paper, but people can't remember them. Use words, not phrases.

2. **Less is more.** People cannot remember phrases, and they cannot remember more than five words that characterize your values. Make your values few in number and high in impact. By limiting yourself to three values, you have an excellent likelihood that everybody will understand, remember, and live them. As my friend Ole Carlson says, "The more laws you create, the more outlaws you create." Three values are excellent, four are good, and five are almost one too many.

3. **The real you.** Take the opportunity to ensure that your values reflect the characteristics that make your organization different. "Be yourself," said Oscar Wilde, "everyone else is already taken."

The case of the technology company whose leaders could not remember their core values caused a bit of a laugh at everyone's expense. The point was clear: If an organization's top leaders can't remember the core values, how do you expect everyone else on your team to remember them?

CHEAP WORDS

Just because your values are easy to remember doesn't mean they are showing up in the character of your organization.

I was hired by a company to improve organizational and individual performance that was being undermined from top to bottom by a lack of trust and collaboration. Even by the admission of the company's senior leaders, this dysfunctional organization was succeeding in spite of itself.

When I walked into the lobby for my first meeting, it was hard to miss the framed poster proclaiming the company's core values. Ironically, "collaboration" was one of four stated values yet they brought me in precisely because leaders were not collaborating with one another in a productive manner.

Character is not what you say, it's who you are and how you behave. In this company, the behavior was out of whack with the nice words on the wall.

We see plenty of people saying one thing and doing another. In sports, Joe Paterno said that "success without honor is an unseasoned dish," then he systemically covered up the child-abuse sex scandal at Penn State. As a seven-time Tour de France cycling winner, Lance Armstrong denied for a decade claims he was using performance-enhancing drugs. When the truth came out, sponsors fled, with many saying that Armstrong "no longer aligns with our company's mission and values."[2]

In business, Walmart's bribery case in Mexico "pitted the company's much-publicized commitment to the highest moral and ethical standards against its relentless pursuit of growth." Investigators hired to pursue the bribery allegations "found a paper trail of hundreds of suspect payments totaling more than $24 million" and "recommended that Walmart expand the investigation." Instead, "Walmart leaders shut it down."[3]

Founder Sam Walton, who had danced the hula on Wall Street in 1984 when associates delivered record profits, was probably doing the twist in his grave.[4]

WORDS MATTER AT THE DELTA COMPANIES

Because The Delta Companies do not manufacture anything, ship anything, or sell products from a brick-and-mortar storefront, CEO Jeff Bowling has been studying, crafting, and perfecting his company's mission and values for years. How these characteristics show up matters because Bowling's business, inside and out, is a people business.

Articulating these characteristics was a challenge because Bowling says being clear about purpose puts the people who matter—customers and employees—in charge. "We had to find the right words to describe what was already there," says Bowling. "Writing some altruistic cliché would have been a snap. But it wouldn't have been right."

After two years of reading, soul-searching, and talking with people inside and outside the organization, Bowling and his team codified the company's character with an elegantly simple statement that was informed by answering this question: What is our reason for existing beyond making money? The answer: "Creating Access for People."

"This may look simple, and it is when you're finished," Bowling told me, "but it was very difficult to nail this idea. Even after we zeroed in on this idea, we had a lot of meetings debating whether the word should be 'for' or 'through.' Each word matters and we had to get it right."

It's a deceptively simply phrase that speaks volumes about the company's commitment to help people succeed in their career at The Delta Companies, to help the people Delta serves (hospital administrators, physicians, and other providers), and to help people in the communities where The Delta Companies do business.

"The Delta Companies exist to enrich people's lives," says Bowling. "Whether it's the lives of employees and their families, our customers and their staffs and patients, our vendor partners, or our local community. The great part of providing staffing solutions within healthcare is we are creating options, opportunities, and freedoms through access to healthcare that didn't exist prior to our performance."

NO MISSION WITHOUT PROFIT

"Profit comes first. People are more important. The paradox recognizes we must first generate profit *and* people matter. Profit means excess. At The Delta Companies, we have excess in fun, rewards, and the intrinsic good that occurs. And monetary profit. There is no mission without a profit," according to Bowling.

As CEO, Bowling understands that the companies can be more profitable if employees are engaged and performing at a high level. So The Delta Companies evaluate overall performance as a staffing company by comparing profitability per employee to that of competitors. The Delta Companies enjoy a larger gross profit margin per employee, suggesting that they are outperforming their competition. "Because of that performance," says Bowling, "we're able to provide more fun, more rewards, and more giving back."

The company's core values have been distilled to two powerful words: *Performance* and *Humanity*. Performance is quantified as profit margin, growth rate, Net Promoter score (a measure of customer satisfaction), and productivity per member (employee).

Humanity is quantified as patient access, employee engagement, philanthropy, and fun.

"In order to enrich others, a balanced approach of performance and humanity is required," Bowling says, and refers to the ancient Chinese who believed in two complementary forces in the universe: yin and yang. One is not better than the other. They are both necessary, and a balance of both is highly desirable.

"For The Delta Companies," says Bowling, "the yang represents our objective to create a high-performance environment. The yin represents our objective to create a fun, rewarding, and respectful environment. While the yin is intangible and subjective, people know fun when they see it. Energy, passion, creativity, philanthropy, respect, and other positive attributes of the yin are equal in importance to the very tangible and objective yang. "At The Delta Companies," Bowling reports, "we have zero tolerance for high-performing jerks that suck the yin out of others."

The Delta Companies hit their financial objectives each year, employees are productive at a rate higher than the industry average, and customer satisfaction level is exceptional with a Net Promoter score averaging 65.1 (in service businesses, world-class scores are 65 and some of the world's most admired companies have Net Promoter scores in a range of 51–57).

Character counts at The Delta Companies.

FIND YOURSELF IN THE IDENTITY PYRAMID

As you move toward the top of the Identity Pyramid, your perspective should gradually shift from a historical perspective to a current perspective and, ultimately, to a future state. The going gets tougher as everyone takes a crack at providing their take on each section.

Our firm developed a list of "100 critical questions" we would ask when companies engaged us to help them with strategy, performance improvement, and other important activities such as new market entries and products launches. In time, our list of questions grew to number in the hundreds. Here are a few questions corresponding to each of the other sections of the Identity Pyramid to get your juices flowing:

Our mission: Our reason for existing beyond making money.

- Why are we in business? What are we trying to accomplish?
- What kind of company are we trying to be?
- What ideas are we fighting for?
- If our company did not exist, what would the world be missing?
- What are we most passionate about today?

What we do best: Our core competencies.

- How do we deliver value to our customers? Would our customers agree?
- Are we financial-driven, sales-driven, operations-driven, or something else? Which of these disciplines puts us in closest touch with the people who use our products or services?
- What are the barriers customers and prospects must overcome to do business with us? What must we do to remove or lower those barriers?

- Where will our future profitable growth come from?
- If we are the "gold standard" in our industry, what must we do to strengthen our position? If we are not, what must we do to become the "gold standard"?

Why people buy from us: Our competitive advantage.

- What causes our customers to select us over our competition?
- What memorable experience are we creating with our customers?
- What are our customers' unmet needs?
- What is our customers' greatest pain? What would reducing or eliminating that pain be worth to our customers?
- Describe the most recent major breakthrough at our company. What has been the impact of that breakthrough?

Our personality: How we show up; our culture.

- If I could choose just three words to describe our culture, what would those words be? How do those words compare to the ones on our website?
- How would our employees describe us? Our customers and prospects?
- If an impartial observer visited our organization, what would that person see, hear, and experience? Are we who we say we are?
- How would this observed behavior align with or vary from the behavior we desire as an organization? What is causing this behavior?
- What happens when behavior does not match our stated values?

Our best customer: Customers we love and who love us.

- What is it about our best customers that we appreciate the most? What can we do to attract more of them?

- What is it about our worst or most difficult customers that we dislike the most? What can we do to turn them into great customers? If we can't convert them, what's our plan for firing them?
- What would happen if we increased our focus on our best customers?
- Do any surprising situations represent an underserved opportunity?
- Who uses our product or service in a way that we did not intend for it to be used?

Answering these questions will tell you a lot about your character.

Let's examine more closely the segment of the Identity Pyramid that reads *How we deliver on promises.*

THE SCHIZOPHRENIC ORGANIZATION

When leaders are asked, *"To whom does your organization make promises?"* they generally respond with *"customers."*

You know you're keeping your promises to your customers and clients by measuring revenue growth, retention, repeat business, and referrals. And you occasionally receive comments, calls, and emails telling you that you've done a great job. Customer satisfaction surveys such as the Net Promoter score can measure quantitatively how well you're doing in keeping your promises to customers.

There's often a "whatever it takes" mindset that comes into play to make sure you're keeping customers happy. It's a big part of who you are—your character—to deliver on those promises.

These promises are important, but they are promises made *outside* the organization.

What about promises being made *inside* your organization? Why do we treat customers one way and colleagues another? That behavior makes for a schizophrenic organization. The promises being made inside the organization, such as deadlines, commitments, and agreements (both spoken and written) made to one another, are broken every day.

Promises are based on trust. When promises are broken, trust is betrayed and such behavior calls into question whether the trust that existed between two individuals can be restored. Broken promises reveal a character flaw.

When a promise to a customer has been broken or is about to be broken, it's often because someone broke a promise to a colleague. When this news reaches you, the usual immediate response is that you, one of your star players, or a special group of team members that you can count on gets busy fixing the problem. I call it the Heroic Event. You may call it fire-fighting. Whatever you call it, your job as the leader is to deliver on the promise that's been made to your customer. It's in your character to do so.

A sign posted between the men's and women's restrooms of a manufacturing company in North Carolina where I was conducting a workshop provides an apt reminder for us to treat our colleagues the way we want to be treated:

> **THERE IS LESS TO FEAR FROM OUTSIDE COMPETITION THAN FROM INSIDE INEFFICIENCY, DISCOURTESY, AND BAD SERVICE.**

In other words, we have met the enemy of underperformance, and it is us.

When assignments are fumbled by your employees, what's happening? Do they not share your sense of urgency? Your sense of responsibility to others in the organization? Your commitment? Your character? Perhaps not.

When these types of events occur inside your organization, they signal an accountability problem. Such problems make it hard to scale your operation because you're managing by exception.

Consider these questions:

- Has an event like this happened in our organization in the last 30 days?
- What was our response?
- What was the cost?
- Could the event have been prevented?

As you calculate the cost of one of these events, bear in mind that more than money is at stake. Your workflow has been disrupted as you moved this particular problem to the head of the line, effectively jeopardizing the timing of other projects for other customers. Your reputation with your customer has been tarnished. Your reputation with your colleagues hangs in the balance as employees wonder why these problems are allowed to continue and why the people who are part of the problem are still on the team. Reputation—the sixth of the Seven Pillars of Accountability—will be examined further in Chapter 9.

FIND THE ROOT CAUSE OF UNDERPERFORMANCE

As you dig into the problem to learn why it happened, the answer to the fourth question—*Could the event have been prevented?*—is usually "yes." Remember the funnel from Chapter 2? It showed two fundamental causes to investigate: People and Processes.

Up to this point, we have examined the idea of character primarily as it relates to the qualities and traits of people. But character can also refer to the qualities and traits of things. So before rushing to blame a person for the problem, reexamine your processes. Is hiring a process or an exercise in individual judgment? Are we hiring the right people, not just for a job, but for our culture? Consider the character of your other processes, including these three:

1. Workflow. What systems are in place to replicate success? Do those systems reflect the way work really gets done? What

steps can be added, deleted, or modified to improve efficiency?

2. **Tools, training, and development.** Do people have the tools they need to be effective? Has the organization provided training and development to help people do their jobs to the best of their abilities? How do we test to ensure people have the tools and training they need? How do we develop soft skills, such as leadership, judgment, and problem solving?

3. **Communications.** Were the expectations of the job clear? Were the expectations related to individual performance clear? Were the direction and feedback provided consistent?

We look more closely at these issues in Chapters 5 and 6.

When you turn to the People component of the Heroic Event, consider the role character plays in these three facets of the human condition:

1. **Skill.** Did the person who made the mistake have the skill to perform the job he or she was asked to do?

2. **Will.** Did the person who made the mistake have a passion for what they're doing or were they just going through the motions? Do they want to improve?

3. **Fear.** Did the person recognize that something wasn't right, but was fearful of bringing a question or problem to the attention of his or her supervisor? If so, was it out of fear because the person believed he or she would be asked to add solving this problem to the long list of tasks already being worked on? Or was the person afraid of a "shoot the messenger" syndrome? Whose character is in question?

Over time, each person in your organization creates a bias about his or her character. For one person, the bias may be one of commitment and dependability. For another, the bias may be one of empty promises and always falling short. In each case, the person's behavior has earned the particular bias.

It's true that top performers may not be fearful of speaking up about problems. But stars who see their colleagues drop the ball and get away with it or who watch their suggestions for improvement fall on deaf ears will decide it's not worth giving their best and may, in the end, decide to jump ship.

The sum of this behavior is your character, and it's on display every day in your organization.

It's your culture. The words you choose to describe your values are important. You have chosen these words to describe your organization's character. Your promises are the actions that speak louder than your words. Are they in alignment?

ACCOUNTABILITY INSIGHT

- Decide what you stand for.
- Talent predicts future results: Hire for values as much as skills.
- Without trust, there's no conflict; without conflict, there's no change; without change, improvement is difficult.

TAKE A FRESH LOOK

Take a fresh look at your organization's values that you say define your character, then reexamine your scores from the Character Pillar of the assessment.

- Are our values in writing?
- Do our values look like everyone else's or do they describe our distinctive personality?
- Are our values easy to understand and simple to remember?
- Do our values reflect our real behavior?
- Do our values serve as a filter for decisions?
- Are we setting the bar too low or just right for our people?
- Do we promote people based on how their performance aligns with the organization's values?

- Do we rely on the organization's values to address under-performance?
- How easy or difficult is it to speak truth to power in our organization?

In high-performing organizations, accountability is a side-to-side process. But accountability starts at the top and is shaped by the character of an organization's leaders.

5

GALVANIZING YOUR TEAM

Unity

Every employee knows and supports our mission, vision, values,
and strategy and knows their role in helping to achieve them.

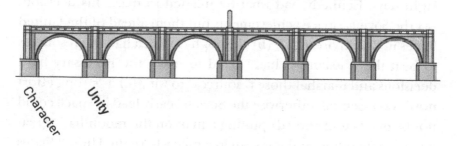

Character   Unity

All for one and one for all!
—Alexandre Dumas,
from *The Three Musketeers*

Standing before 40,000 men, women, and school children at Rice University Stadium on a warm, sunny September day in 1962, President John F. Kennedy declared, "We choose to go to the moon."

A series of events—played out on the world stage like a high-stakes game of chicken—had led to this moment.

On April 12, 1961, Soviet cosmonaut Yuri Gagarin became the first human in space when he orbited the earth.

The Space Race was on. Space leadership had become a measure of world leadership. And America was already behind.

So eight days after Gagarin's orbit, Kennedy responded to the Soviet achievement by doing what the best chief executives do. He posed the key question to his leaders who were overseeing America's budding space program: "Is there any . . . space program which promises dramatic results in which we could win?"[1]

Experts scrambled to answer this question, and after another eight days, Kennedy had what he needed to make his decision: (a) the Soviets' space achievements put them ahead of the United States in "world prestige"; (b) although America had the resources to beat the Russians, it had "failed to make the necessary hard decisions and marshal those resources" to win; (c) a "strong effort now" was essential, otherwise the Soviets' early lead in space could not be overtaken; and (d) putting a man on the moon had "great propaganda value" and was seen as a race where the United States "may be able to be first."[2]

Armed with this assessment, Kennedy weighed the costs, the risks, and the benefits of overtaking the Soviets in the Space Race and made the first of many "hard decisions" related to America's space program. On May 25, 1961, speaking before a joint session of Congress, President Kennedy challenged America with the goal of "landing a man on the moon and returning him safely to the earth." He wanted it done "before this decade is out." And he wanted to beat the Russians.

PLAYING TO WIN

Kennedy cast a bold vision: if the United States was going to play the game, competing was not enough. The United States would play to win, and so beating the Russians to the moon became the overarching objective of America's space program. Everything else was secondary.

Perhaps Peter Schutz learned from Kennedy. When Schutz was named CEO of Porsche in 1981, he became the first non-German to lead the German car manufacturer. The drastic move to hire an American engineer was prompted by the company's decline in prestige and sales. Porsche was no longer winning races. Porsche was also losing money.

I met Peter Schutz in 2007 when he spoke to a group of CEOs in Dallas about achieving extraordinary results from ordinary people. Schutz shares his experience in his book, *The Driving Force*, and it's the story of his early days at Porsche he shared that day with us.

Upon his arrival at Porsche, Schutz found himself participating in a tradition where about 40 of the company's top managers gathered for lunch every Monday. Talk around the table, he remembers, was "fairly dull," so during a break in the conversation Schutz asked, "What is happening at Porsche today that is so exciting that you can hardly wait to run and tell our customers and dealers about it?"

The silence was deafening.

With that simple question, Schutz pinpointed a "fundamental problem that would not show up on a financial statement." Schutz realized that "Porsche needed an exciting challenge to power its turnaround. It lacked the driving force of motivated people working on something that truly energized them."

Confronted with this realization, Schutz convened a meeting of everyone at Porsche who was involved in racing and asked,

"What is the most important race of the year?" The 24-hour race in Le Mans, France, he was told. The race would take place 62 days from that day.

"What are our chances of winning?" Schutz asked.

Just as Kennedy received a blunt assessment in response to his question about the chances of winning the Space Race, so, too, did Schutz receive a bleak forecast for winning the Le Mans race. He was told that Porsche's cars "would give a good account of themselves," but there was "no chance of these cars winning the overall race."

Hearing this assessment, Schutz later said that he "thought about their response for about 10 seconds" and then replied: "Let me explain something. As long as I am in charge of this company, we will never go to any race without the objective of winning. Let's get to work and go racing."[3]

In each case, the chief executives:

- Cast a vision to engage, unify, and inspire people. Aristotle said, "The soul never thinks without a picture," and King Solomon said, "Without a vision, the people perish." Great leaders think big and inspire people to rally around a cause that's bigger than themselves.

- Understood that competing was not enough. Playing to win creates purpose. Purpose sparks unity. Some leaders confuse making money with their organization's purpose and then wonder why their employees are less than enthusiastic about meeting performance objectives.

- Challenged their team to accomplish an objective most thought was unattainable. NASA and Porsche started from a position well behind the competition with the odds stacked heavily against them. In casting their high risk/high reward vision, each executive surrendered day-to-day decision making, effectively motivating his colleagues to solve their own problems. Owning the outcome galvanized commitment and drove peer accountability.

- **Made the challenge public.** Public commitments drive personal and organizational accountability. Declaring your intentions to others increases the likelihood that you will do what you say you will do. The people you are counting on and those who are counting on you know where you stand. For people of strong character, falling short is an embarrassment, which is perhaps the most undesirable of consequences.

Schutz and Kennedy won their races. But in 1961, plenty of people doubted that what Kennedy was saying could or would be done.

GAIN YOUR INNER
CIRCLE'S COMMITMENT

To achieve great results, leaders must first earn the commitment of their inner circle.

As debates continued within the White House and NASA around the purpose, strategy, cost, schedule, safety, and scientific agenda related to a trip to the moon, Kennedy did not waiver from his objective of beating the Russians nor from his conviction that the objective could be accomplished.

As a responsible chief executive, Kennedy sought the counsel of experts. As an extraordinary leader, he persuaded his team to commit to and achieve an objective they first believed was unattainable.

In a private meeting between President Kennedy, NASA chief administrator James Webb, and eight other staff members, JFK asked if getting a man to the moon was the top priority of NASA. The transcript clearly indicates a lack of commitment from the scientists. Indeed, the team was divided.

"Everything we do," Kennedy says, "ought to really be tied into getting onto the moon ahead of the Russians."

"Why," NASA chief administrator James Webb starts to ask, "can't it be tied to preeminence in space, which are your own. . . ."[4]

Does this ever happen to you? You studied the facts and searched your mind and your heart. You made a hard decision and committed to that decision. You cast a clear vision of what it will take to win, and you're determined to do what's necessary to win. Now someone on your team wants to water down the vision. Hedge bets. Play not to lose. There's a time for debate and a time for action. The time for debate was past. Kennedy's vision of sending a man to the moon was already public.

What's more, JFK understands that a vision of "preeminence in space," which is how the NASA scientists want to reframe the vision, is ambiguous and therefore weak. NASA wants to achieve a scientific objective. Kennedy wants to win the top prize. Like any good leader, Kennedy understands the need for an unambiguous target and knows that "preeminence"—even though he's used that very word—doesn't mean much to most Americans.

For this reason, your organization's mission (its purpose beyond making money) and vision (where you're going) are especially important. They must translate beyond the financial performance of the organization. They must matter to everyone on your team and inspire people to show up every day and give their best to achieve a goal that is bigger than any individual. It is how great organizations drive accountability.

People want to win. Winning requires unity, commitment, and accountability. Leaders unify their colleagues and put them in position to win.

CONVICTION AND CLARITY

It is natural for an organization's budget meetings, like this one with Kennedy, to morph into an examination of an organization's purpose and priorities. In Kennedy's case, the president and his team must agree on a clear vision and allocate the necessary resources to achieve it. The resources to be successful in space were absent because the conviction to make the hard decisions had been avoided. When it is time to decide, if your vision is important, you must put your money where your mouth is.

Kennedy is willing to do that, and he knows he needs everyone's commitment to win, starting with those in his inner circle.

So as the meeting continues, Kennedy works to gain their commitment to achieve the public vision (landing a man on the moon) and the implicit vision that has yet to be announced (beating the Russians).

JFK challenges the scientists to "get really clear that the policy ought to be that [landing a man on the moon and returning him safely to the earth] is the top-priority program of [NASA], and . . . except for defense, *the* top priority of the United States government . . . otherwise we shouldn't be spending this kind of money because I'm not that interested in space. The only justification for it . . . is because we hope to beat [the Russians] and demonstrate that starting behind, as we did by a couple of years, by God, we passed them."[5]

It's a remarkable admission by Kennedy that he's "not that interested in space." Kennedy's clarity and conviction around his vision is based on his recognition that beating the Russians to the moon translates into "world prestige" for the United States. Kennedy is working to persuade NASA's leaders to look beyond the scientific objective of "preeminence" to the emotional objective of beating the Russians.

To achieve something so big, so risky, and so improbably difficult requires singleness of purpose. It requires unity. Winning teams have no room for doubters, naysayers, and handwringers.

COMMITMENT FORGED BY CONFLICT

Unity does not mean absence of conflict. A certain amount of tension is inevitable because conflict is the price of individuality.

The key to unity is being able to answer *Yes!* to the question, *Are we in agreement on the big issues?*

The price of unity is too high when you and your colleagues suppress your true character in pursuit of a false harmony. People of strong character and high intelligence will consider points of view that conflict with their own from people they respect. For this reason, character counts. High-performing teams achieve unity by talking through concerns, questions, and doubts, and committing to the strategy, the action, and allocation of resources required to achieve the vision. And then they hold one another accountable to their shared commitment.

The more passionate the debate, the greater the need to walk out of a meeting unified once conflict is resolved.

In the meeting with Kennedy and Webb, the give-and-take discussion reaches resolution as JFK establishes the idea that beating the Russians to the moon is America's, and therefore NASA's, top priority. As the meeting concludes, Kennedy does three significant things as the ultimate leader who will be held accountable for the success or failure of achieving this vision.

First, like any good leader, JFK doesn't undermine Webb in front of his team, so Kennedy takes the high road to communicate that the required unity to achieve this objective is close at hand, while acknowledging there's still a gap: "I know we're not that far apart," says the president. "But I do think at least we're in words somewhat far apart."[6]

Second, because words matter, JFK asks for Webb to articulate his views in writing, away from the heat of the meeting. Doing so gives Webb time to think about Kennedy's position and work through the issues. Kennedy understands that unity on this huge project starts with NASA's Webb, and Kennedy wants them reading from the same script. Says Kennedy, "I'd like to get those words just the same. How about you writing me and telling how you assign these priorities."[7]

Third, Kennedy agrees to do likewise, saying, "and perhaps I could write my own."[8] This generous offer comes from the man whose bold vision for his country has already made him vulnerable to a skeptical American public.

CONVINCING A SKEPTICAL PUBLIC

That meeting with JFK, Webb, and the others was tough sledding. And those people were among JFK's inner circle. They had to be convinced. Once they were convinced, the NASA officials committed their exceptional talent and energy and that of their teams to beating the Russians to the moon.

Meanwhile, the American public was in a doubting mood. On the one hand, pride mattered: *"If we're so good, why didn't we get to space first?"* On the other hand, practicality was at stake: *"Who cares about space? This program is going to cost a fortune in taxes."* And human life hung in the balance: *"Even if we spend the money, can we get our guys to the moon and back alive?"*

Doubts continued to simmer.

So 16 months after delivering his speech to Congress, Kennedy was using his considerable powers of persuasion to take his case for a moon race against the Russians to the American people, 40,000 of whom had assembled at a football stadium in Houston, hometown of the newly formed National Aeronautics and Space Administration, or NASA.

Kennedy's September 12, 1962, speech—his "We choose to go to the Moon" speech—is easily accessible on the Internet, and its power resonates today. Kennedy's speech provides a blueprint for any executive seeking to unify a group of people in order to accomplish a difficult task:

- Seize attention. "We meet at a college known for knowledge, in a city noted for progress, in a state noted for strength, and we stand in need of all three. For we meet in an hour of change and challenge, in a decade of hope and fear, and an age of both knowledge and ignorance."
- Describe the situation and the motivation for action. "The exploration of space will go ahead, whether we join in it or not. [N]o nation which expects to be the leader of other nations can expect to stay behind in this race for space. We mean to

be a part of it. We mean to lead it. Yet the vows of this nation can only be fulfilled if we in this nation are first. And therefore we intend to be first."

- **Appeal to shared values.** "Surely the opening vistas of space promise high costs and hardships as well as high reward. So it is not surprising that some would have us stay where we are a little longer, to rest, to wait. But this city of Houston, this state of Texas, this country of the United States was not built by those who waited and rested and wished to look behind them. We choose to go to the moon in this decade and do the other things not because they are easy but because they are hard. Because that goal will serve to organize and measure the best of our energies and our skills. Because that challenge is one that we are willing to accept, one we are unwilling to postpone, and one that we intend to win."

- **Acknowledge difficulties and provide context.** "To be sure, we are behind, and may be behind for some time. But we do not intend to stay behind. And in this decade we intend to make up and move ahead. [A]ll this costs us all a good deal of money. This year's space budget is three times what it was in January 1961 . . . a staggering sum, though somewhat less than we pay for cigarettes and cigars every year."

- **Paint the vision, show commitment, mix with humor.** "We have given this program a high national priority, even though I realize that this is . . . an act of faith and vision, for we do not now know what benefits await us. But if I were to say, my fellow citizens, that we shall send to the moon, 240,000 miles away from the control station in Houston, a giant rocket, more than 300 feet tall, the length of this football field, made of new metal alloys, some of which have not yet been invented, capable of standing heat and stresses, several times more than have ever been experienced, fitted together with a precision better than the finest watch, carrying all the equipment needed for propulsion, guidance, control, communication, food, and survival, on an untried mission, to an unknown celestial body, and then return it safely to earth, reentering the atmosphere at speeds of over 25,000 miles per hour, causing heat about half that the temperature of the sun—almost as hot as it is here today—and do all this and do it right and do it first before this decade is out, then we must be bold. And I think we must pay what needs to be paid. I don't think we ought to waste any money, but I think we ought to do the job."

- **Be specific.** "During the next five years, the National Aeronautic and Space Administration expects to double the number of scientists and engineers in this area, to increase its outlays for salaries and expenses to $60 million a year, to invest some $200 million in plants and laboratory facilities, and to direct or contract for new space efforts over $1 billion from this center in this city."

- **Leave them inspired.** "Many years ago, the great British explorer George Mallory, who was to die on Mt. Everest, was asked why did he want to climb it, and he said 'Because it is there.' Well, space is there, and we're going to climb it. And the moon and the planets are there. And new hopes for knowledge and peace are there. And therefore as we set sail, we ask God's blessing on the most hazardous and dangerous and greatest adventure on which man has ever embarked. Thank you."[9]

Whatever you think of Kennedy, he undoubtedly inspired an entire generation of Americans to think big and get on board for the space race. He made public his vision of beating the Russians to the moon. And he held NASA accountable for winning the race.

INSPIRATION IS CONTAGIOUS

One of those inspired Americans was The Container Store founder and CEO Kip Tindell.

"I was a big fan of JFK, even at age 10," Tindell told me. "I certainly remember watching on television his ability to communicate so effectively, his charm, his leadership. And I was spellbound. The Camelot thing worked on me."

In 1978, a 25-year-old Kip Tindell founded The Container Store with Garrett Boone and John Mullen.

Their commitment to culture, undergirded by a set of Foundation Principles, has earned The Container Store the distinction as one of the retail industry's greatest success stories. The company has appeared on *Fortune* magazine's list of "Best Places to Work" 15 consecutive years, twice earning the number two position and twice ranked number one.

TALENT IS THE WHOLE BALLGAME

"Talent is the whole ball game," says Tindell. "One of our Foundation Principles is 'one great employee can easily deliver the business productivity of three good employees,' and that's an understatement."

The Container Store not only finds and hires great people, it holds on to them. The Container Store's employee turnover rate averages 6 percent in an industry in which average annual turnover exceeds 100 percent.

Tindell's roommate at the University of Texas was John Mackey, founder of Whole Foods and co-author of *Conscious Capitalism*. "Kip, along with John Mackey," says Casey Shilling, "is one of the big proponents of conscious capitalism, getting the movement going."

"The nice thing about conscious capitalism," says Tindell, "is it's unabashedly in favor of making money. There's nothing wrong with profit. It's good. When you have a company that operates that way, the universe conspires to assist you. Everybody wants to see you win."

GREAT TALENT COSTS MORE

The Container Store pays its employees 50–100 percent above the industry average, and Tindell says "it takes a lot of bravery to pay great people well." He's "not an advocate of paying mediocre people well, just great people. Our salespeople today make what our store managers of several years ago made. This type of purposeful rapid rising of salary has allowed us to compete effectively for great talent."

Tindell believes this approach rewards everyone. The employee wins, who's getting paid two times what someone else is willing to pay. The company wins, because it's getting three times the productivity at two times the payroll cost. And customers win because they are interacting with great people who provide great service.

Are willing workers in short supply? Don't baby boomers complain that Millennials just don't want to work?

Baby boomers comprise 36 percent of the The Container Store's workforce; Generation X, 34 percent; and Millennials, 30 percent.

"I don't think you can indict a whole generation," says Tindell. "That notion denies the spirit of humanity. People want to go to work in the morning, and they want to work with great people. And they want to accomplish great things and then they want to go home at night feeling wonderful about what they've accomplished. We're much more excited when we do our best.

"There have been studies," continues Tindell, "that indicate the first 25 percent of an employee's productivity is voluntary. That next 75 percent depends entirely on how employees feel about their boss, their product, the company. So I think the reason that The Container Store has done so well is because the productivity of our employees is just off the charts. It's much more fun to be in a company that's a super-high achiever than one that's mediocre."

A company's reputation starts with its employees. "The two most important underpinnings of our company's culture," says Tindell, "are being able to work with people that you think are really great, really motivated, really talented. That's 1A. Then 1B is 'communication and leadership are the same thing.' And that's a pretty profound thing if you really believe it and you act on it."

Kip Tindell was big on *transparency* long before that word was used to describe a communications style. It's a style that has served him well.

"Even when I was in high school," Tindell says, "transparency was how I chose friends. The more you know about something or somebody, the closer you get and the more you can love it or them. People who are not transparent are usually afraid, they have deep-seated insecurities. I choose employees the same way I chose friends: based largely on how transparent they are. Transparency and integrity—those are two things I look for most."

PURPOSE IS CURRENCY

What value do you place on purpose? On excelling at something meaningful?

Wouldn't accountability be less difficult and high performance more of a natural outcome if the people on your team all were genuinely passionate about what they were doing? These questions turned Jeff Hook into an entrepreneur.

Hook began his career at Hallmark Cards, consulted in two "Big Six" accounting firms, next led the Dallas office for Oracle Consulting, and then served as a senior leader at i2 Technologies. Despite his success, Hook found himself searching for something more fulfilling.

So in 2004, Hook and a small group of developers founded Fellowship Technologies, and created Fellowship One, the industry-leading web-based church management software that helps churches become more effective in ministry and more efficient in administration. In 2009, FT was named to the Inc. 5000 list, climbed the list the following year, and in 2011 was purchased by Active Network.

The early days of FT were much like any other start-up. It was a roller coaster ride: up with wins and down when a big deal slipped away. Yet FT quickly won 26 of the 100 largest churches in the United States and grew quickly. "We had a lot of fun," Hook told me, "and we achieved enormous success because we had a committed group of people trying to get something off the ground."

Right from the start, Hook focused on culture. He and his team developed a document, "Culture on Purpose," that was used as a "guideline for creating a culture of worship, leadership, innovation, service, and authenticity. We live by these core values toward one another, our customers, and our partners. We talk about these core values, we reward performance based off of these core values, and we frequently celebrate them. They are an everyday part of our life at Fellowship Technologies."[10]

Hook says two primary reasons fueled his belief that culture was important. "First," Hook says, "I'll use a sports analogy: you see great players play for a certain coach and a certain team and the dynamics are so great the organization gets the most out of that player, and they're a winner. And when that player is traded to a different organization with a different coach with bad dynamics, the person isn't worth the salary. So for us, working in the faith market, we knew how important this market is to a lot of people who work here. It caused me to think, 'If we're going to be successful instead of just be another company, we have to emphasize the faith aspect within the lives of our employees.' Doing that contributed to our culture because it meant we attracted people who really wanted to work here."

Second, while that approach narrowed FT's selection pool of talent, it also created a filter for hiring people who were passionate about the company's mission and vision. "We could hire motivated, dedicated, and productive people for less than market rate," says Hook, "because they wanted to be on our team."

Hook also subscribes to the idea that money follows passion, and not vice versa. "Everybody knows," he says, "though most people don't follow it, that if you want to make a lot of money, go find what you're passionate about and do that. Over time, because of the quality of the work you do, because of your passion, you will make money. Don't go looking for some career that makes you money, because in the end you'll be unhappy and you'll probably walk away from it. The practical side of this approach is that we were able to attract some really talented people who were willing to take a bit of a cut in pay to be part of a young, vibrant company that was doing meaningful work."

By using purpose as currency, Hook attracted experienced people who helped get FT out of the gates fast while staying within its budget.

Today, Fellowship Technologies serves 46 of the 100 largest U.S. churches and also supports churches in other countries. Like Kip Tindell of The Container Store, Hook attributes FT's success to a team of people who want to work with great people and who are unified around a bigger purpose.

"Strategy is important," said Hook, "but you can have the best strategy in the world and if you don't have a culture of execution and respect you are not going to be successful over the long term. You create and sustain that type of culture from people who are inspired about their work."

He believes you can incent behavior, but you can't incent passion. "It's my job," he says, "to help people distance themselves from their pettiness and the minutia going on in their lives. People have their lives at home. So in order to perform as an organization, your people must be motivated enough to exceed their own expectations, which often are quite modest. It's the leader's job to bring the right people on board and then bring out the best in each of them."

CLARITY CREATES CONFIDENCE

To bring out the best from the people on your team, you must tell them what you expect. They, in turn, want to know that what they are doing contributes to the greater goal. So setting clear expectations is an essential component in driving accountability throughout the organization.

Setting clear expectations at every level in the organization is one of the simplest and most effective steps leaders can and should take to drive performance. And yet it's a step that's ignored, assumed, or botched by most leaders. In my survey of leaders, only 43 percent "strongly agree" or "agree" that "every role in the organization is clearly defined and communicated." The implication: more than half the employees are not clear about what is expected of them.

You must be clear about what you expect of yourself, your organization, and those who work for you. You must communicate those expectations. People can't hear you think. Don't make your colleagues guess what you want them to do. Unspoken expectations lead to resentment.

Likewise, the clearer you can be about what you *don't* want and what is *not* acceptable, the less time you'll waste.

As you set expectations, keep in mind that it is not enough to simply tell people what you expect of them. Expectations that are dictated rather than discussed and negotiated before commitments are made are essentially empty promises. Without genuine commitment from all parties involved, the expected performance may not happen.

Just as clarity creates confidence in you and those that work with and for you, the opposite is also true: confusion causes chaos. Ambiguity creates a high likelihood that work is being duplicated, ignored, or performed poorly.

Your operating (or strategic) plan should ensure that everyone is clear about:

- Where we are (Point A)
- Where we're going (Point B)
- How we'll get there
- Who's responsible and will be held accountable for specific tasks

- Deadlines for commitments
- Rewards and penalties related to performance

A few thoughts about deadlines: they are powerful motivators for getting things done, yet they are an under-appreciated (or oft-ignored) element in helping drive accountability (the power of deadlines is examined further in Chapter 7).

My wife, Janet, says that if you want to get something done around the house, throw a party. As the date of the party approaches it's amazing how much gets accomplished. The same is true of due dates in the workplace. For this reason, the planning sessions I lead for leadership teams include a one-day follow-up session four to six months after the initial two-day session. What happens between the original two-day session and the one-day follow-up session is up to you and your team. The one-day follow-up session is the party.

When your plan includes the above-mentioned components, it becomes your contract at the leadership level. And the basis of your accountability model.

THE UP-FRONT CONTRACT

At the individual level, expectations should be established as an up-front contract with an if/then component.

The power of the if/then component is its simplicity, its clarity, and the fact that it is discussed and agreed to—as the name of the contract says—up front. "If you do this, then you will get this. If you do not do this, then this is what will happen." Clear expectations and clear consequences for both sets of behaviors are indicated.

Accountability breaks down and emotions swirl when clear expectations are not established up front.

Keep your plan simple. Don't spend time writing a plan with dozens of pages. Spend your time gaining commitment among your leadership team on what must be accomplished.

Invest the time you save in the planning process on execution because executing your plan will take everything you've got. I developed a one-page template called the Migration Chart™ for use in strategic planning sessions to help leaders convert their ideas into the priorities the organization must address as it "migrates" from Point A to Point B (see Appendix, page 265).

In my book, *Lead the Way*, I examine the planning and execution process. After leading more than 165 strategic planning sessions, I have observed 10 benefits of effective planning you should expect your planning sessions to deliver (see Appendix, pages 267–269).

HOW MUCH INFORMATION WILL WE SHARE?

A purpose, vision, and plan that are clearly and consistently communicated forge solidarity, inspire confidence, and drive performance. Clarity about every significant aspect of your organization, from what you believe to where you are going and the role each person plays, unifies employees.

The key question you must answer is: *How much information will we share?*

The Container Store shares everything except individual salaries, including board meeting presentations, sales reports, store comps, everything. Nothing is edited, nothing is held back, and people know that. "People know that we are telling them everything," says Casey Shilling, "and so everybody feels a part of this team."

Has sharing all of that information ever backfired? What if the information you share falls into your competitors' hands?

"People occasionally say that I share too much information," says founder Kip Tindell. "I believe the companies of tomorrow that will dominate are the ones that understand *team* and understand *transparency*. Communicating the way we do adds up to a competitive advantage that so far offsets any little fragments of information falling into the wrong hands. The benefits of communicating are fifty-fold to one over withholding information."

The Container Store communicates future site locations, which no other retailer does. The company communicates price promotions. Customers, employees, and even other retailers can see that information. "I honestly can't remember an incident where that came back and bit us at all," says Tindell. "So we are pretty fanatical about it. It's pretty hard to talk us out of it."

The Container Store approach is not for everyone. That's not the point. The point is that if you've got the right people on your team, they want to know what's going on and how they can help. Nature abhors a vacuum, so if you don't tell them what's going on, people will fill the void with their own information. The likelihood of that information being accurate is pretty small. So you can either give them the opportunity to make up inaccurate stuff or give them the real scoop yourself.

What's more, most of the information being communicated is not a secret. The secret? A unified team that out-executes your competition.

OVERCOMMUNICATING IS NEXT TO IMPOSSIBLE

Effective leaders understand that communicating truthfully in a confident style that is authentic to them and that connects with all employees is equivalent to the rebar that supports each of the seven pillars of their bridge that will carry the organization from Point A, across the abyss, and safely to Point B.

Nucor's Ray Napolitan calls it "the continual drumbeat." He believes that a leader can say something 10 times, but the employee will hear it just once. Napolitan illustrates the importance of the drumbeat to reinforce another key Nucor concept: the repeat sales team. Nucor has riggers, welders, detailers, people responsible for shop drawings, people who load and ship the material, and drivers. Each person, Nucor believes, is part of the repeat sales team.

"What happens," Napolitan will ask employees on the shop floor, "if Detailing details the project correctly, the riggers do everything correctly, welders have perfect welds, loaders load material safely, and our delivery is late? Is this repeat sales? And they'll say, 'No.' So it's up to the leader to put things in terms everyone can understand. As a leader, you've got to believe in your people and help them understand how they fit and are a key part of our mission. It takes all of us working together to succeed."

Southwest Airlines believes in overcommunicating. "You cannot send a message one time via one vehicle," says Elizabeth Bryant. "You've got to look at daily communication, weekly, monthly, face-to-face, news lines, newsletters, emails, web-based communiques, handwritten notes from leaders. Whatever it takes to help our employees understand where we are, where we're going, and why their role in that journey needs to happen."

It's one thing to tell someone something and expect them to know it, and quite another for them to actually get it. "If we really want to make sure that people understand something," says Herman Miller's Tony Cortese, "we have to craft that message and deliver it in multiple fashions, through multiple channels time and time again. That's something I've learned the hard way over the years."

Herman Miller has learned that communicating with people requires a deliberate process. "We want to hold people accountable and we want to see everything move forward," says Cortese, "so we need to clearly articulate a vision for them and we need to keep finding different ways to show them that vision, and show them how that vision ties in to what it is that they do."

COMMUNICATING CHANGE TAKES EVEN MORE EFFORT

Overcommunication is even more important when it comes to informing your employees of significant changes in the organization.

Senior leaders are required to look to the future, consider a variety of strategies and options, and then think through the implications of implementing their decision. You may weigh key decisions for weeks or months and share your thoughts with only a few of your trusted inner circle. You read a lot, talk to senior leaders outside your company, consult your key people, and engage outside experts. Most of your people are not looking, imagining, and thinking as far on the horizon as you. So don't expect your colleagues to embrace what you say the first time you say it. Although you have been living your decision for weeks, they are hearing it for the first time.

"By the time I make a decision that will carry us forward for the coming years," says CEO Jeff Bowling of The Delta Companies, "I'm totally convinced that the decision I'm making is the correct one. I understand the logic, the context, the risks, the benefits. I've been thinking about it 24/7 for weeks, maybe months."

Don't expect understanding, much less consensus, the first time you announce a new initiative.

"It finally dawned on me that I was six to nine months ahead of my team," says Bowling. "Now, we have communications game plans for those types of changes."

One rule of thumb for internal communication: by the time you are sick of talking about something is about the time your employees are starting to embrace what you have been telling them.

MARRIOTT'S STELLAR PERFORMANCE

If this perspective about purpose, communications, and unity seems like pixie dust, unicorns, and rainbows, consider this: a Gallup study of more than 1,000 working adults indicates the cost of America's disengaged workforce exceeds "$300 billion in lost productivity annually."[11]

Companies on *Fortune* magazine's "100 Best Companies to Work For" list report lower turnover and higher levels of productivity. Publicly traded companies on this list have seen their stock price increase an average of 10.8 percent.[12]

Marriott International, for example, is both a Most Admired company and a Best Places to Work company, and its stock gained 28 percent in the most recent measurement period.

Bill Minnock, senior vice president of global quality at Marriott International, told me the company's consistent high performance can be attributed to living the "values and principles of our founder, J. W. Marriott, Sr.: 'If you take great care of your employees, they'll take good care of the guests and the guests will return again and again.' We commit to our associates—our employees—and we set stretch goals to drive superior performance, and we communicate consistently. What we do inspires people to stay for a long period of time. I've been with the company 30 years."

With more than 3,700 properties and 18 brands in 73 countries and territories, Marriott International offers the most powerful portfolio of hotels and resorts in the world. Every day the staff at every single Marriott property convenes for a "daily stand-up meeting."

The daily stand-up meetings reinforce the company's vision, values, and essential daily activities. "The best of the best at this," says Minnock, "is the Ritz-Carlton organization. They're remarkably spectacular at this. So when you start every day like that, it shows commitment, and that commitment will deliver the results we—and, more important—our guests expect."

THE COST OF DISENGAGEMENT

The flip side of a great customer experience can be traced to a culture where employees are disgruntled, disengaged, and dysfunctional. The results can be measured in high levels of customer dissatisfaction, class action lawsuits, and workforce strikes and disruptions.

As American Airlines and US Airways considered merging, American's workers rebelled at their company's initial rebuff of US Airways' interests because they supported the merger. In its filing with the Securities and Exchange Commission, American Airlines attributed lost revenue of $45 million due to "operational disruptions that affected bookings"—nearly twice the impact of lost bookings caused by Superstorm Sandy. The problems "started a day after American outlined the new terms of employment it would impose on its pilots."[13] Coincidence?

I experienced this "disruption" firsthand. While traveling in February from Dallas to Harrisburg, Pennsylvania, I made connections in Chicago's O'Hare Airport. I anticipated a weather delay, and soon learned that the Chicago to Harrisburg flight would be delayed 30 minutes. When time came to board, the gate agent announced that the previous crew had failed to communicate to the incoming crew a problem with the de-icing equipment. The previous crew had written the report, but didn't inform the next crew. Passengers and crew moved to a different plane at a different gate, and we lost another 40 minutes. When we finally boarded the substitute plane, we sat for another 30 minutes because the ground crew had loaded all of the baggage on the first plane, had to unload it, and then move it to the new plane. Total lost time: 1 hour, 40 minutes.

Was this disruption an isolated incident? Not according to American Airlines. Were these actions deliberate? I doubt it. But the incident illuminates the negative impact a handful of employees had on a planeload of paying customers.

It's ironic that accountability is a problem for so many airlines, when they require that passengers agree to the if/then contract before takeoff. If you are sitting in a seat on the emergency exit row, you will be asked to perform the functions in the event of an emergency. "If you cannot perform or do not wish to perform the function, then a flight attendant will be happy to reseat you."

Why do so many airlines expect one set of behaviors from customers but not from themselves?

WHAT IS DYSFUNCTION COSTING YOU?

Disengagement, disruption, and dysfunction are not limited to a particular age, geography, industry, or size of an organization.

I once led a strategic planning session for a firm where the tension among the leaders was so palpable I marveled at this company's success. I recalled the company had a set of core values its CEO held in high regard, so we pulled up the company website on the Internet, and then I asked each of the dozen leaders to pull out a blank piece of paper and, without writing their name on the page, to assign a number on a scale of 1 to 10 with 10 being excellent and 1 being lousy for each of the company values. When the leaders finished, I wrote the core value on a flip chart and then wrote the numbers each of the leaders had assigned that value. There were a lot of 3s, 4s, and 5s; no 10s; and only a few 8s and 9s. Not much unity.

I shared with them an African proverb that says, "I take no joy that the hole is in your end of the boat" and then I told them they were in a leaky boat that appeared to be on the verge of sinking. We completed the planning session, and several weeks later I learned that about one-third of the executives in the room that day had since left the firm of their own volition or had been terminated.

Plenty of dysfunctional companies manage to be successful. How much more successful could you be if everyone was unified around the mission, vision, and values of your organization?

10 WARNING SIGNS OF DISENGAGEMENT

Most of us recognize that life provides no absolutes. And when it comes to employee disengagement, the shades of gray are infinite.

You need to watch for the telltale signs to determine whether your colleagues have checked out or, worse, are wreaking havoc within your organization. In descending order, here are 10 warning signs of employee disengagement:

10. **Information pipeline dries up.** Leaders are the last to know what's really happening.
9. **Employee complaints increase.** Grumbling about perceived injustices (large and small) is the order of the day.
8. **Absenteeism increases.** Sick days and PTO days are maxed out.
7. **Turnover increases.** Employees are leaving almost as fast as you can hire new ones.
6. **Shrinkage and theft increase.** "Where did that tool go?"
5. **Productivity declines.** It takes more people longer to complete assignments.
4. **Silos and discourtesy are pronounced.** "That's not my job."
3. **Broken commitments increase.** Tomorrow never comes.
2. **Quality of service and products declines.** "We have more returns and canceled orders than ever."
1. **Brand erosion occurs.** "Remember when we were the preferred provider in our industry?"

Any one of these issues can dilute productivity and profitability, and the top three can kill an organization if left unchecked.

Have you observed any of these warning signs in your organization?

CRYSTAL CLEAR EXPECTATIONS

The thought behind "clarity creates confidence" is that setting clear expectations is at the root of achieving high levels of accountability in your organization.

Too often leaders are in such a hurry to reach Point B they assume everyone understands a word ("success," "excellence"), a vision ("to be the best," "the preferred provider"), or a value ("integrity," "results-oriented"), so spending time ensuring that everyone is clear on those words and ideas can seem like a waste of time.

My experience is that without specificity around those words, you leave room for each person to interpret those words differently based on their perceptions, biases, and experiences.

During a meeting with the two founding partners of a firm, the subject of work-family balance came up.

"Work-family balance is important to us," said one partner. "That's a big part of who we are."

"Then why do so many people work such long hours?" asked the other partner.

The two partners agreed on their firm's values at a 30,000-foot level, but not at a down-in-the-trenches level. If work-family balance was viewed as a color, both would agree the color was blue. The problem is that one partner saw "blue" as "navy" while the other saw it as "turquoise."

Without clarity, each partner brought a different view—with different measures and different results—to their expectations, creating inconsistencies in holding those that worked for them accountable. That conversation exposed other fundamental difference and the partners later split.

EXPECT GREAT RESULTS FROM GREAT PEOPLE

All of the leaders I spoke with emphasized the importance of setting clear expectations.

"High performance," said Ernst & Young's David Alexander, "starts with hiring great people and then communicating expectations. It's important for that tone at the top to be established, so the people in our geographic area of Ernst & Young need to hear that from me in terms of setting expectations. We work hard to give a consistent message on our expectations to establish accountability—both individual accountability and team accountability."

Herman Miller's Tony Cortese says, "We share the belief that if we hold people to a high standard, they tend to deliver. It's our belief that people tend to rise to whatever the expectation is, so we try to create a fairly high bar for people and they continually amaze us with their high performance."

"We don't have very many rules," said Southwest's Elizabeth Bryant. "We do receive mandates from the FAA and there are a lot of different organizations that cause us to make certain decisions in one way. When it comes to our people, we have very clear expectations that are defined for every employee and three of those expectations are around the values of our organization."

For some companies, the relationship between management and unions is anything but unified. At Southwest Airlines, where more than 85 percent of the workforce is represented by a union, the relationship is considered a partnership. "There are times that you disagree, that's absolutely true," says Bryant. "You don't always see eye-to-eye on what the result is going to be, but we always agree that we want what's best for the employees and, ultimately, our customers. Having this foundation has led to very positive relationships with all of our unions."

At Nucor, the key to great execution and great results is being clear about what's expected at every level in the organization. "The way to do that," says Ray Napolitan, "is to start with talented folks, provide tools and training, and set clear expectations to hold people accountable. A culture of high performance starts with hiring the right people, and then changing behavior with clear expectations. If you don't change behavior, you won't change your culture. We make sure that we connect the mission and vision of the company—the big arrow, so to speak—to the employees' day to day performance."

Focusing on a few must-win priorities and being clear about individual, departmental, and organizational expectations related to those priorities increases effectiveness at every level of the organization. Directing an employee to "focus" on 10, 12, or 20 areas for improvement is not focus at all. A simple test for employee productivity is to determine if every employee can say whether they've had a successful day at work.

Do your employees know what is required of them to produce great results for the company? If employees struggle to answer this question, it's time to get more specific about what's expected.

UNDERSTAND WHAT MOTIVATES PEOPLE

To galvanize unity and drive high performance, people need to know what you want them to do and what's in it for them when they do it.

Most of the time it's money, but often it's something else.

Jeff Hook at Fellowship Technologies proved that people were willing to earn a bit less in their paychecks in exchange for contributing to a cause they found meaningful. The Container Store hires great people who want to work with other winners. And Southwest Airlines accepts only those people who are eager to rally around their cause of connecting people to what matters most in their lives.

Scientific data derived from Maslow's hierarchy of needs identify a total of six motivators that drive people to high levels of performance, sometimes sacrificing other benefits along the way. The six drivers, in no particular order, are:

- Economic—an interest in money
- Regulatory—an interest in tradition, process, and order
- Political—an interest in power, though not necessarily politics
- Theoretical—an interest in learning, logic, and reason
- Aesthetic—an interest in form and harmony
- Social—an interest in helping people[14]

It would be foolish, however, to think that money doesn't matter to employees, because it does. It's not always the first consideration, but it's always an important consideration.

NUCOR'S PAY-FOR-PERFORMANCE MODEL

Nucor's pay-for-performance model is well-regarded for its fairness and flexibility, its practical approach of aligning employees' interests at every level in the organization, and connecting the work people are asked to do with the rewards they receive for a job well done.

By sharing risks and rewarding productivity at every level of the company, Nucor drives performance at every level. And while Nucor's base pay at all levels is anywhere from 25 to 50 percent lower than a comparable employee at another steel producer, Nucor's model fosters safety, quality, productivity, and accountability, and enables Nucor employees to out-earn their peers nearly every year.

Every Nucor employee has a five-part compensation plan that starts with a base pay.

Second, every employee has some type of incentive bonus program. "In some cases," says Nucor's Ray Napolitan, "you definitely want different incentive programs because you will get the behavior that you incent." Nucor's fabricated products field sales people work on a sales commission plan. Production personnel are paid weekly on a shop bonus based on productivity and quality improvements. Office personnel, such as engineers, designers, detailers, and so on, are paid on a return-on-assets-type bonus as are the department managers (sales, engineering, production, builder services, customer service) so they focus on maximizing profitability. "We're aligned as a management team," says Napolitan, "instead of having the sales manager focused on sales volume and the manufacturing manager focused on labor-hours per ton. All of the managers are focused on returning the most to the corporation, return on assets. So instead of a conflict, the managers' missions are aligned through compensation."

The third part of Nucor's five-part compensation plan is a 401(k) match.

The fourth part is a profit-sharing plan that calls for 10 percent of Nucor's pretax earnings to be distributed to employees based on their annual earnings and the annual earnings of the corporation.

And the fifth part of the five-part compensation plan is the employee matching stock investment plan (EMSIP), where for every $1 of Nucor stock that an employee purchases, the company matches an additional 10 percent.

Service anniversaries are also celebrated, so after five years of service, a Nucor employee receives fives shares of Nucor stock.

A nonfinancial aspect contributes to Nucor's success, as it does at The Container Store, Southwest, and Fellowship Technologies. "There's a lot of pride in a Nucor teammate," says Napolitan. "Nucor takes care of its employees and really walks the talk, and in return the employees recognize that. We're so proud to work for this company that we want to work harder and smarter and return more and pay it forward back to the company."

Because a number of ways can be employed to lead people, savvy leaders do well to understand the motives of those they are leading in order to get more of the behavior they expect.

THE MYTH OF CONSEQUENCES

Somewhere along the way, consequences have come to be viewed as unfavorable.

The first part of the myth of consequences is that a consequence is only negative when the truth is that it can be either positive or negative.

The origin of the word *consequence* is two Latin words: *con* (originally *com*), meaning "together" and *sequens,* meaning "to follow." It is a neutral word meaning "something that logically or naturally follows from an action or condition."

The second part of the myth of consequences is that people don't like them. Again, the discomfort has its roots in the mistaken belief that a consequence is code for "punishment" when the word can also mean "rewards." In my experience, the people who don't like consequences are those who consistently underperform in their jobs. Stars, on the other hand, love consequences because to them the word is synonymous with a prize.

Accountability is hard work. Nothing will sap your team's energy quicker than casting a bold vision, gaining commitment, and then not following through. During every planning session, the leadership team confirms an existing strategic direction or agrees on a new one and then establishes three, four, or five must-win priorities to complete in order to move the organization from Point A to Point B.

When those priorities have been set, I divide the leadership team into sets of smaller groups and give them 30 minutes to answer these questions:

1. How will we ensure accountability?
2. What will be our rewards for achieving our objective?
3. What will be our response to underperformance?

When the groups reassemble, answers are shared.

Proceeding with the specifics of the plan is rather pointless until these three questions have been answered and everyone is committed to the collective response.

Accountability will live or die in the day-to-day operations of an organization.

I also give CEOs the option of having everyone sign a Pledge of Accountability at the conclusion of a planning session (see Appendix, page 266).

I admit to the CEOs that it is corny, but I also tell them it's powerful. Why?

First, it's a contract. The leadership team has just agreed that achievements will be recognized and substandard performance will be penalized. The reality is that peer pressure will be the motivating factor for each participant to carry out his or her commitment. Leaders don't want to let their peers down. Or themselves.

Second, the Pledge of Accountability is a visible symbol of the team's unity and commitment to execute the plan that is developed. Organizations display the signed Pledge of Accountability prominently in their workplace: employee break rooms, by time clocks, on the shop floor, in training areas, conference rooms, and sometimes in the lobby.

Wherever you decide to place it, the Pledge of Accountability is a constant reminder of the leadership team's unity and each leader's individual commitment to do his or her part and hold one another accountable.

ALL OF US MUST DO OUR PART

Knowledge is the currency of forward-thinking organizations.

Honest, consistent communication within your workplace can be the make-or-break difference between a divided, dysfunctional, and underachieving organization, and a unified team that is committed to accomplishing great things.

ACCOUNTABILITY INSIGHT

- People need a purpose that's bigger than themselves.
- It's almost impossible to overcommunicate.
- Clarity creates confidence.

TAKE A FRESH LOOK

Reexamine your score from the Unity Pillar of the assessment, and then consider these questions:

- Have we been clear about our purpose beyond making money?
- Does our vision focus only on numbers, or does it give our people something to cheer for?

- In what areas are we not doing the best that we can do? How will we respond?
- Are we setting organizational and individual performance bars high enough? How can we expect to attract other winners to our organization if we aren't committed to being the best we can be?
- Do we have the talent we need to win? Who else do we need? What will it take to attract the people we need to win?
- Are people trying to join our organization or trying to leave it?
- Is everyone committed to winning? Does everyone know what is expected of them to help us be successful? How can we tell?
- Are our people capable of overcoming incredible challenges? If not, what or who is holding them back?
- How much information will we share? What information will we not share?
- How often will we communicate information and provide progress updates? How much time do I spend communicating? What should it be? What changes in how I invest my time or changes in the messages I'm delivering would increase the likelihood that every employee knows exactly where we're going and what's expected of them?
- How do our teams handle their disagreements? What steps can I take to increase the trust level so that real issues are brought out in the open and addressed? Where can people go for help?
- What methods of communication are most effective for our different stakeholders?
- Is the behavior we expect from our employees aligned with the rewards and penalties of performance? Are our managers' compensation plans aligned to ensure that we are working toward a common goal?
- When did we last reexamine our compensation plan? Does our comp plan allow for the variable of a down market? Does our comp plan include financial and nonfinancial incentives?
- Do we know how individual employees want to be rewarded?

Without the unified and enthusiastic support of everyone in your organization, accountability will be an uphill battle and high performance will remain beyond your grasp.

To accomplish great things, the employees of an organization must be unified around a common goal, and each person in the organization must believe that what they do will affect whether that goal is reached.

"In a very real sense," said John Kennedy, "it will not be one man going to the moon, it will be an entire nation. For all of us must work to put him there."

6

GREEN AND GROWING

Learning

We are committed to continuous learning so we invest in ongoing training and development.

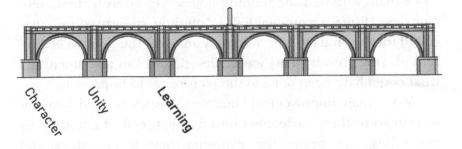

Character · Unity · Learning

> The illiterate of the future are not
> those who cannot read or write.
> They are those who cannot learn,
> unlearn, and relearn.
> —Alvin Toffler

With Christmas just around the corner, a man whom kids all over the world counted on to delight them was busy in his workshop.

On December 23, 1935, Walt Disney was at his desk typing an eight-page memo to Don Graham, who had been brought on board at Walt Disney Productions to turn cartoonists into animators.

Snow White and the Seven Dwarfs was in the early phases of development and already was being labeled "Disney's Folly" because of Walt's ambition to turn this work into the first-ever feature-length animated film. Disney was undaunted by the talk sweeping Tinsel Town, but he recognized that the animation he demanded for *Snow White* required something more, something new. Those who had been drawing Mickey Mouse were now going to be asked to elevate their game. "Some of our established animators," Disney wrote Graham, "are lacking in many things."[1]

To shore up this deficiency, Disney spelled out in great detail to Graham a "systematic training course" to address these deficiencies. Disney recommended a "method of procedure" that called for the animators to "minutely analyze" the "idea to be presented, [the] result [that] was achieved, and [an assessment of] what could have been done to the picture . . . to improve it."[2]

More than improvement, however, Disney wanted Graham to transform these cartoonists into a new breed of animator by expanding their perspective, exposing them to new styles, and teaching them new skills. Graham's pupils would need to unlearn what had brought them to the pinnacle of their career and then learn a whole new way of thinking and drawing. And they would have to do it quickly.

A COMMITMENT
TO LEARNING

Walt Disney's commitment to create a structured program within his studio for his most valuable team of employees is remarkable on two levels: First, Disney sought to bring a disciplined process to creativity. He was "convinced that there is a scientific approach to this business," and he did not want to rest until "we have found out all we can about how to teach these young fellows the business."[3]

Second, the investment Disney made in his teachers, employees, and the films he produced constituted a significant financial bet, particularly when his move to institutionalize learning within his studio coincided with the depths of the Great Depression when nearly 20 percent of Americans were unemployed and the country's industry was climbing out of a deep hole after hitting bottom just two years earlier.[4] Disney mortgaged his home to finance the work of 750 animators who produced the 1 million images that became the film *Snow White*.[5]

It's clear from Walt's memo—from his sense of urgency and insight into the qualities that make a good animator, to his insistence that these techniques be learned and applied by "young and old as well"—that not every animator would make the jump.[6]

Walt Disney was giving animators the tools, the training, and the opportunity to develop the new skills that would be needed as the Golden Age of Animation was dawning. The company was doing its part.

Those on the receiving end of Disney's investment in their learning and development would be held accountable for doing theirs.

GREEN AND GROWING

Halfway across America in Oak Park, Illinois, a young man who had met Walt Disney when they served in the same ambulance-driving regiment during World War I was trying to figure out what he wanted to be when he grew up.

It took him awhile, but, at age 52, Ray Kroc made the best decision of his life when he purchased a small hamburger operation from Dick and Mac McDonald and changed forever the way the world eats. "I was an overnight success all right," Kroc later recalled, "but 30 years is a long, long night."[7]

Three years after founding McDonald's, the company had sold its 100 millionth hamburger, and three years later in 1961, Kroc launched a program he later called Hamburger University, whose sole purpose was to train operators and franchisees "in the scientific methods of running a successful McDonald's." This institution of higher learning boasts more than 80,000 graduates.[8]

Like Disney—and like you—Kroc needed a team to achieve his vision. Kroc envisioned a "restaurant system" stretching from coast to coast and, later, around the world that could churn out burgers, fries, and drinks so consistently they would taste the same in Peoria, Illinois, as in Paris, France. And like Disney, Kroc believed in the power of learning through systematic training for his most promising employees in order to improve individually and organizationally. Learning, training, and development were key ingredients in McDonald's success. "If you aren't green and growing," Kroc often said, "you're ripe and rotting."[9]

Investing time and money in developing your team has always been important to leaders of high-performing companies.

LEARNING BEGINS IN YOUR BACKYARD

Learning continues to be exceedingly important because the pace of change has never been faster; and it will never again be as slow as it is today. Research from the University of Southern California estimates the average person produces the equivalent of six newspaper pages of information every day, compared with one-third that amount 24 years ago.[10]

So it's understandable if you are drowning in the tidal wave of information that's washing ashore in your business. How can you and your team keep up with learning all that you need to know? How do you know what you need to learn to do the job you're supposed to do?

You are wise to look beyond your four walls to learn from changes occurring in the competitive, political, regulatory, cultural, technological, and financial arenas that will make an impact on your business.

But before you look outside your organization, first look inside.

When you do, you likely will find things happening in your organization—under your nose and behind your back—that will surprise you. Learning does not have to be expensive, but not learning can cost you a fortune.

WANT IMPROVEMENT? ASK YOUR EMPLOYEES

Before I conduct a strategic planning session with a company's leadership team, one of the decisions the CEO must make is determining the participants. *Where do we draw the line on who attends and who doesn't?* I'm often asked.

It depends, though the easy answer is that all of the CEO's direct reports must attend. There may be a second level of leaders that should also participate, and the CEO and I discuss that option.

Are there people on your team whose input you'd like but who cannot attend the planning session? I ask. *If so, I'll call them. We'll be learning something from this next tier of employees.*

Here's how it works. The CEO sends an email advising the leaders who will not attend the planning session that I will be calling, and that (a) no preparation is required; (b) everything said during the call is confidential; and (c) the call will take just 15 minutes.

When I call, I ask these four questions:

1. **What's working well at your organization?** I hear what sounds like the company line of "good products," "dependable services," "good people," and "solid financials." No surprise.
2. **What's not working?** Typically, the employees begin to unload . . . to a complete stranger. By the time I've talked

with half the people to be called, I can anticipate with accuracy what I will hear on subsequent calls. What's the learning? First, it's an indication of a pent-up demand among your employees to be asked and to share. Second, it's an indication of issues that are either unknown or underestimated. Third, it could be the indication not of a problem, but of a lack of communication around a particular program, policy, or person. Communication, training, and accountability regularly top the list of what's not working in most companies.

3. **If you were in charge, what decision would you be making?** This question moves the person from complainer to problem solver. Again, I'm looking for patterns of problems or opportunities to address. Frequent feedback is a need for more communication from the CEO about where we're going, how we'll get there, and how we're doing. Another is getting rid of underperformers. (More on that topic is found in Chapters 7 and 9.)

4. **What's one thing the organization can do to make you more effective?** You might be surprised by the suggestions for simple fixes this question prompts. *"Stop making salaried employees punch a time clock! Don't you trust us?"* And *"By having me report to two different people, I'm often working on competing projects with competing deadlines."* And *"Why can't we invest in an admin? For every penny they think they're saving on salary, they're burning a nickel of my time doing work that's not my primary focus."*

A CEO in Toronto told me that going through this process was a waste of time. "I already know what my people think," he told me. "Besides, we can't possibly implement everything that you hear on these calls."

"You're right," I responded, "we can't do it all, but we can pick one or two of the biggest issues we uncover and work on those. Plus, just because you don't ask them doesn't mean they're not thinking about this stuff."

When I completed the calls and made my report, the CEO was surprised to learn that he was not as plugged in as he thought, and we went to work on an issue strangling his organization's effectiveness.

Remember the results of my survey of the 82 leadership teams in Chapter 2? Your position in the organization will give you a biased view of performance. The higher your position, the more optimistic your view of how things are going.

Once you learn the truth—or the perception of the truth—it's your job to eliminate or minimize the obstacles that make it harder for your colleagues to meet your expectations. That's why I tell leaders they are in the barrier removal business.

One more thought on who to invite to your planning session: I advise against inviting board members (though I've done it), because one of the purposes of the session is to build trust. Trust building is accomplished when the team addresses meaty issues, including lack of accountability among peers, and it's often difficult to get these issues on the table among those who work together; it's even harder with outside board members present.

Learning doesn't just come from the top. Nor does it come only from experts conveying information and training to your employees. Learning can and should be bottom to top and side to side, just like accountability in high-performing organizations.

If you don't want to improve, don't ask your people for their feedback. Ignorance may be bliss, but its price can be costly, as the following example illustrates.

WHEN LEARNING IS A SURPRISE

As noted previously, I spend a significant portion of each month serving as a coach, consultant, and confidant to 32 CEOs and 16 key executives who are leading successful organizations in a variety of industries. Once a month, I facilitate a meeting for a group of CEOs in noncompeting businesses who act as a sounding board for each other. They discuss problems and opportunities, question decisions before they're made, and then hold one another accountable to implement the decisions made in the meeting. Between the monthly meetings, I conduct private coaching sessions with these executives to ensure that accountability becomes reality.

At one of these monthly CEO meetings that I lead, the executives had gathered for their regular meeting. The host was given 30 minutes to present his business update. The CEO had told us month after month how great things were going. He'd told me the same thing in our private sessions. Key new talent was being added, he'd told us. Plans to move to a new, larger building were moving forward. An acquisition was pending. Life was grand, or so we were told.

During his presentation, the CEO shared his financials. Imagine our surprise to see that sales were down. Expenses were up. Cash was tight. Yikes!

Was the CEO embarrassed to tell us the truth? What role had I played in not creating a safe space for the CEO to share this information? What questions had I and the other CEOs failed to ask month after month? Or were these problems blind spots for this CEO?

Who knows? It didn't matter. What the CEOs learned was that simply taking a person at his or her word was no longer enough. The surprise learning prompted the CEOs of that group to make a significant decision that day.

FORM A SWAT TEAM

The CEOs of my group—stunned to learn the facts from a peer whose financials showed he would have a terrible year—made the decision that day to minimize future surprises.

Here's the process we use in my two CEO groups, and it's a form of learning you can use in your organization: Before a CEO hosts a meeting, four CEO peers visit the hosting CEO's company. We call this process "a SWAT team visit" (i.e., special weapons and tactics units), not to be confused with a SWOT (strengths, weaknesses, opportunities, and threats).

The SWAT team members meet privately with the CEO's employees without any boss being present. The SWAT team asks questions, compares notes with one another, and, based on what they learn, makes recommendations to the CEO.

When we started the SWAT team visits, the process initially was viewed as the most feared day in the life of the CEOs because they realized that any masquerading on their part was about to come to an end once the SWAT team completed its visit.

Now the process is considered an incredibly valuable day because of the learning everyone—not just the host CEO—receives, and because of the recommendations to capitalize on opportunities and fix problems based on feedback from a group of peers. It's also a huge accountability tool.

You don't have to belong to a Vistage group to gain the benefits of a SWAT team experience. Find four noncompeting business executives you trust and whose only motive is your success. You must be willing to learn the truth, or the perceived truth, of how your colleagues believe you're running your business. If you enjoy those kinds of relationships and you can deploy them on a SWAT team visit, it often prompts invaluable learning.

HIRE FOR VALUES, TRAIN FOR SKILL

The leaders of companies I work with have been inoculated against a deadly disease plaguing many organizations.

The disease is known as *unique-itus*. Leaders can be a carrier of this disease without realizing they're infected.

The chronic symptom is a belief that the technical skills and experience required to contribute to their business are so different, so special, so unique, that only people who have spent years in their industry are the best fit for their organization. With the exception of doctors, lawyers, and scientists, most of the work we're asking our colleagues to do can be taught and learned on the job.

Yet we often hire or promote people largely because of who they used to be. We are mesmerized by their past. So we scrutinize a candidate's résumé, examine past experience and accomplishments, check references as best as we can, and ask candidates to take some type of assessment that largely confirms what we already sensed: That this candidate is a Driver, an Analytic, or some other personality type. We then attempt to project that historical personality and performance into the future. We'd do well to remember the disclaimer wealth management firms use: Past performance is no guarantee of future results.

When things don't work out with the person we hired, it well may be because of underperformance and accountability-related issues.

Just as often, however, people are fired because of who they are. And for this reason, character counts. Character is more than a personality trait; it's a deep-seated set of values. And our values are revealed during times of adversity.

The next time you hire or promote someone, look beyond technical capability and take a closer look at the person's character. Are this person's values and beliefs consistent with ours? A deeper dive may reveal an abusive sales exec, a manager who blames others for problems they helped cause, or a person who is unwilling or unable to talk about tough issues.

These people are unlikely to change their behavior. That's who they really are, and we ignore those characteristics at the peril of our culture and, ultimately, our success.

Your team is one of the best predictors of future performance. Are you evaluating your team based on who they *were* or who they *are*?

Even when you hire great people with values that match your own and who share your enthusiasm for the work, you still need to invest time, money, and patience to help them reach their full potential in your organization. Of the executives I surveyed,

67 percent said, "We view ongoing training as an investment, not an expense," and 74 percent said "We give our employees the tools and training they need to succeed."

Hire for values. Develop skills.

ONBOARDING AT SOUTHWEST

When Southwest Airlines decides you're a good fit for the company, it uses a comprehensive process to ensure new hires understand what it means to be a member of this elite club. The company receives more than 100,000 résumés each year for about 2,000 positions, so the competition is pretty stiff.

Once a person is identified as a good fit for Southwest, they are asked to participate in several different activities to immerse them in the company's culture. "We want to ensure that employees are having a consistent experience whether they're in Los Angeles or Baltimore," says Elizabeth Bryant. So every employee comes to Dallas for a new hire class called Freedom, LUV and You, or FLY, for a full day of learning around the company's history, values, and culture, and to understand what's expected of them.

Employees are asked to view their role not just as a job or even a career but as a cause. "Our employees," says Bryant, "are providing Americans the freedom to go, see, and do when they may not have been able to do that before. We rally them around this cause we have at Southwest Airlines, and we ask them to commit to that."

From there, new employees experience multiple connections with the company, ranging from lunch with senior leaders to a variety of company-wide events and celebrations. "We want to ensure new employees understand what it means to be part of Southwest Airlines," Bryant says.

Many companies throw a small party for an employee's last day on the job. What changes would occur—in commitment, in culture, in performance—if you threw a party on a new employee's first day?

RNDC'S THIRST FOR TALENT

Republic National Distributing Company (RNDC) is one of the biggest companies most people have never heard of. Yet most of us consume what they sell.

At $6.5 billion in annual sales and 7,900 employees, RNDC is the second largest premium wine and spirits distributor in the United States with wholly owned operations in 22 states and the District of Columbia; it's the thirteenth largest company in the world based on alcohol revenue.[11]

Bob Hendrickson is RNDC's executive vice president of operations in the Americas, and like other leaders I spoke with, Hendrickson has made a successful career for himself in a company he "fell in love with" shortly after graduating from college.

"By the time I'd graduated from college," Hendrickson told me, "I already had some of the best training for the industry I chose.

"I was in a fraternity," he jokes.

Hendrickson was recruited by Gallo in Los Angeles as part of its college training program and spent about three-and-a-half years with Gallo. Gallo placed Hendrickson in one of their distributors that became part of RNDC with the idea that he would work in this Dallas distributor for a two-year assignment and then return to California to continue his employment with Gallo. "So 29 years later," says Hendrickson, "I'm still waiting for that phone call."

Hendrickson has been one of the driving forces behind RNDC's growth. His early focus was on sales and he still spends 70 percent of his time on the road, but as his responsibility grew he made talent development a priority.

Of RNDC's 7,900 employees, about 65 percent are in sales, with associates in operations and administration comprising the other 35 percent. About 45 percent of RNDC's employees are Gen Xers, about 28 percent are baby boomers, and about 27 percent are Millennials. Identifying, attracting, developing, and retaining talent, especially among the Millennials, is an essential component of RNDC's success.

RNDC recruits most of its talent at the college level, talking with deans of business schools and recruiting on campus. RNDC brings the best candidates to Dallas for a day of extensive interviews then sends them out in the field so they understand what their job is going to be.

"When I joined in 1986," says Hendrickson, "I remember hitting $100 million in sales and thought, 'We've hit the big time,' and now we're over $6 billion. Our average annual revenue growth the last five years is nearly 15 percent, and we bring on board about 100 new employees every year. So our thirst for talent is never-ending."

RNDC's approach to learning and development reached a new level of focus in May 2007 when National Distributing Co. (NDC) and Republic Beverage Co. (RBC) merged to create RNDC. The two companies had enjoyed considerable success on their own, but their respective leaders understood that consolidation was the name of the game in the beverage industry, and they wanted to lead the field, not fall behind.

The two companies shared similar values and similar operating cultures, and these similarities have been the foundation of the merged company's continued success. This merger of equals resulted in a rare blend of a family-owned company whose owners are actively involved in the business that's managed by outside executives like Hendrickson who were the key players in the two legacy businesses. RNDC's operating approach is markedly different from other companies in the alcohol beverage industry: RNDC's leaders effectively created a culture, structure, and operating system that look and act more like a public company while retaining the values and strength of a family-owned business.

INVESTING IN TALENT

Lorraine Luke joined RNDC as the company's vice president of human resources 16 months before the NDC and RBC merger, bringing considerable training and development experience from her 20 years working at YUM Brands, parent company of KFC,

Pizza Hut, and Taco Bell. Once the merger was completed, Luke and her team worked with RNDC's senior executives to assimilate the two companies' compensation and benefits program, then developed a long-range plan to address recruiting, retention, and development.

Hendrickson, Luke, and other RNDC executives made two significant talent-related commitments. First, RNDC enhanced its process to identify and bring on board top talent effectively and efficiently. Second, the company committed to developing its people so that they're three or four people deep in every key position.

"We were doing a pretty good job in both areas, but we knew we had to get better," says Hendrickson. "For example, we expect Texas to push past $2 billion in sales. Texas is a great model of a deep talent pool where we focus purposefully on the professional development of our associates. It's important they understand what it means to be part of the RNDC culture, from job expectations to standards of operations and best practices. As a result, Texas has become a strong exporter of top talent, bringing best practices to other markets."

Although these two priorities of onboarding and development were clear to RNDC's leaders, implementing the changes was a two-year process.

As leaders analyzed turnover metrics, they saw that most of the turnover occurred in the "backside of the house" versus the "front side of the house" and it was occurring within the first 90 days on the job.

"We expected this to be the case," says Lorraine Luke, "because we have night crew, day crew, and merchandisers, and those jobs require physical work. A lot of these are entry-level positions, non-college requirements, and so these people can go across the street and work for similar wages. But that turnover is disruptive, wasteful, and not good for our reputation, so we worked to compress the onboarding experience from six months to 90 days through more structured training, heavy involvement of the manager, and a lot of follow-up."

The most significant new piece added to the onboarding process was assigning a mentor to new hires. The mentor is generally outside the new hire's scope of responsibility so the new hire can talk to this mentor without any repercussions in terms of the chain of command. RNDC also provided more communication and coaching around a new hire's development path.

"The quicker we can get new hires on board," says Hendrickson, "the quicker we can help them understand what it takes to be successful with us and show that we are taking responsibility for training them, the better it is for us and for those who choose to stay."

Development is evaluated as an investment, not an expense. "If there's a training need," says Hendrickson, "for the most part it's not a question of finance, it's a question of *Do we need to do it? How is that training going to help our organization?* If those two questions are answered positively, then we proceed. If we start viewing our talent development as a financial issue then we are going backwards."

Just as accountability is a two-way street—*Can I count on you? Can you count on me?*—so, too, is learning. What's good for the employee is usually good for the company.

Successful companies understand they can learn from their employees, so they survey their workforce to learn how employees feel about the company, to measure employee engagement, and to assess whether the company's training, development, and communication initiatives are working.

RNDC's internal survey shows that "92.7% rated their overall satisfaction with RNDC as good," and "97.4% of associates were motivated on the success of RNDC."[12]

CAREER DEVELOPMENT AT RNDC

As part of RNDC's focus on improving employee retention, a renewed emphasis was placed on career development.

The company learned through exit interviews that some people were leaving because they didn't know what lay ahead for them, so Luke developed a program where managers nominated their associates to participate in an extensive career development program.

"You don't really punch a clock around here, so you really have to like what you do," says Hendrickson. "If that passion shows up in their performance, an associate will be presented to the management team and be given the chance to participate in our formal succession planning program."

Managers present their top talent in person and then the management team is excused so executives can discuss who will be selected as bench players for key roles. "It's not a slam-dunk to get into this program," says Hendrickson, "although the success rate is close to 90 percent of associates we identify as 'top talent' moving their career forward two or more positions within five years." The talent review continues with presentations by district managers, area managers, division managers, VPs, and EVPs who are each presenting to the senior leadership team. "It's a great day for us," says Hendrickson, "because we know where our talent is, and—just as important—our associates know where they stand."

Strengths are praised and weaknesses are coached, so when a promotion becomes available, these up-and-comers are well positioned to interview for that job.

RNDC's career development process also means leaders had to learn how to have difficult conversations about an employee's ability to learn and perform. Fact-based conversations minimize the emotional component of the feedback process. "This process," says Hendrickson, "has given us a venue to sit down with an employee and say, 'Here is what you're doing well, and here's what you need to do to improve.' At first, our managers were scared to have that conversation. It's human nature not to want to have that conversation. But you have to have those conversations so that your people have a clear understanding of their path with us."

Most RNDC managers believed they would lose people by having honest conversations with them about their performance. "The reality," says Hendrickson, "is that we didn't lose anybody because, if anything, the people who needed to improve appreciated the fact that they knew where they stood."

"Not everybody wants to move forward in their career," says Lorraine Luke. "A lot of people are happy with what they're doing, and we're glad to learn that about them because it helps us in our decision making. On the other side of that coin, we have an 85 to 90 percent promote-from-within rate, which is tremendous."

ADVICE FROM STANLEY MARCUS

The Container Store's culture determines how it hires, who it hires, and how it develops people. "We'll hold out forever to hire the right person," says Kip Tindell. "It's not easy, but it can be done—even in retail. You must first believe that it's possible. I've found most people have truly given up on that notion. You can hire great people, but it takes astronomically higher levels of HR resources to attract, recruit, hire, train, and retain great people.

"We put our money where our mouth is, so we pay 50 to 100 percent more than most in the retail category," he says. "How can you afford not to do that if you're hiring winners? We commit to a 10 percent-per-store payroll versus 3 percent industry average. We don't take economy of scale on wages; we look for savings in other areas. Everybody wants to see you win. We treat our vendors just like we treat our employees. They love us. And we get the best price in the country. We buy stuff cheaper than mass merchants even though we buy 5 percent of the volume that they do, but we have a much better relationship than those big retailers do. You can't beat them on volume so let's beat them on relationship. That's easier."

To get this winning performance, Tindell says, "we invest in training and training and more training."

Stanley Marcus was the CEO of luxury retailer Neiman-Marcus, the store his parents founded. "He was my hero," says Tindell, who scheduled several visits with the legendary retailer.

"He once said to me, 'You have the best people in the business. How do you do it?' So I told him about our training, and he listened in his gentlemanly way and then said, 'Mr. Tindell, you train bears and seals, you educate people.' With apologies to Stanley Marcus, we still call it training, but I learned a lot from our conversations because he's right: it's about educating people and arming them to the fullest."

Tindell recalls the story of Albert Einstein sitting on a train and watching a parallel track as another train was pulling away. It appeared the other train's wheels were spinning backward. Einstein immediately conceived the theory of relativity. His mind was prepared for that flash of intuition.

"Intuition," says Tindell, "does not come to an unprepared mind. You must train to make it happen. Intuition is the sum total of one's life's experience. Yet we're taught that intuition has no place in business—just logic. Why would you leave intuition at home when you come to work?

"You can't imagine how hard it is to get an employee to leverage that intuition," Tindell continues. "The key to high-performing, problem-solving employees is preparing them to use their intuition, not training them to act."

It's cliché for companies to say "our employees are our greatest asset." Companies invest millions of dollars in equipment then skimp on salaries and shortchange people when it comes to their development. High-performing companies believe that great people are hungry for learning, so they feed that hunger.

"Every first-year employee receives about 263 hours of training versus eight hours that most retailers provide, and most of that is video training," says The Container Store's Casey Shilling. "We provide video training and web-based training. But most of our training is eyeball-to-eyeball because you're having conversations with your employee, and you can gauge if they're getting it. So we establish expectations for accountability, and then we circle back with employees to make sure they're applying what we've taught them." The company has full-time sales trainers in each store and provides ongoing training not just on product and operations, but also on its Foundation Principles, Conscious Capitalism, and leadership.

"A lot of people don't take the time to train the way we train because it costs SG&A [selling, general, and administrative] dollars," Shilling continues. "The Container Store's SG&A budget is probably about 48 percent of our sales, and that's really high. But we believe that when you communicate, you train, and you make sure that you've got a high-performance culture, people want to stay here. Obviously that training pays off when you're not having to hire people over and over again. That's core to our business."

OMNICOM UNIVERSITY

Learning takes many forms at high-performing companies.

Learning is not limited to training, though training is certainly a big component. Talent development includes workshops to help employees improve their specialized skills and can be conducted by outside consultants and specialists as well as by internal subject matter experts (SMEs). Remember, the so-called theoretical driver described in Chapter 5? These individuals, who may be on your team, are fulfilled by the opportunity to continually learn and then share their learning by leading workshops for their colleagues. By tapping in to the talent of your own people, you are honoring them as they help their colleagues learn and develop.

My wife, Janet, led the Dallas office of DDB Worldwide, the international advertising agency whose longtime client is McDonald's. The best companies can learn from anyone, and DDB's holding company, Omnicom, followed McDonald's lead by establishing Omnicom University in 1995. Janet attended Omnicom University in Boston with other agency leaders from around the world where case studies and courses on leadership and other subjects were taught by professors from Harvard as well as by other well-regarded instructors. A lot of the learning occurred outside the classes. Janet brought what she learned back to the Dallas office and shared it with her colleagues.

Your organization can provide funding to allow employees to become certified or receive continuing education credits in finance-, engineering-, technology-, and legal-related courses, or to pursue a postgraduate degree.

Learning can include forming cross-functional teams from different departments or business units to attack inefficiencies and to brainstorm ideas for new products and services based on observations and feedback from customers. Or to streamline workflow and minimize inefficiencies to improve time-to-market execution, reduce waste, and boost profits.

More than anything, learning is an attitude and it's a way of thwarting complacency, attacking problems, and spurring intellectual, skill-based, and, ultimately, financial growth.

"One of the best tests of an organization, particularly in a challenging economy, is how it invests in its people," says Ernst & Young's David Alexander. "Are you really, truly committed to your people? I don't think you can hold yourself out as having that commitment unless you sustain training over time, especially in challenging times. Sure, there's some things that you can do to help slow down the spending in training in challenging economic times, but if your people sense that you really don't have that commitment, and the only time that you're willing to spend on training programs for your people are during the good economic times, then they will quickly sense that and realize that you're not committed to their continued development throughout their career."

EMPLOYEES OWN THEIR CAREER

Leaders of high-performing companies share an expectation that the company will do its part to provide training, tools, and development opportunities, and the employees will do their part.

"Accountability," says Nucor's Ray Napolitan, "starts with a personal commitment to do what you say you're going to do, when you said you'd do it. It's also about continual improvement, continuing learning, and focusing on results, not just activities. We provide tools and training, and it's the teammates' obligation to also develop tools and help train themselves. This allows us to set common and clear expectations and then require accountability for getting great results. So, that's the model. One of our goals as leaders is to help our people succeed."

"When we hire somebody," says Southwest Airlines' Elizabeth Bryant, "we want them to grow with this company. So we've got to invest in them and provide them with development opportunities throughout their career at Southwest.

"We also send a pretty strong message to employees that they own their career. As an employee of Southwest Airlines, if I want to grow within this organization, what's my responsibility around that? So instead of waiting for a leader to approach me about an assignment, what can I do to get involved? What classes can I take? What mentor can I seek out to help me develop this skill? Let me focus on my individual development plan, and sit down with my leader and talk about my short- and long-term goals and come up with a plan together on how I might be able to get there."

Talented employees want to grow, and that doesn't always translate into a promotion. Growth can be a stretch assignment, an opportunity to learn something new, an opportunity to work on an assignment with a person outside of their daily work environment. Growth can mean participating in an outside learning seminar or spending a day with another employee in the office to better understand that side of the business. Or reading a book and sharing the learning with others. Numerous ways can help you keep your people "green and growing."

"My response to a leader—regardless of company size—who says a career path is just not feasible," says Elizabeth Bryant, "is 'Plan on having a robust recruiting arm, because you're going to lose those employees.' It's the responsibility of the leader to provide an environment for learning, and it's the responsibility of the employee to seek out those opportunities for learning and growth."

Like everything else in the accountability equation, the responsibility for learning is shared equally.

LEARNING AT ERNST & YOUNG

Long before David Alexander became a vice chair of Ernst & Young, overseeing a 10-state region with approximately 250 partners and another 3,000 employees, he was a client-serving accountant in the firm.

Accounting requires a lot of technical expertise and the firm has training programs to help people achieve that goal. Yet Alexander watched some people get so removed from the academic side of the profession by serving clients that they didn't take the time to study and pass the rigorous CPA exam. "You can't go anywhere in public accounting without that certification," Alexander told me, "and you can be told 100 times that you need to pass the CPA exam, but it's up to you to prepare for it, take it, and pass it. I quickly realized that unless I passed my CPA exam it would be a short career, so getting my certificate was goal number one for me coming out of college."

Every professional services firm has a career path. In Alexander's case, after passing the CPA exam, the next step on that path—and it was a long next step—was eight years of 60- to 70-hour weeks serving clients in the firm's Lexington, Kentucky, office, topped off by 40 hours a year of mandatory continuing education.

Even with this workload, Alexander made two critical decisions that required additional investments of his time. Those decisions helped his development, and they also propelled his career to the top of Ernst & Young.

TWO CRITICAL DECISIONS

When you're working long hours, the last thing on your mind might be deciding to volunteer for activities that require even more of your time. But volunteer he did. "A lot of people were so exhausted by their client commitments that they didn't have anything left in the tank," Alexander says. "I was always the first to raise my hand for community activity. I thought volunteering and giving back was the right thing for the firm, and I also thought it was a good way to demonstrate leadership." Alexander volunteered for United Way responsibilities, recruiting activities, and anything else that didn't require a partner's presence. "A lot of it was grunt work," Alexander recalls, "but after a while, the partners started noticing what I was doing and I took on even more responsibility."

Alexander next was asked to move to EY's national office for a three-year assignment. He served as a consultant to all of the EY offices that relied on Alexander for research and advice on complex accounting matters and disclosure issues. "I later realized," says Alexander, "that I was being groomed for a regional director position."

Taking on responsibility was starting to pay off.

Alexander's second critical decision was seeking out mentors. "I've always been a big fan of mentoring programs, but I think that some of the most effective mentoring happens informally, by gravitating toward people you admire and respect. That's one thing I always tell our people: 'Seek out mentors.'"

It was Alexander's early mentors—first, Bob Lee in Lexington, and then Bob Guido in the national office—who helped prepare him for the tough journey and the tough people decisions he would need to make as he continued moving up the firm's ladder where, increasingly, he was charged with holding people accountable.

While in the national office Alexander was named a partner in the firm and was asked to move again, this time to Nashville where he was named partner-in-charge of the national office's Entrepreneurial Services group.

It was in Nashville that Alexander reached the lowest point in his career from a work-family balance standpoint. He was still working 60 to 70 hours a week in a stressful work environment with constant regulatory deadlines and difficult client demands, and this schedule was hampering his role as husband and father.

"I was working for a managing partner who was difficult and someone that I didn't respect personally or professionally," Alexander says. "I found it ironic because I believed I could make a positive influence in peoples' lives, plus I'd worked so hard for so long to achieve my dream of becoming a partner at EY. Now I was so discouraged that I considered leaving not just the firm but the profession. Thankfully, I had another mentor in Nashville, Bob Whelan, who was a steadying influence and urged me not to make a decision that I would later regret."

A Saturday morning phone call from Ray Eanes, the Southeast managing partner in Atlanta, changed Alexander's career—and life.

The long hours, quality work, and an attitude of placing the firm first resulted in Alexander being offered a position as the firm's Southeast regional director of human resources, reporting directly to the firm's vice chair. Not only did this opportunity allow Alexander to exit Nashville gracefully, it meant he could begin putting his stamp on the firm's people policies and procedures, which is where his career interests lay.

THE LEADERSHIP REVOLUTION

It's natural for a global professional services firm to claim talent development as a priority. In Ernst & Young's case, the firm's commitment to learning has been validated regularly by *Training* magazine, where EY is in the Hall of Fame, and by MAKE (Most

Admired Knowledge Enterprise), whose global MAKE panel has named Ernst & Young for 14 consecutive years as one of the world's top learning organizations. Should learning be viewed as a necessary expense or a great investment? What's the payoff? Although Ernst & Young is a private firm, its NYSE-traded peers—also recognized along with EY as 2012 Global MAKE Winners—delivered impressive results:

- For the 10-year period 2002–2011, total return to shareholders (TRS) was 19.7 percent, nearly three times the average Fortune 500 company median.
- Return on revenues (ROR) was 12 percent, 3.2 times that of the Fortune 500 ROR median.
- Return on assets (ROA) was 9.9 percent, nearly four times that of the Fortune 500 ROA median.[13]

"We all know about the Industrial Revolution," says Alexander. "In the mid-1980s, we started going through what we began calling a 'Leadership Revolution.' We realized that there were a lot of requisite leadership skills that partners weren't fully equipped to handle. For example, how do you go from being a client-serving technical partner to a leader of a practice? At the time, we didn't have any formal leadership development training. Back in those days, the firm would say, 'You're going to be the managing partner. Good luck.'"

Alexander needed more than luck when he was named regional managing partner of the firm's Southwest region in 1993. He inherited a region fueled by energy, technology, and real estate and those industries faced huge challenges, which had a negative impact on the firm's Southwest operations. Even worse, Alexander's predecessor had abdicated some of the tough decisions, costing the predecessor his job.

Upon being named to his new role, Alexander made the difficult decision that the Southwest practice was overstaffed by 10 partners and 100 staff members. "I lost a lot of sleep over that decision to let so many people go," says Alexander, "and it affected my personality because I knew whatever decision I made was going to impact not only their career but also their families' lives. It was an ugly situation. I had hoped to be on an early 'honeymoon' with my new partners. There wasn't anything else to be done but make the cuts, so everybody was scared of me. And that just wasn't my style."

Alexander needed to rebuild trust, so he asked a senior partner for feedback after he'd given the partner his review. "I asked, 'What do you think I could do better?' And he said, 'You know, David, you could focus more on ministering to the partners.' I said, 'What are you talking about?' And he said, 'Get to know them, get to know their families. Get to know their issues, their challenges, their stresses. Figure out how you can help them bring the whole person to the workplace.'"

That candid conversation helped David Alexander realize that it was now time to develop a more systematic approach to applying the lessons he'd learned over the years from his mentors.

FIVE LIFE LESSONS

David Alexander brought in Charlie Baker, a former ordained minister, and together they began to change the culture of the firm's Southwest region.

They started with a new leadership development program with a fitness module and paid a trainer to work with five partners on a trial basis. Other modules were offered and included nutrition and work-family balance. At the core of this leadership development program was the desire to build trust so that meaningful conversations about challenging issues could occur.

"Initially I got some strange looks from my partners," Alexander says, "and they started thinking that maybe Charlie was my spy, but I said, 'No, Charlie doesn't report back to me on any of his conversations. It will be more effective if those conversations are treated as confidential.' The partners didn't trust Charlie at first, but pretty soon they were telling him their life story."

Alexander also realized the firm was losing some talented partners because spouses didn't fully understand what their spouse was experiencing at the firm. Next up: Baker began talking with spouses. "That was sort of out-of-the-box," says Alexander, "and, after a while, people could see that we really did care. When I became regional managing partner, I instinctively began putting into action things that would rebuild trust and confidence. I decided that there were a lot more things that I was interested in and that we would measure other than technical capabilities and the operations of the firm."

The pilot program worked so well that the program ultimately was offered to the entire partner group over a period of years.

David Alexander's character—reinforced by his mentors—shaped the learning and development programs he initiated as he continued to live out and teach others by example:

1. **The principle of influence.** "When I taught training courses for the firm," Alexander says, "I would tell our people, 'The firm needs you to be a leader from day one.' And they'd say, 'We can't be a leader, we're not in charge.' And I would say 'Not everyone can be *the* leader, but everyone can be *a* leader.' Your influence affects others to the degree that you place their interests first."

2. **The principle of others.** "I watched my first mentor as we would attend events, and he would call everyone by their first name. I said, 'Bob, how do you do that?' He said, 'Before every event I attend I make it a point to get the attendance list, and I study it, and I've trained myself to have name/face recognition.' Every person you meet is worthy of your best."

3. **The principle of vision.** "Always help others see the promise of a better tomorrow. I had a different explanation of my CEO title. I always told my partners it didn't stand for chief

executive officer, but rather chief encouragement officer. They liked that."

4. **The principle of positivity.** "My mother contracted a severe case of polio when she was eight months pregnant with me, and she wasn't expected to live. She became paralyzed. Despite her physical handicap, she never had a bad day. She was always positive, and she never said 'Why me?' When life presents roadblocks—and I've had my share—I would think about her. As a leader, it's up to you to stay positive so you can encourage your colleagues."

5. **The principle of mission.** "Live a life with integrity and with an emphasis on relationships. There's a saying that 'People don't care how much you know until they know how much you care.' No matter what business you're in, when you care for people and build relationships, when you have something to say, they will listen."

Three years after being promoted to regional managing partner and right-sizing the practice, Alexander fully gained the trust of his colleagues. His next career milestone included being named America's Managing Partner of Regional Practices. He next was asked to join EY's board as a vice chair of the firm.

The leadership lessons that David Alexander learned from his mentors transcended the technical training Ernst & Young provided to help develop great CPAs. As a result, the firm began to focus increasingly more time and money on helping its employees become better leaders, and, ultimately, more fulfilled human beings. Not surprisingly, the firm's performance also soared.

WATCH, LISTEN, AND LEARN

"On one of my first client meetings with my mentor," says Alexander, "I asked, 'What role do you want me to play in this meeting, Bob?' And he said, 'I don't want you to play a role. I want you to watch and listen and learn.' So I would watch and listen and learn, and I might interject a comment or answer a question. I learned how to ask the right questions, and I learned how to interact with people. This is a skill, an art, really, that is lost on many people because those are soft skills, and there's a tendency to lean on technology rather than conduct business face-to-face."

Because talent is a key predictor of future performance, reexamine the time, money, and energy you are investing in your single greatest asset: your people.

Not all employees are good managers. And not all managers are good leaders.

When times are good, effective managers keep the machine—your business—running smoothly, cranking out products or services on time and on budget. When times are tough, a person's character and competence are revealed. The worst global recession in 80 years tested seasoned and new managers alike. As tough times continued, some managers were expected to do something for which they were unprepared. They were expected to lead.

In talking with EY associates, what I hear repeatedly is a marked difference in how work gets done at EY versus other firms. At other firms, hierarchy is important so supervisors tell associates what to do and the associates do it. The EY culture is one of showing people what to do, giving them the responsibility to execute, and then holding them accountable.

If you want to grow your business, you must grow your people. And the gap you and they are facing often is not a skill gap. It's a leadership gap. Lieutenants who are smart enough and skilled enough often lack vision, confidence, interpersonal dexterity, and judgment. The gap must be closed as you move from Point A to Point B.

ACCOUNTABILITY INSIGHT

- Top performers want to improve; ask "What's working?," "What's not?," and "How can I help?"

- Learning does not need to be expensive; not learning can cost you a fortune.
- Employees own their careers; mentors help.

TAKE A FRESH LOOK

Reexamine your score from the Learning Pillar of the assessment, and then consider these questions:

- To what extent do our employees demonstrate a natural curiosity? A desire to learn, improve, and increase their value to our organization?
- What's our plan for developing talent? Are we preparing the path for our colleagues, or preparing our colleagues for the path?
- With what regularity do we ask our employees what they need to be more effective? If leaders are in the barrier removal business, when was the last time leaders asked their colleagues about the barriers standing in their way and then removed those barriers to help colleagues meet the expectations set for them?
- Do our employees understand that we will give them the environment, the tools, training, and opportunity to be successful, but that it's up to them to own their careers? What's our approach to mentoring our employees?
- What has been our most effective approach to attracting, training, engaging, and retaining people?
- What are we doing to encourage the best ideas from the most people? Do our people feel challenged? Are they having fun? Are they growing? Are they fulfilled?
- As I think about my direct reports, how would I rate their effectiveness for the last month? The last quarter? What can I do to help them increase their effectiveness?
- What's the product of our management team?
- How do we determine the qualifications for the talent we'll need in the future? What's the basis of being a great colleague in our organization?
- How do we produce leaders? What's our process for battle-testing leaders before they go into battle?

Stanley Marcus told Kip Tindell that training was for bears and seals. David Alexander recognized the need to develop leaders, not just accountants. Whether you call it training, development, or learning, on-the-job education involves people and that makes it difficult.

Roger Enrico was the brand manager who helped introduce Frito-Lay's Doritos chips to the world, and he eventually became the CEO of Frito-Lay's parent company, PepsiCo. "The soft stuff," he noted, "is the hard stuff."

7

WHAT YOUR BEST EMPLOYEES WANT

Tracking

We have reliable, established systems to measure
the things that are most important to us.

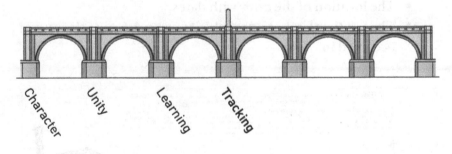

Character   Unity   Learning   Tracking

Facts do not cease to exist
because they are ignored.
—Aldous Huxley

It has been called "the best statistical graphic ever drawn"[1] depicting one of "the most lethal military operations in world history."[2]

"It" is a chart, or, more precisely, a flow map.

The subject is Napoleon's disastrous invasion of Russia of 1812, known in Russia as "The Patriotic War of 1812," and commemorated by Tchaikovsky's "1812 Overture" and by Tolstoy's *War and Peace.*

This flow map was conceived and designed by French civil engineer Charles Joseph Minard and published in 1869. Known as *Carte figurative des pertes successives en hommes de l'Armée Française dans la campagne de Russie 1812–1813*, the chart, said photography pioneer Étienne-Jules Marey, "defies the pen of the historian in its brutal eloquence." With one image, the graphic indicates:

- The size of Napoleon's army
- The geographical coordinates of the army
- The direction of movement, both as it advanced and then in retreat
- The location of the army with dates
- The weather temperature, which was key because the retreat occurred in winter

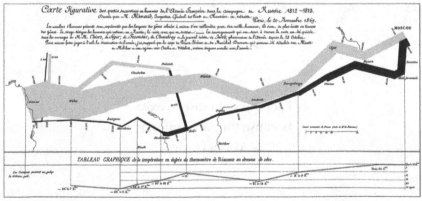

Source: http:en.wikipedia.org/wiki/File:Minard.png

Figure 7.1 Charles Joseph Minard's Flow Map of Napoleon's Russian Campaign

Accounts differ on whether Napoleon was leading as many as 600,000 men or as few as 350,000 men, though most historians place the number at about 450,000 men and Minard's flow chart indicates 422,000 men. All experts agree that the number represents one of the largest armies ever assembled for a wartime campaign.

Napoleon finished his disastrous six-month Russian campaign with 10,000 men.

He had fought two skirmishes and one major battle at Borodino and captured an abandoned Moscow. He lost 10 times more men to disease, desertion, suicide, and starvation than he did to the Russians. Napoleon also lost his dream to rule the world, and 14 months later he was exiled to Elba.

Like many leaders, Napoleon was defeated in the end not by his competition, in this case an opposing army, but by his own hubris. "Those who failed to oppose me . . . who readily agreed with me and accepted all my views," Napoleon once said, "were those who did me the most injury." If Napoleon really practiced what he preached, what accounts for the staggering loss of men, reputation, and power?

The map of Napoleon's Russian campaign prompts these questions:

- Who *inside* the organization holds the organization's top leader accountable for his or her performance?
- What indicators will we track? What indicators are less meaningful?
- How will we communicate performance?

Napoleon marched to Moscow, and you are crossing a bridge to reach Point B. Save the spreadsheets for the financial guys and make sure the information you share with your troops is something they understand, care about, and can influence.

Would Napoleon have made different decisions if he had considered the weather, the condition of his troops, and the impact on morale of invading an empty city?

COMMUNICATION: THE SECRET INGREDIENT

Each of the Seven Pillars is of equal importance, and each pillar shares one feature that—if absent, abused, or weakened—will cause every pillar to crumble and your bridge to collapse. Don't look now, but you and your team are halfway across the bridge over a deep river.

Ancient Roman engineers built their bridges to last. Their bridges were well-designed and well-built, and volcanic ash was a key ingredient that, when added to their version of concrete, produced a durability that could withstand decay. Modern engineers reinforce their concrete with steel rebar. For our purpose, an organization's cultural equivalent of volcanic ash and steel rebar is communication.

The Unity Pillar and Tracking Pillar are linked by benefit of what each communicates about accountability to your employees.

Recall the key components of the Unity Pillar are:

- Deciding how much information to share
- Ensuring that everyone knows what's expected of them
- Aligning rewards and penalties with performance

Human beings crave communication. We want it as affirmation, information, instruction, and entertainment. "We think that just about anything can be solved with communication," says The Container Store's Kip Tindell.

With the right people, this belief is true. With the wrong people, communication can be used as a delaying tactic when a commitment is not honored. Excuses comprise the language of losers. When you tolerate excuses, you may find yourself in deep water struggling to hold people accountable.

The key components of the Tracking Pillar are:

- Deciding what performance indicators to track and what increments to use
- Ensuring that what's being tracked is shared widely and connects with your employees intellectually, operationally, emotionally, and financially
- Making the tracking timely, accurate, consistent, and visible

The key to *what* and *how* you track is making certain your employees understand *why* you're tracking performance. If you use tracking as a stick that's wielded to drive performance, you are a fool with a tool. If, however, you believe—and, just as important, your employees believe—tracking helps people make better decisions, improve performance, and celebrate milestones, then tracking will be an essential component in your quest to drive accountability at every level of your organization.

Tracking performance and making this information visible throughout the organization are crucial for driving high performance because they provide the feedback mechanism that enables leaders to remove much of the subjectivity, emotion, and excuses associated with underperformance. Although extenuating circumstances occur in even the best organizations, they are rare.

Tracking performance allows the facts to speak for themselves and do the heavy lifting of holding people accountable.

FLYING BLIND

You and your team have achieved your current level of success because you know what matters, you keep your eye on it, and you do your best to deliver it.

More times than not, what matters most is sales, or revenue or profits, and for some, safety, units shipped (a form of revenue), and billable hours (another form of revenue) make the list. These items are appropriate, and it is appropriate that performance in these areas is tracked closely.

Of the executives I surveyed, 63 percent "strongly agreed" or "agreed" that "we have systems to measure the things that are important to us," and 66 percent said "we base decisions on logical, factual information, and not on emotion."

But what is being measured?

Tracking sales or profit indicators alone won't tell you the entire story as Peter Schutz discovered at Porsche. And the survey numbers for tracking drop when other key tracking-related questions are asked. Even though 61 percent of the executives said "we align individual objectives with company objectives," only 51 percent said "everyone knows what's expected of them"—a 10 percent gap. Only 43 percent of the executives "we have a system in place for gathering customer feedback"; only 42 percent "share progress against key performance indicators (KPIs) with all employees"; and only 33 percent said they "review individual performance with every employee in writing at least two times per year."

These numbers indicate that as few as one-third and, at best, half of employees at these successful organizations know what's expected of them and how they're doing against those expectations. Do your employees know the measures being used to hold them accountable?

Running a business without tracking nonfinancial indicators, without gathering data directly from your customers, or without providing performance feedback with your employees is like piloting an airplane from the aft galley without any gauges to help you. You're flying blind.

The CEO of a successful engineering firm completed the accountability assessment, and when I reviewed his results I was surprised to see that his Tracking scores were lower than I expected so I asked him how an engineer who loves data could have such low scores. "We track a number of things," he told me "such as safety, our sales pipeline, job status, and profits. But the assessment asked about tracking customer satisfaction, and we don't do it systematically, so I gave us a 1. It asked about tracking employee satisfaction, and we don't do it beyond informal conversations, so I gave us a 1. It asked about sharing company data with all employees, and we don't do it frequently or consistently, so I gave us a 2. Pretty soon, you end up with a low score. The good news is we're now tracking those things, and it's helped our morale, our productivity, and our performance."

I find plenty of opportunities for leaders to enhance tracking, and these enhancements lead to more productive (and happier) employees, less workplace drama, and, ultimately, to improved overall performance.

The use of the word *tracking* is deliberate. Yes, the "T" in tracking helps spell "CULTURE" in the Seven Pillars of Accountability, but more important, *tracking* provides a broader term for gauging performance.

NOT EVERYTHING CAN BE COUNTED

Your first decision about tracking performance is determining what to track.

"I regularly remind myself," say Nucor's Ray Napolitan, "of the quote, 'Not everything that can be counted counts, and not everything that counts can be counted.'

"So while we track lots of information, we don't want to get hung up too much on metrics because we can measure some things quantifiably and some things not so much."

Does the personal development of your employees matter? How do you track it? What about other intangibles such as employee engagement, morale, and pride?

"People want to be a part of something successful, something big," says Napolitan. "Consider a welder, for instance, and he or she understands that what they do really does make a difference. If that welder makes a mistake—it could hurt or kill someone—and that's making a difference in a negative way. And when they see that they play a role in providing roof structures and floor structures, that's a positive difference. How does their work fit into a project so that it's not just a product on a welding table? It's our job as leaders to connect that. We explain 'the why.' Taking time to help people understand why we do what we do and track what we track is hard work. But it's fun."

Sales, revenue, and profitability indicators are important for any company. High-performing companies track sales, they share those numbers enterprise-wide, and they watch other indicators to gauge the mood of the troops.

The Container Store provides sales information every day to every employee, posting daily reports company-wide. The company owns the elfa manufacturing business in Sweden, which accounts for about 24 percent of annual sales, so sales of that best-selling product are measured every day. Turnover, sales per payroll hour, and conversion rates also are tracked.

Having fun is a big part of The Container Store's success. "We also watch things that aren't on a spreadsheet," says Casey Shilling. "We call it the fun-o-meter. Walking around and having conversations with people measures a lot. You can tell a lot about an organization by how people are feeling when you sit down with them, have an open door policy, and look people in the eye."

THE ORGANIZATION'S SOUL

What "soft indicators" are you currently not factoring into what you are tracking? Consider this exercise to help you think about your organization as a person. When you track activities, behaviors, and outcomes as though these things are part of a body, you may discover new performance measures to track that resonate with your employees.

You may be able to quantify the soul of your organization.

Use the "Soul Man" model to approach tracking from a fresh perspective, which will help you rethink what you are tracking, how it connects to the work being done, and how—if at all—you are making that behavior visible. Here are four "soft indicators" we have already examined and assigned a place on the "Soul Man."

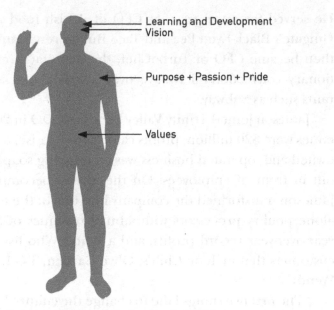

Figure 7.2 The Organization's Soul: Overlooked KPIs

- **Purpose.** Do you and your employees have the heart for the work you are doing?
- **Values.** What feeling do you get in the pit of your stomach about a particular person or situation?
- **Vision.** Can everyone see where we're going and how we're doing?
- **Learning.** What is our organizational IQ?

Compare your thinking to the version in the Appendix, page 274.

All organizations are living organisms. All companies have souls. Your company and its culture are a reflection of your people and their behavior.

Are you measuring everything that matters to them?

THE TRINITY VALLEY FOODS TURNAROUND

Dennis Jameson cut his teeth in the restaurant business working as a financial analyst at Long John Silver's Seafood Shoppes.

He served for seven years as CFO of British food manufacturer Unigate's Black-Eyed Pea and Taco Bueno restaurant chains, and then became CFO of TurboChef, the manufacturer of a revolutionary convection-microwave oven used in quick-serve restaurants such as Subway.

Jameson joined Trinity Valley Foods as COO in 2001 when revenues were $20 million, profits came as a surprise, and the family-owned and -operated business was an ongoing soap opera played out in front of employees. On the way to becoming president, Jameson transformed the company into one of the top U.S. stand-alone poultry processors with annual revenues of $178 million, year-over-year record profits, and a Who's Who list of restaurant customers that include Chili's, Olive Garden, T.G.I. Friday's, and Wendy's.

"The first two things I did to change the culture," Jameson told me, "were to create a growth vision for the company and remove the negative emotion from the equation. I was intentional about replacing a negative emotion with a positive emotion."

Jameson moved quickly to understand the business model in order to establish a pricing system, and then began to develop relationships with suppliers to procure poultry with predictable supply at competitive prices. These moves allowed Trinity Valley Foods to pursue national accounts, and those new, big customers fueled the company's growth.

"The softer side of our business—the people part where hopes, fears, likes, and dislikes come into play—took longer to change than the technical aspects of our business, the purchasing, processing, and shipping part of what we do," says Jameson. Changing the culture from one of mediocrity to one of high performance is a continuous journey, and Jameson estimates it took at least three years before people trusted the changes they were experiencing and believed that the changes being made were here to stay.

The company's model, while complex to manage, has a short list of controllable elements, and because its raw material—in this case, chicken breast meat—is 90 percent of its cost of goods sold, identifying immediate opportunities was not difficult. The difficulty, Jameson quickly realized, was that the timeliness and accuracy of company data posed big problems.

"We would accumulate our KPIs for a financial period," Jameson says, "and the KPIs would indicate we beat all of our benchmarks for cost, yields, throughput, and productivity. And then the financial statement would come out and we would fall short of the profit forecast by a significant amount. We were spending 75 percent of our time in meetings trying to determine if the data were accurate."

Without reliable data, decision making was guesswork and the idea of holding someone accountable was next to impossible because the data were inaccurate, inconsistent, and inconclusive.

FOUR STEPS TO IMPROVE PERFORMANCE

The company took four key steps to address the tracking and performance issues:

1. Upgraded staffing. "It all starts with having the right people," Jameson says. "We terminated employees who weren't receptive to learning, added a financial analyst for each of our five lines, upgraded our first-line supervisors, and added an experienced director of operations because these people have the greatest opportunity to affect the business all day long. They're where the rubber meets the road."

2. Initiated training. "We helped people understand the five metrics that matter: safety, quality, yield, attendance, and throughput. We taught employees Six Sigma principles and where to look for waste. Our hourly workers had never been exposed to these concepts. You can only do so much out on the plant floor, so we made significant investments in getting 300 hourly workers off the plant floor and into 90-minute on-site training classes on a regular basis to understand that these five metrics were everyone's report card."

3. **Upgraded tools.** "We purchased new equipment, and initially everyone was nervous about losing their job until they saw how this equipment would help them be more productive and make more money. We converted our reporting from an Excel spreadsheet to an Access database and added a full-time data-entry person and financial analyst. We established control points that were checked several times each shift to track 1 million pounds of chicken a week being processed in our plant. We improved our data collection."

4. **Created a sense of urgency.** "The daily report cards are posted publicly so each department can compare its results against its peers. When we started posting the numbers I asked, 'Who would like to make a dollar more per hour?' and of course everyone wanted to make more. My commitment was that a score of 90 percent or better on their report card earns you one dollar per hour more in pay, recognition in front of your peers, and a paid day off. Tracking created urgency."

In high-performing organizations, accountability is not just top-down. It's bottom-up and side-to-side.

When he initiated this tracking process, Jameson was concerned these moves might foster competition, but the culture has been a supportive one. "We don't compete with each other," says Jameson, "we compete against the metric. We compete for the prize. We show up, put our head down, and do our jobs. There's not a lot of rah-rah. We all know the job. That's been made clear. We are each accountable for getting ourselves to work and being safe. We are selectively accountable for hitting the financial measures on the job. And our people have chosen to be accountable to themselves and to each other. Our people understand our accountability contract and they're motivated by it. When people, starting with me right down to the plant floor, do what they've agreed to do, that's accountability. That behavior builds trust. It takes time. But it's absolutely worth it."

BASEBALL STATS AND
THE DELTA COMPANIES

If you watch a baseball game for any length of time, you soon see that statistics are kept for everything. Other sports track performance, but baseball was the first to obsess over statistics.

The stat story can often sound something like this:

TV Announcer: "Rangers second baseman Ian Kinsler is batting first in the lineup and his average is .320 against left-handed pitchers with runners in scoring position in home games played at night."

That's a ton of information when all we really want to know is, "Can he hit?"

If you've seen the film *Moneyball*, based on the best-selling book of the same name by Michael Lewis, you learned that most teams were measuring batting average when the better predictor of runs scored was the player's ability to reach first base safely, whether beating out throws to first or by drawing walks from opposing pitchers. When the Oakland A's started looking at different indicators, they started signing different players who, more times than not, commanded smaller salaries.

Leaders frequently get carried away tracking activities that are meaningless to most employees. And sometimes what is being tracked is meaningless to the company's performance.

Jeff Bowling, CEO of The Delta Companies, played baseball in college. Although it's not surprising that his healthcare staffing company tracks lots of activity, he balances the information he tracks with the information he shares.

"From a management perspective, I don't know that you can track too many things," Bowling told me. "Leaders should look for clues where they can. There are a lot of things we look at as indicators in the business that we don't share and that we don't hold people accountable to doing on a daily basis. Sharing everything is something I used to do, and I found it was counterproductive because I had a tendency to look at the negative things. Plus, if you're looking at everything without context, then that information is not particularly helpful for you or your employees."

Every leader I interviewed said their company tracks hundreds of indicators but has figured out those two or three measures that are important to the individual for driving performance.

"Knowing what those important indicators are," says Bowling, "is the difference in 'key' performance indicators and what we call NKIs, or non-key indicators. Our leaders are most focused on sales, our Net Promoter score that measures customer satisfaction, and employee retention."

SOUTHWEST'S FOUR MAGIC NUMBERS

Southwest Airlines measures performance at every level, and the company is known for its "triple bottom line" of "Performance, People, and Planet." Every employee watches customer satisfaction, on-time arrivals, and baggage handling because the Department of Transportation tracks that data, which are important performance features to customers.

Southwest's Elizabeth Bryant calls net income, net income margin, return on invested capital, and cost per available seat mile the "four magic numbers." "Each department has their own initiatives and their own scoreboard that they post," she says, "and these scoreboards show how a team performed compared to another station or another center or another department, and how we performed against ourselves the previous month. All the way down to the individual who has performance metrics to help each employee answer the question, 'How am I doing today based on the objectives I set at the beginning of the year?' If you're going to make decisions as an owner," she says, "you need to understand how your choices impact our company."

Nucor tracks and shares safety, quality, and productivity data with all employees. Ernst & Young tracks market leadership, client-related quality, and people development. The Container Store shares everything except personal salaries, though its "bread and butter" is sales, conversion rates, and employee retention.

Of all the things you track, which two or three indicators should be emphasized repeatedly, communicated continuously, and then celebrated when significant milestones are reached?

TRACKING TOO MUCH STUFF

If you have the right employees, they will tell you what information they need to be effective and to feel like the work they're doing is meaningful.

What CEOs want to track and what employees want to see tracked are not always the same.

Of the 82 leadership teams that completed the assessments, the overall Tracking score among all CEOs was an average of 12 percentage points higher (58 percent versus 46 percent) than the score of the other executives on his or her team.

The CEO of a Wisconsin distribution company completed the accountability assessment and his tracking scores were high. His leadership team—his direct reports and their direct reports, about 20 people in all—then completed the assessment. I reviewed all the assessments and provided a composite score to the CEO summarizing the results in each of the Seven Pillars. Among other things, the Tracking scores were low, and this result surprised the CEO because his scores had been off-the-charts high.

When the CEO and I reviewed the composite score, he said, "We track a lot of information, and we do a really good job of tracking." I asked him a few questions, then suggested he meet with his leaders and ask what had caused them to score Tracking the way they did. We agreed to speak again after the meeting.

When the CEO called back, he said his leaders told him the company was tracking too many things that were not meaningful to them. "What we heard," the CEO said, "was that we track a lot of things, but they tend to be very financial- and efficiency-oriented.

We also heard that we may not be tracking other things that are important from an accountability perspective."

Additionally, the company had been tracking certain things for so long no one could remember why they were being tracked. "Somebody asked for a report years ago, and that report kept getting produced, but no one really knows why and no one really uses it. But we produce it, it takes time to produce, and when we don't use it, the people who produced it are frustrated and we've wasted time on meaningless activity."

The company has since focused on the most important indicators, eliminated superfluous reporting, and improved performance.

Although it's true that what gets measured is what gets done, it's also true that your accountability and performance will improve when what you measure connects to the work you're asking your people to do.

ACCOUNTABILITY IS NOT MICROMANAGEMENT

High-performing companies track performance a variety of ways. They watch a variety of different indicators. And they find a variety of ways to communicate what's being tracked. The key is knowing what information is helpful to share and—even more important— knowing how to use that information to set expectations and to hold people accountable.

A big part of leading is communicating the right way. A big part of micromanaging is communicating the wrong way.

When Jeff Bowling bought out the founder of The Delta Companies in 2003 to become CEO, he was both excited and worried. "We were a fraction of the size we are now," Bowling says, "and I remember very clearly that there was no safety net. If I didn't start doing a much better job holding people accountable, we weren't going to make it as an organization."

The Delta Companies have come a long way since that purchase and so has Bowling. Under his leadership, the company achieved record-setting revenue growth for nine of Bowling's

10 years as CEO, averaging 29.1 percent growth per year as it went from $8 million per year to $85 million. The company's head-count has grown six-fold, and it's been named repeatedly to *Texas Monthly*'s "Best Places to Work in Texas" list.

But when Bowling took over as CEO, the company was adrift. "We looked like a lot of organizations," he says. "We were moder-ately successful, had good intentions, and we talked about things directionally, but nothing got documented, and nothing got fol-lowed up on."

Progress was slow and Bowling calculates it took three years to change the culture. Continual follow-up—he calls it "rigorous inspection"—was a big piece of accomplishing that change.

When Bowling bought the company he was still a recruiter on the floor and he quickly realized he had to get out of produc-tion. He needed to make time in his schedule to follow up on what people were committing to get done. "Following up takes a lot more time than people think," says Bowling. "It requires self-discipline. And that's one of the reasons it doesn't happen in most companies. Leaders don't make it a priority."

At first, Bowling figures he overdid it and was micromanaging. "When I think about micromanagement," says Bowling, "I think in terms of the frequency and nature of the follow-up. I don't recall that our follow-up became more frequent, but I believe due dates became much clearer, and people were more conscious of the importance and the weight of those deadlines. We got a lot more clarity, and the two together—more clarity about the expectation, more consistent follow-up on the performance—changed our cul-ture and our results for the better."

COACHING FOR GREAT RESULTS

As an athlete and as a successful CEO, Jeff Bowling has benefited from effective coaching.

He's a big believer in coaching, keeping score, and winning.

The Delta Companies rely on the Up-Front Contract described in Chapter 5 to set performance expectations with all of its employees, and this contract specifies desired outcomes and what will and won't be measured. This accountability contract also includes:

- Actions/Behavior required
- Time required
- Skill required
- What not to do
- What the person is likely to feel as he/she performs the work
- Mistakes others have made and how to avoid them
- The if/then component

The power of the if/then component is its simplicity, its clarity, and that fact that it is discussed and agreed to—as the name of the contract says—up front: "If you do this, then you will get this. If you do not do this, then this is what will happen." Clear expectations and clear consequences are set for both sets of behaviors.

Bowling's advice to leaders who say their colleagues are not making their commitments is to shorten the frequency of the follow-up and provide coaching.

"Follow-up without coaching is micromanaging," he believes. "Follow-up with coaching is helping the person succeed. So if performance is lagging, go to daily follow-ups instead of weekly. If that doesn't work, go twice a day. If that doesn't work, go hourly, and make them come to you and check in with you. If that doesn't work, then you have a different performance issue to address. That's why the if/then component is essential."

Bowling works to remove subjectivity from tracking. "We keep score," he says, "we make it visible, and we celebrate wins."

TRACK WHAT MATTERS MOST

"Part of what makes accountability so hard," says Bowling, "is that life is too fast or we're too busy or we ask for too much. I see it all the time in parenting, and I'm guilty of it, too."

Bowling realized the more metrics he puts in place, particularly if they're used as a stick, the more follow-up he's going to be doing. Using metrics as punishment is not fun or inspiring and requires a lot of follow-up to ensure the consequences of breaking a commitment are enforced.

"As a parent," says Bowling, "accountability becomes an encumbrance on me to get my daughter to where she needs to be, or removing one of her privileges. I don't want that burden. I'd rather coach her on a few things and take a more positive approach to help her succeed. It's the same at work. I think it's an error when leaders track and share too much stuff because if you say that all of this stuff matters, then you've got to track every single thing every time with every person. And the first time you don't go back and follow up, you've discredited yourself as being trustworthy."

Bowling admits making mistakes at work early on and says he shared "whatever information was impressive, and that information was magnified in bad times. I wanted to provide a sense of confidence to people when times were bad. I never want to mislead anyone. I knew we would make it through the tough times and I simply wanted folks to feel secure. Had I just come out and said, 'Here is where we are and it's not all pretty,' I believe we would have gotten out of the jam quicker. People really want to help. Today, we're using the same metrics to show how the company is doing, but we created a context for those metrics around our purpose and a larger set of goals."

Making the connection between the person, their performance, and the organization's purpose is essential. Discipline without purpose is drudgery.

WINNERS LOVE TRACKING

Clarity is a great motivator. Ambiguity is a great demotivator, at least to your high-performing employees.

Tracking is your mechanism for communicating clearly and unambiguously the performance that is occurring at the enterprise, business unit, departmental, and individual levels.

It's what your best employees want. They want to know how they are doing against their individual objectives and they want to know how their performance is helping the organization achieve its larger objectives. "Is the work I'm doing getting us closer to Point B?"

Research confirms that "making progress in meaningful work" is "the single most important" way to keep your team engaged, accountable, and moving forward.[3]

Underperformers don't like clarity, and they fear tracking because it leaves them no place to hide.

One of the most important deliverables of a strategic planning session is the written plan that shows clearly who will do what by when. Although the person whose name is listed alongside an action item may enlist the help of others from his or her team to complete the task, only one person will be answering to their peers for delivering on the commitment.

Your operating plan should be clear about who is doing what, by when for what expected outcome. Eliminate places to hide, so performance is simple to track.

Winners love tracking; losers don't.

If you have the right people on your team, peer pressure is a powerful accountability force.

NUCOR'S TEAM SCOREBOARD

Business leaders use sports analogies frequently because in sports there are rules, score-keeping, and, barring the occasional tie, winners.

"Tracking is a scoreboard," says Nucor's Ray Napolitan, "but if you're playing basketball and you're standing at center court and all you're doing is looking at the scoreboard, what do you think your chances are of winning the game? None. You have to track performance, but you've got to get in there, execute with excellence, and play to win the game."

Nucor tracks a lot things and works to keep things simple. "I get dashboard reports every Monday morning," Napolitan says, "that show me backward-looking and forward-looking data, and in 30 minutes I get a snapshot of how our group did for the week and how we're doing for the month. We view these metrics—safety, quality, productivity, sales, profitability—as one important method for measuring continual improvement.

"When we send out our quality charts, if there's one division where quality is out of line with others, I don't have to call them," he says. "The managers see it, they know it, and they're all over it. Regarding our dashboard reports, they will typically email, call, or meet with me, saying 'You'll see reduced bookings this week and here's why.'"

Napolitan views his job as helping GMs ensure execution. Like Jeff Bowling, Ray Napolitan draws a fine line between helping and micromanaging. "If I see a trend, I'll talk with the GM and he'll help me understand what's going on. Most of the time the GMs have an answer, and it's not an excuse. You can tell if it's an excuse. If it's the same answer over and over again, then it is an excuse and it becomes a problem."

At Nucor, excuses are rare. Performance is discussed, displayed, and used as a determining factor in every employee's compensation. The conversations and scoreboarding are daily, weekly, quarterly. Performance is reviewed in regularly scheduled meetings and informal visits. Tracking is shared with all employees, not just a few.

"We put things in common terms," says Napolitan, "so, for example, if someone earns 5 percent on their return on assets bonus, that may not sound like a lot, but when you tell them it's two-and-a-half-week's pay, and this bonus was paid because we controlled our inventory and receivables, we reduced scrap, we reduced waste, then we have connected that employee's day-to-day performance to the company's performance, and how that performance shows up in their paycheck. Everyone's compensation is heavily incented toward achieving high-performance metrics. And, of course, if there's no profit, then that bonus can be calculated precisely as zero. It's predictable, and it's tied directly to performance."

At the plant floor level, performance around safety, productivity, and quality are tracked, displayed, and understood by most, if not all, employees. Production metrics are calculated daily and posted publicly that evening. Weekly performance is then totaled and the bonus is paid the following week.

"Our employees understand how the formulas work," says Napolitan. "Some folks have such a good understanding of our tracking system they can tell you that if they run so many tons in a week their bonus is going to be so many dollars the next week.

"There's also an 'add' for catching internal quality errors," he says, "so if our production folks catch an error where our office folks misdetailed an order, they get a gain in their bonus. And if the production folks make a mistake, if they ship something incorrectly to a customer, there's a deduction to the entire line to that week's bonus." Safety is tracked in seconds. "It only takes a fraction of a second to have a life-changing incident," says Napolitan. "Most of our divisions have a green light indicating a safe day, a yellow light indicating a 'near hit,' and a red light if there's been a recordable incident."

Individual learning and development are also tracked. "Nucor provides its leaders a lot of autonomy, and some divisions use an annual performance review and some divisions, such as ours, do not," says Napolitan. "We have a series of goals and objectives that are unique to each person for operational, production, and personal development objectives. Personal development for a production teammate might be 'visit two customers this quarter' or 'read a book on leadership'; then we'll sit down in person or over the phone at least every other month for 60 to 90 minutes and track progress against these objectives and see where I can help.

"For each of the three to five areas, we have two or no more than three priorities or action plans. If you get much more than that it gets convoluted. That's the official sit-down," he says. "The real mentoring happens every day."

When tracking is treated as a scoreboard for continuous improvement and a method of recognizing and rewarding high performance, it's a positive rather than a punitive tool. Tracking takes the guesswork out of confirming those who are performing and those who are not, enabling leaders to give credit where it is due and corrective action where it is warranted.

"We need two of everything," Noah called to one of his sons from the ark, "and as many scapegoats as you can find."

At high-performing companies, scapegoats are rare breeds.

ACT ON WHAT YOU TRACK

What often confounds leaders is that the failure to honor a commitment is discovered as a deadline draws near. The revelation that a commitment to a customer, client, or colleague is about to be broken adds to a leader's stress because the surprise limits both the amount of time to deal with the issue and the options available to correct it.

These types of surprises lead to the Heroic Event examined in Chapter 4.

When faced with a commitment that is about to be broken, leaders have only five options in their decision-making arsenal:

1. Miss the commitment. This option is usually the least palatable. You can renegotiate the deadline, but you've still missed the deadline, broken your original promise, and taken a goodwill hit in the eyes of your customer, client, or colleague.
2. Remove other activities to focus 100-percent effort on commitment. This option requires the person responsible for

completing the task to stop working on anything or with anyone that's not of the primary task.

3. **Add talent to the task to meet the commitment.** As the opposite of Option 2, this approach asks other colleagues to stop whatever they're doing to pitch in on this project and bring it across the finish line.

4. **Add money to the task to meet the commitment.** Whether through the addition of new tools (from equipment to software to training) or outside talent (from temps to contract workers to consultants), this option often sounds like "Let's throw some more money at the problem."

5. **Add time (extend the deadline) to meet the commitment.** A variant of Option 1, it's also the easiest and most popular of the five options. It's also why deadlines drag on and projects are not completed.

Tracking helps eliminate these surprises and arms leaders with a tool for making better decisions during the life of a project and not just at the end, when it's often too late.

At the outset of a project when performance expectations are set between two or more colleagues, it's critical all parties ask and agree on the answer to three fundamental questions: "What is to be done?," "By when?," and "Who is accountable for completing this activity?"

This handoff or delegation of the work to be performed is where many leaders stumble. Three other questions must be asked, answered, and agreed to in order to drive accountability and deliver the expected outcome:

1. **Track for clarity—agree on the up-front contract with the if/ then component.** Are the expectations we've set clear? Are the consequences?

2. **Track for responsibility—be clear about roles, responsibilities, and authority.** Is your role in this task to analyze and recommend, to observe and inform, or to take charge and act?

3. Track for follow-up—establish a plan for follow-up before the deadline. What will be our schedule for reviewing progress on this task?

Failure to ask these questions and make the answers part of the performance expectations may have you answering another question: Whose job am I doing today?

EVIDENCE, NOT EMOTION

When shots rang out on the night of March 5, 1770, and the musket smoke cleared, five men lay dead on Boston's King Street.

In the days leading up to the outbreak of the American Revolution, public sentiment was running high against the British, and the "Boston Massacre" further heightened American resentment against King George and his troops garrisoned in Boston. Future president John Adams was approached about defending the eight British soldiers and their captain when other American lawyers had refused to accept the case.

Adams, then 34 years old, weighed the risk to his reputation. As a patriot, he joined his countrymen in the outrage over the killings. As a lawyer, he held himself accountable to his belief that all men were entitled to a fair trial.

Adams's character trumped his emotions, and he took on the defense of the British soldiers. As Adams dug into the case, the facts emerged: A mob of civilians had incited the soldiers, throwing snowballs, trash, and punches. Evidence suggested someone in the mob yelled, "Fire!"

"Facts are stubborn things," Adams told the jury, "and whatever may be our wishes, our inclinations or the dictums of our passions, they cannot alter the state of facts and evidence."

In Boston's hostile environment, where passions were decidedly against the soldiers, facts emerged and the captain and six of the eight soldiers were acquitted. The remaining two soldiers, though found guilty of manslaughter, were punished with only brands to their thumbs.

Holding people accountable at the workplace is rarely a matter of life and death.

When you have established performance expectations and have agreed on how performance will be tracked, the emotional pain often associated with holding employees accountable can be minimized if not eliminated. The data—not emotion, not excuses, not position or power—serve as the clear, consistent, and impartial evidence of a person's performance.

ACCOUNTABILITY INSIGHT

- Tracking performance does the heavy lifting of accountability.
- Connect what you're tracking to what people are doing.
- People want to see progress: Make tracking visible.

TAKE A FRESH LOOK

Reexamine your score from the Tracking Pillar of the assessment, and then consider these questions:

- Are we measuring what matters? How do we measure our organization's effectiveness?
- Have we agreed on the terms of measurement (time frames and increments)?
- What would we look like if every person was doing everything right the first time? Why is there never enough time to do something right the first time but always enough time to go back and fix our mistakes? What changes must we make to reduce our mistakes?
- What soft indicators should we consider tracking? What tangible measures have we assigned to our most intangible organizational goals?
- Do our systems convert data into timely, accurate, and actionable information?

- Have we established checkpoints to track progress in the life of a task, project, or priority?
- How do we communicate organizational performance? Individual performance? Do our employees connect what they're doing to what we're tracking? Operationally? Financially? Emotionally?
- What picture of our performance would be worth 1,000 words to our employees?
- If our management team was on a desert island, what key performance indicators (KPIs) would we consider vital in order to run our business on a daily or weekly basis?
- What are all of the strategic levers that drive our business?
- Where is the Pareto principle at work in our company? What is the 20 percent of activity that produces 80 percent of the results?

Do we have a system in place for regularly measuring customer or client satisfaction? When did we last measure satisfaction? What did it show? What did we learn? What action will we take?

Your best employees want to know what's expected of them, and they want to see progress.

Yes, you trust these employees, and you strengthen that trust when you track performance.

At the December 8, 1987, signing of the Intermediate-Range Nuclear Forces Treaty between America and the Soviet Union, President Ronald Reagan reminded Soviet General Secretary Gorbachev of an old Russian maxim that is the essence of tracking: "Trust, but verify."

8

INSTILLING A SENSE OF URGENCY

Urgency

We make decisions and act on them with a sense of urgency.

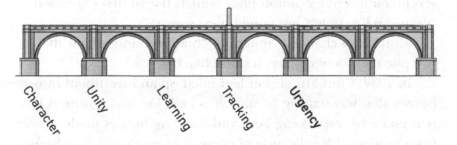

Character   Unity   Learning   Tracking   Urgency

Rise early. Work hard. Strike oil.

—J. Paul Getty

When J. Paul Getty died in 1976, he was worth more than $2 billion and one of the richest men in the world.

Ever the overachiever, Getty reminded a reporter that "a billion dollars isn't worth what it used to be."[1]

Getty earned his wealth in the oil business as a shrewd, hardworking man who spoke four languages fluently, was conversational in four others, and could read Latin and ancient Greek. His collection of essays on success became his book, *How to Be Rich.* In it, he wrote that he believed most executives were "dedicated to serving the complex rituals of memorandum and buck-passing."[2] In contrast, Getty had incredibly high expectations, starting with himself, and he held himself accountable to the urgent pursuit and achievement of his goals. There's no evidence Getty ever met Clint Murchison, Sr., another member of the elite oil wildcatters club, but both men hijacked, paraphrased, and then regularly used as though it was theirs a quote about money that seventeenth-century philosopher Francis Bacon first expressed as "money is like muck, not good unless spread."

Murchison changed "muck" to "manure" and added that "if you pile it up in one place, it stinks like hell."

In 1944, Clint Murchison had piled up an investment in new houses that was starting to stink like hell. He had ventured into real estate by purchasing land and building houses made mostly from products his collection of companies produced. The houses were reasonably priced, well designed, and well built. But they weren't selling. Murchison was growing impatient.

He had admired from a distance a spunky young hat shop owner whose best customer was Murchison's wife, Virginia. "The next time you visit your friend who sells the crazy hats," Clint suggested to Virginia, "ask her if she has any ideas how to sell my crazy houses."[3]

Virginia Murchison picked up her hat-shop friend Ebby Halliday, and they drove over to look at Clint's houses. Three weeks later, Ebby had secured her real estate license, sold all three of Murchison's houses, sold her thriving hat business to her partner, and started a new business.

Today, Dallas-based Ebby Halliday, REALTORS is the largest independently owned residential real estate company in Texas and ranks twelfth in the United States with approximately 1,500 sales associates and staff in 25 offices. In 2012, the company participated in almost 16,000 property transactions with a sales volume of approximately $4.8 billion. The firm's website, ebby.com, averages more than 16,000 visits daily.[4]

THE FIRST LADY OF REAL ESTATE

Everyone calls her Ebby, and in residential real estate circles, everyone knows who you're talking about. Ebby Halliday is the first lady of real estate.

Her business grew year after year, and she became an outspoken advocate for business and for women. Ebby was invited to the White House in 1975 to share her views on business, and was named by *Realtor Magazine* one of the 25 most influential people in the industry. She has served the city of Dallas in a variety of leadership positions in and out of real estate, and, from her first days in business, has traveled the globe in a tightly packed speaking schedule as an indefatigable cheerleader for Dallas and as a savvy business-woman spreading the word that successful businesses are built by serving your customer, serving your community, and serving your industry. Ebby received the prestigious Horatio Alger Award for her "remarkable achievements accomplished through honesty, hard work, self-reliance, and perseverance over adversity."[5]

I first met Ebby Halliday when I invited her to speak at a breakfast for executives whose companies had recently joined the ranks of the Dallas 100, the top fastest-growing companies in Dallas.

She had just turned 91, but hadn't slowed down. She had plenty of energy, generosity, and great advice for leaders looking to grow themselves and their business. I watched these leaders—successful in their own right—as they took notes to capture Ebby Halliday's life lessons, her perspective on a range of issues, and her wisdom.

Ebby's path of upward trajectory is the story of guts, urgency, and knowing what makes people tick.

A LEGACY OF FIRSTS

Like other successful leaders I spoke with, Ebby Halliday has rock-solid values, uncanny instincts, and an incredible work ethic. She worked after hours and weekends during her high school years in Abilene, Kansas, selling hats in the basement of a department store "at a time people could barely afford to eat," she told me. "When you develop an ethic where if you don't work, you don't eat, you have a leg up on anything else that happens in your life."

She graduated in 1929, the year every bank in America closed. "The Great Depression was in full swing with bread lines around the corner," she says, "but I kept moving." Ebby moved to Dallas and began selling hats at W. A. Green Department Store across from Neiman Marcus. In seven years, she had accumulated $1,000—"quite a sum in those days"—and, during an appointment to have her tonsils removed, asked her doctor for advice on speculating in the stock market. "I told him I wanted to become an entrepreneur," she remembers. "He suggested cotton futures, and cotton was king in Texas, so that's where I invested my money."

Ebby's gutsy decision to invest her entire net worth of $1,000 became $12,000 in three months, and she opened her own hat shop. Months later she had sold Clint Murchison's houses and launched a pioneering career in residential real estate. By the time of Ebby's 1965 marriage to Maurice Acers, a former FBI agent and lawyer, she had assembled an impressive list of industry-changing innovations that she either created or popularized.

When Ebby and I met for our final interview, she recalled with a sense of accomplishment and gratitude the results of her life's work. She and Michael Poss tell her inspiring story in *Ebby Halliday: The First Lady of Real Estate,* and here are just a handful of her notable achievements:

- **Created the first display homes.** Clint Murchison's houses may have been sturdy, but "they were ugly," Ebby told me. "So I decorated them and they became the first display homes. And I sold them."
- **Leveraged MLS information.** Dallas was slow to adopt Multiple Listing Service; Ebby was the city's first broker to complete a transaction in 1953.[6]
- **Championed women's causes.** In 1955, Ebby formed the Dallas chapter of the National Association of Real Estate Boards (NAREB) Women's Council at a time when those boards consisted almost entirely of men; two years later she was elected president of the national council.[7] A familiar theme in her speeches was, "Know your business . . . ask no special favors, and act like a lady but do business like a man."[8]
- **Created the first national referral service.** Established a network in 1960 enabling brokers to buy, sell, and inventory houses coast-to-coast.[9]
- **Led the way among realtors to harness technology.** In 1970, she put technology to use in order to share up-to-the-minute information about home listings.[10]
- **Established three separate companies to handle leasing, mortgages, and titles.** Using this portfolio approach provided the company with alternative revenue streams that insulated it from market swings.[11]
- **Created an in-house resource: Ebby Ink.** This outlet allowed her to write, publish, and print sales and home listing literature for her sales associates.[12]
- **Established a corporate relocation program.** This program played an important role in helping big companies like Dresser Industries, Associates Corporation of North America, Lennox Industries, Celanese Chemical, American Airlines, and Diamond Shamrock relocate their headquarters.[13]

Ebby Halliday has been a keen observer of the world around her. She brought fresh, creative approaches and took calculated risks to keep her company moving forward. But great ideas are worthless without practical application and relentless execution, and Ebby held herself and those around her accountable to make things happen. By whatever name you choose to call it—persistence or passion, stubbornness or stamina, drive or determination—Ebby Halliday, like all great leaders, demonstrates an urgent will to win.

TURNING KNOWLEDGE INTO PERFORMANCE

The ability to pause and reflect on organizational and individual learning is perhaps the single greatest talent of exceptional leaders. As the leader, you don't have to be the one solving the problems, but you must identify them and then act on them.

Balancing reflection with action is one of the hallmarks of a great leader. Thinking things through can make a good plan better. Effective execution of a good plan can make your company great. Retailers remind us that their sale events are "For a limited time only" for a reason: Great opportunities don't last forever.

Just as the Unity Pillar and Tracking Pillar are linked by virtue of what each communicates about expectations and progress against those expectations, the Learning Pillar, Urgency Pillar, and Evolving Pillar are linked because the characteristics shared by these three pillars embody the approach exceptional companies take to harness, apply, and benefit from knowledge.

The Urgency Pillar converts learning into high performance by:

- Sustaining a laser-like focus on improving processes to drive productivity
- Minimizing red tape to create a sense of urgency and a bias for action
- Recognizing mistakes and moving quickly to address problems

Large companies and small businesses alike recognize the impact produced by a sense of urgency in the workplace.

Among the executives completing the accountability assessment, 76 percent "strongly agreed" or "agreed" that decisions are acted on "in a timely manner," and 79 percent "strongly agreed" or "agreed" that "we recognize our mistakes and move quickly to address problems."

Minimizing red tape was a factor in driving performance among 61 percent of the executives, and making "decisions with less than 100 percent of the data" was "strongly agreed" and "agreed" to by 57 percent of the executives.

Ray Napolitan of Nucor characterizes this type of decision making as a "commonsense approach" to leading people and projects. "We'll go down a path and we will think through how best to approach a particular problem or opportunity," he says. "We'll get 60–70 percent of the analytical part that we'll mix with a gut feel for whether something will be successful, and then make a decision to implement our decision, understanding that we're going to make adjustments based on a commonsense approach. So if something doesn't work, we change it. We'll move quickly to tweak things. We don't get caught up in paralysis by analysis."

GREAT RESULTS COME STEP BY STEP

Ebby Halliday's successful career and her company's upward trajectory have been bracketed on the front end by the Great Depression of 1929 and the Great Recession of 2008–2009, with 10 recessions in between.

"We've been up and down in our six decades of business," Ebby says, "but we've been resilient, we've built our reserves, and we keep progressing, even when the market is dipping, so we're prepared for the end of a downturn."

The decade of the 1960s, for example, started and ended with a recession, and while these two recessions didn't slow sales for Ebby and her growing team, they stretched cash. During that decade, Ebby said she once paid out "every cent" she saved to her employees. She credits her longtime CFO Ron Burgert with "keeping us solvent," though Ebby was the force behind those character-building decisions, and her disciplined focus on serving customers helped her small, growing company overcome disaster. By 1971, Ebby Halliday Realtors had achieved its twenty-sixth consecutive year of sales increases.[14]

Ebby Halliday loves football, and she compares business to her favorite sport. "You want to play in the Super Bowl," she told me, "but first things first. When you're down, you can't always try to score a touchdown. You have to make a first down. Then another one, and another one, and another one. Make enough first downs, you'll eventually score your touchdown. Make enough touchdowns, you win the game. Win enough games, you play in the Super Bowl. There's a lot of blocking and tackling in between. It's not all glamorous. The important thing is to not give up."

Leaders at exceptional companies initially were interviewed during the depths of the worst global recession in 80 years. Follow-up interviews were conducted as the economy recovered. In the five years between recession and recovery, all of these companies changed their practices but none of them changed their principles, and none of these companies permanently eliminated any jobs other than for individual performance issues. How did they do it?

They doubled down on serving their customers, made tough decisions, and then acted with a sense of urgency to implement them.

Don't confuse urgency with lots of change. People can handle only so much change because it's stressful. And don't equate urgency with rash, hasty decision making and execution. Urgency for these high-performing companies is the disciplined focus on a handful of compelling priorities that are executed with purpose, commitment, and immediacy.

GOOD PERFORMANCE
IN BAD TIMES

"We certainly share the long-term vision with our people," says Herman Miller's Tony Cortese, "and there's a matter of flexibility and practicality also. We talk frequently about where we're at now. Former Herman Miller CEO Max De Pree was famous for saying, 'One of the biggest responsibilities for a leader is to tell their people what time it is.' And that means getting out there on a regular basis and saying, 'Here's where we are.' So every month all the employees are exposed to where we are with respect to our annual goals. Where we are with respect to large contracts or issues that we're contending with."

Even in the best companies problems arise. When that happens at Herman Miller, leaders take immediate action. That may mean that a plant manager calls his people together to discuss and resolve an issue in real time. "We recognize that we've got to get the word out and we have to talk to people on a regular basis," says Cortese, "and that can mean morning huddles with work teams to say, 'Here's what we've got today. And we've got to get this delivered by Monday, and that means that we're going to work this weekend and here's what we need to do.' It's our belief that if the employees don't understand what it is that we're asking of them, then we can't expect them to deliver the results we need. So we overcommunicate."

Smart people crave communication, and smart companies deliver. Yet there's always room for improvement.

"It's an exhaustive process," says Cortese, "and there are times when it's much easier to say, 'Yeah, we've told them that, now let's turn our attention to something else.' You can't do that. You have to be ever-diligent with communication. That's probably one of our biggest takeaways over the years at Herman Miller: we overcommunicate, and that's one of the things that makes us different from other companies."

Each executive I interviewed made it clear that every person—from the CEO to the hourly worker—was sharing the financial and emotional pain of the tough measures prompted by the recession. The decisive action taken by the leaders of these exceptional companies saw their companies emerge from the recession stronger than ever.

URGENCY IS A COMPETITIVE ADVANTAGE

As the recession worsened, urgency became a competitive advantage for well-run companies.

At The Container Store, the continuing sales decline brought what Casey Shilling calls "a laser-like focus on expense management." The solution was obvious, but in a company where "one great employee equals three good employees," the execution was painful. The company cut some employee benefits to prevent layoffs.

In good times, exceptional companies build trust. In tough times, trust is tested.

The Container Store was performing better than other retailers, but the recession hit the company, so executives moved quickly to bring expenses in line. "Our biggest financial commitment, as it is in most organizations," says Shilling, "is in our investment in people. So we initiated a salary freeze and stopped our 401(k) match. Those are yucky conversations to communicate to 6,000 employees. But our people overwhelmingly supported those decisions because of the culture we've created over the last 35 years."

Emerging from the recession, The Container Store increased its head count to 6,000 employees from 4,000 in 2008, and in 2012 alone opened stores in five new markets in California, Florida, and Virginia, recorded revenues of $707.5 million and expects to join the billion-dollar club in a few short years. Not bad for a company that started in a 1,600-square-foot warehouse.

While the Great Recession of 2008–2009 touched virtually every business on the planet, some industries were hit harder than others. *Fortune* magazine called 2008 "a historic year of red ink," and listed airlines and hotels "among the worst hit."[15]

Southwest Airlines reported 2008 revenues of $11.023 billion and, though its profits were off 72 percent from the previous year, Southwest was the only major airline to make money and continue its run of what has become 40 consecutive years of turning a profit.[16] The following year was even worse for airlines, and Southwest's revenues dropped to $10.35 billion, yet the company still earned a profit.[17] Despite punishing market conditions, Southwest continued to execute its vision of becoming the "World's Most Loved, Most Flown, Most Profitable Airline," and it closed on its acquisition of AirTran in 2011 while other companies were closing their doors.

People weren't traveling, so they weren't booking hotel rooms. In the spring of 2009, things weren't too sunny when Marriott International reported a 29 percent decline in operations from the previous year. "Despite the downturn," said CEO J. W. Marriott, Jr., "we're moving ahead," and he confirmed the company was maintaining its urgency on a range of initiatives to stay "on track to open over 30,000 rooms in 2009."[18]

As Southwest Airlines and Marriott navigated the recession's stormy seas, Nucor was on its way to achieving revenues of $23.66 billion, $1.83 billion in net earnings, and producing 25.18 million tons of steel. But hard times were just around the corner for America's biggest steel producer.

The pay-for-performance compensation model Nucor's Ray Napolitan describes in Chapter 5 was established in the mid-1980s, so it had been battle-tested during a 30-year span that included domestic recessions and international currency manipulations that created an unlevel playing field for U.S. manufacturers.

When the bottom fell out in 2009, Nucor was ready, but that didn't make the decisions any easier or any more palatable.

COURAGE IN TOUGH TIMES

Nucor's sales plummeted to $11.19 billion, a decline of 53 percent. Nucor suffered a $293 million loss and produced 17.57 million tons of steel. All Nucor employees, including those at the top, earned less money, yet the company did not lay off a single employee due to lack of work.[19]

"As expected," Nucor CEO Dan Damico told his shareholders, "2009 proved to be the most challenging year we have ever faced. The recession severely deepened in late 2008, significantly reducing demand for our products, particularly in the first half of the year. The past 18 months have been a time of hardship and difficulty for all 20,400 on our team."[20]

"It's easy to be courageous in the good times," says Nucor's Ray Napolitan. "It's very difficult to have courage and commitment when times are tough." Yes, Nucor employees made less money during the Great Recession, but the company's 40-year no-layoff practice continued. "Our goal during difficult times," says Napolitan, "is to train our folks, develop techniques, improve our processes, and get ready so that we will emerge stronger when the market turns."

Nucor was ready for the downturn, and its leaders and workforce were well positioned to lead the recovery in manufacturing. In 2010, Nucor's steel production rose, and rose again in 2011, and again in 2012, when the company recorded 23.09 million tons of steel.[21]

"We bring a sense of urgency to our daily work," says Napolitan, "but Nucor has always focused on the longer-term view. We're all about continual improvement and long-term thinking, and that's what separates us from our competitors."

COMMUNICATING URGENCY

During the Great Recession, air travel and hotel bookings were down, steel production was down, and commercial construction was down.

In Edmonton, Alberta, in Canada, Clark Builders began feeling the recession about a year behind the United States.

Founded in 1974, Clark Builders had grown to $473 million by 2008, and gained a reputation for delivering great results in cold climate construction.

Brian Lacey joined the company in 1990, and today he's one of Clark's eight partners. He spent his first eight years at Clark working 12- to 14-hour days seven days a week at remote locations, first in the Canadian high arctic and later in Siberia.

He was 23 years old when he received his first remote posting, and he admits that he "didn't have a lot of formal management training; it was pretty much trial by fire." Working in brutally cold temperatures, Lacey learned a lot about himself, about what it takes to keep a project on schedule and on budget, and about accountability.

"Accountability is a trait," he told me, "and it's critical to achieving large-scale success, which is typically achieved as a sum of small successes.

"What I've found is that people tend to want to do well, and I've learned that communication is key to helping them succeed. Like any process, communication can have a weak link, and when that weak link breaks the chain in your critical path you can find yourself in trouble."

Lacey identifies his top performers to handle the critical items on a project. He creates a sense of urgency, charges them with the responsibility for the outcome, and sets the up-front contract so expectations for accountability are clear.

"When you provide good people enough information to operate well, they're going to strive to meet or exceed your requirements," Lacey says.

"If a project team comes back at the end of a job and a manager says, 'They weren't very successful on their production, and our productivities are on the line,' the first questions to the manager are 'Did you advise them of the metrics? Were they aware of our production goals?' And more often than not I find the necessary information wasn't communicated, it wasn't measured, and it wasn't managed.

"I often use this analogy: If you ask somebody to go for a run and when he comes back you say, 'I wasn't very happy with your performance,' but you haven't told him if he's doing the 100-yard dash or a 26-mile marathon, then you're really not being true to him out of the gate."

"SAY, STAY, AND STRIVE"

In 2009, Clark grew to $537 million, and then, says Lacey, "the wheels fell off the economy so we dropped to $506 million." The company has reinstalled the wheels and is cruising toward revenues of $650 million.

Despite the challenging market fluctuations, the team at Clark has achieved consistent growth in employee engagement among its 900 employees who operate out of four offices in the three Canadian provinces of Alberta, Saskatchewan, and Northwest Territories.

For five consecutive years, including during the challenging economic downturn, Clark Builders has been named one of the top 50 employers in Canada. "A small number of companies have achieved this distinction two or three times in consecutive years," says Lacey, "but earning the distinction five straight years is a rare accomplishment."

Clark is benchmarked against other Canadian companies as well as other construction companies by Aon Hewitt, the international human resources and consulting firm. Among all participating construction companies, only Clark drove the survey down to its field staff. "Where I come from," says Lacey, "it's pretty easy to create a good work environment. When it's hot outside you've got your air-conditioned office, and when it's cold outside you've got the heat turned on. But when you're driving your culture down to the guys who are getting mud on their boots and are struggling through everything from rain to sleet and snow and we have those levels of engagement, that's pretty gratifying."

The Aon Hewitt study measures three metrics: "Say, stay, strive." What do your employees "say" about the company to colleagues or friends or others? What's the likelihood they will "stay" with the company for the long term relative to market competitiveness? And what's the likelihood they will "strive" to go above expectations?

Lacey is responsible for all field construction, everything that happens outside of the office, which involves 700 workers. "Any rating above 80 percent is considered high engagement," says Lacey, "so I was pretty happy that our team achieved a 97 percent engagement rating."

Clark Builders has created a culture by design, not by default. The company is intentional about its culture, and the employees know it and appreciate it. Only 3 percent of Clark's employees were considered "passive" and none of the employees were considered "disengaged," an extraordinary achievement compared with other studies that indicate 30–50 percent of the workforce of many organizations are disengaged. The overall engagement for Clark Builders in 2009 was 74 percent; in 2010, it was 76 percent; in 2011, it was 78 percent; and in 2012, it was 80 percent, earning Clark Builders the distinction of being ranked the thirty-second best place in all of Canada to work.[22] Lacey told me "the average 2013 score in North America was 63 percent, the average score in Canada was 79 percent, and the average for construction and engineering was 74 percent." In 2013, Clark posted its fifth consecutive year of being named to the list of the 50 best employers in Canada, achieving a new level of employee engagement of 81 percent.

ACTING ON THE DATA

When achievement of any kind is recognized, some people will celebrate, sit back, and think, "We've arrived." Others will celebrate and then get back to work.

"I think there are a lot of companies that are named to the 50 Best list that probably get the report and they're pretty darned proud about being named, and they consider that they've arrived," says Lacey. "We celebrated, of course. And then we analyzed the data. We found areas that we could improve upon, starting with the low-hanging fruit. What were the areas across the business where people had the most concerns?"

Lacey and his team categorized the issues, then he went into the field to visit with employees in groups of 10 people, asking for feedback on the report. They listened, made changes based on the feedback, and then communicated the changes to the employees.

One consistent piece of feedback was the desire for communication about the day-to-day business from a management perspective. So every quarter Clark holds a town hall meeting, shutting down job sites at 3:00 p.m. so that employees can attend and get an overview of the business.

MEDIOCRITY IS NOT ACCEPTABLE

The Merit Contractors Association in the Canadian province of Alberta is comprised of approximately 1,400 contractor member firms that employ more than 45,000 people in commercial, institutional, and industrial construction sectors.

The association bestowed on Clark Builders the Willard Patrick Training Award as the top firm in Alberta for training its employees. Clark Builders' investment in training and development is a direct result of its first engagement study.

"We've got a pretty intensive training opportunity for our people," says Lacey, and Clark's training curriculum includes a career development path.

"I created a graphic with a guy I call 'New Boots' who's never been on a project before, and he shows up in those brand-new boots." Lacey charts various career paths from bottom to top. "We track and manage their development," says Lacey, "and we make it clear that not everybody is going to get there. And not everybody aspires for that, so if you're happy at a particular level, by all means stay there. We communicate that we'll provide the opportunities. What they do with that opportunity is completely up to them.

"People appreciate that we're giving them the opportunity to be successful, and they appreciate that we recognize their hard work. They know we're not going to settle for mediocrity."

The moment I stepped into Lacey's Edmonton office it was apparent he loves golf. Lacey equates Clark's results and desire for continuous improvement to a golf score. "If you're shooting 130," says Lacey, "it doesn't take much effort to get down to 120. That score is like our first year of the study. There was low-hanging fruit. But if you're consistently shooting 80, it's pretty tough to get to 75. So as we continue going through this process, we're really dialing in to the details. We understand that our challenge is going to be sustaining our high performance. There's not that much room to improve. It's all in the details."

As it always seems to be for the best leaders at the best companies.

THE NEED FOR SPEED

"We sell celebration," says Bob Hendrickson of RNDC, the world's thirteenth largest distributor of fine wine and spirits.

But 2009 didn't offer a lot to celebrate, nor were people buying much fine wine and spirits in a down economy, so RNDC's upward trajectory of year-over-year growth declined. The following year RNDC rebounded with double-digit growth, and one reason was the sense of urgency that Hendrickson created inside the organization. It was urgency, Hendrickson recalls, that his board of directors noticed because of the speed in which he dealt with underperforming managers.

RNDC, as noted in Chapter 6, hires and promotes hundreds of people every year.

When Hendrickson was promoted into his current position, he became responsible for RNDC's eastern half of the United States, picking up 12 new states. In three years, Hendrickson upgraded and promoted talent at the most senior levels of the company.

"We're continually upgrading our talent," says Hendrickson, "and we're able to do that—even in top-flight jobs, which is hard to do—because our bench is deep enough to allow us to make those kinds of moves internally. It's important that we have internal growth, and I believe it's important that we look outside the company with every fifth or sixth hire so that we can get some fresh blood and different thinking. So I believe it's healthy to promote from within, and we do plenty of that, and I believe it's just as healthy to bring in people from the outside every so often to continue to mix up the gene pool."

PERSISTENCE PAYS

People can purchase most anything they want these days from more than one source. If you don't like the brands of fine wines and spirits RNDC is selling, you likely can buy the same sort of product from another supplier elsewhere. So while Bob Hendrickson says RNDC "sells celebration," he's also selling accountability. His customers depend on RNDC to deliver what they promise.

When it comes to getting a sense of who's performing and who's not, "I'm a little bit old-school," says Hendrickson, a youthful 53. Yes, he receives and analyzes plenty of reports, but nothing beats face time.

Hendrickson hops on a flight as soon as he's given new territories and he works with the mid-level managers for two or three days before meeting the state president. "I'm on the road every week and out of the office about 70 percent of the time," he says. "When you get those mid-level managers in a car and you're going around to different accounts, they are apt to tell you a lot more about the truth of what's going on—good or bad—than a guy who's looking at it from 30,000 feet.

"In just about every case, these mid-level guys know who I am. But they open up because I spend a lot of time talking to them, being persistent about the marketplace, our associates, and what engages them. I am genuinely interested in them. I want them to understand that I used to have their job. I'm no different than them. I want to help them succeed, and I want to make the organization better. And you can sense when people are holding back. So my persistent approach ultimately pays off, and eventually they open up and provide insights that help me understand how to define success with them."

Hendrickson judges a person's ability to run a high-performing unit by how their people are being developed. He examines a manager's skill set, how they manage in the market, manage their business, and manage their bottom line. He also factors in extenuating circumstances when a manager is losing money because of market conditions.

"For the most part," says Hendrickson, "I think you can sense a manager through his leadership ability, how people view him, and how he carries himself around his organization.

"I'm a big believer in telling a person what your expectation is. If they don't understand how to do it, train them how to do it. And if they can't do it, you need to make the decision about whether they're a good fit for RNDC."

RNDC's state presidents are tenured leaders, so training is rarely the issue. "The state presidents who have been replaced," says Hendrickson, "have years of experience in the job. When I sense that an experienced manager is not successful and I have given them due warning and told them what the expectation is and they have not met that expectation, they need to pursue their career elsewhere."

The idea of holding long-time employees to the same high standards as the rest of the organization has not always been comfortable for the board, even when it's clear performance is not measuring up and the underperformers have been given months to improve.

"I move quicker than the board might like me to move," says Hendrickson, "because they view things in the context of a personal relationship. But because I'm being held accountable by the board to deliver the numbers, this is where the discussion ends.

I say, 'If you hold me accountable for running the field organization, for the revenues, and for the bottom line, then you need to let me put the right team on the field.' The board has deferred to that approach in most instances."

Terminating employees—especially those with long ties to the organization—is never easy. But leaders must address underperforming employees regardless of their level and tenure in the organization, and sometimes that means terminating people you helped hire, employees who have become friends, and even relatives.

A CEO once reported to his peers in one of my Vistage groups that he had terminated an executive who also was a family friend after giving this person every chance to succeed. Hearing this news, a fellow CEO remarked, "Congratulations on your business successes and condolences for the tough personnel decision. I am afraid it comes with the territory."

When was the last time you dove down two or three levels into your organization to find out what's really going on? Is there any bad news you're pretending not to know? Are you bringing a sense of urgency to your decision making?

When truth can be spoken to those in power without fear of retribution, then listening to those around you will tell you what you need to hear. How you act on this information defines your culture and drives your performance.

FACTS AND TRUTH CAN DIFFER

Ken Polk and Fran McCann didn't start Polk Mechanical Company from the ground up.

They bought a company out of bankruptcy in 2003, inheriting $50 million in contracts, 1,000 employees, and hundreds of jobs that needed to be completed.

They had two immediate challenges: First, they had to downsize quickly because the business wasn't sustainable at that size;

second, while making this transition, they had to figure out what kind of company Polk Mechanical was going to become.

The situation appeared grim: The economy was bad. Polk Mechanical was a start-up company working out of the same office, with the same people, working in the same markets, for the same customers, doing the same kind of work as the prior bankrupt entity.

Looking at the facts, a person could argue, "This isn't a new business. It's an old business with all the stuff that didn't work the first time. What makes you think it's going to work the second time?"

McCann believes truth is different from facts. "Those might be the facts," says McCann, "but the truth is those facts didn't dictate our future. We were going to build a different kind of business."

They quickly went to work restructuring the business to look the way they wanted it to look. This team believed that the clearer the picture you have of what you want, the greater the chance you'll find what you're looking for, so they challenged themselves to have absolute clarity about what they wanted and then to look for the good in every situation. Ken Polk and Fran McCann offloaded offices, lines of business, and projects that weren't a core part of their service to their best customers, weren't generating positive results, or were too small and not scalable. They also terminated underperformers.

Putting more things on their "stop doing" list kept them focused. "It's counterintuitive," says McCann, "that the more tightly focused in on what a target customer or target project looked like, the more we narrowed our definition of success, the more the opportunities expanded."

In five years, that focused approach helped Polk Mechanical achieve record revenues and profits. "We thought we were pretty invincible," says McCann. "I remember preparing our 2009 budget, planning the next five years. And each year was showing growth above our prior record year. Then 2009 hit, and that was the start of the recession for us. We went from 'invincible' to flying so close to the trees on our banking covenants that we were concerned about overall performance."

The firm had reliable indicators warning of the downturn, but management wasn't connecting the dots of the subtle changes happening right in front of them. "The good news," says McCann, "is we had the right tools. The bad news is we weren't interpreting the tools correctly. We know how to interpret them now."

McCann and his team had never been through anything like the Great Recession but says, "That experience strengthened our character muscles, because you do get tested in the tough times. That's where you get to see what you're really made of."

McCann and his team passed the test, leading Polk Mechanical through its toughest year to performance that exceeded its prerecession record-setting year. He did it by reshaping his company's culture.

RESHAPING POLK'S CULTURE

What should a company look and act like?

That was the question Fran McCann had to answer. "At Polk," says McCann, "we work hard to make sure our culture doesn't feel so bureaucratic. I don't want to map out every step an employee can and can't take because that limits what we're here to accomplish in terms of delivering service to our customers."

This philosophy is in stark contrast to the culture McCann inherited. The predecessor company had banners on the walls saying, "We are the provider of choice, the employer of choice, and we deliver great customer service." However, its culture said otherwise: internal processes were so restrictive and cumbersome that delivering service to customers required multiple approvals; if a customer called with an emergency, by the time the required approvals were secured the customer had hired a competing firm. The old company trained employees not to think but instead to follow blindly "the rules," even if the rules were not appropriate for the situation.

"At Polk," says McCann, "we expect our employees to deliver exceptional customer service consistently. As leaders, we must do our job: removing, not creating, obstacles that could impede our team's ability to deliver that service. We are confident that if we hire the right people, we don't need bureaucracy to cause them to make the right decisions about how to do what's right for our customers and our company.

"Part of building a company culture that feels less like a corporation and more like a community is a by-product of growing up in a big family," says McCann. As one of seven kids with 31 people in his extended family, he recognizes and appreciates that with a large family comes great diversity in opinions and beliefs, whether about raising kids or politics or sports. Despite those differences, their family was raised with an underlying set of strong core values.

"A business is really no different," says McCann. "If we look at our employees as part of our extended family, we will appreciate the benefit of differing opinions and approaches as long as we are all rooted in a common set of values. This family feel will cause us to be a stronger company because as we get better at caring for each other, we will get better at caring for our customers and that will ultimately show up on the bottom line."

RESCUE IS ROBBERY

During the recession, Polk's employees depended on the leaders to make decisions and give answers. Effective leaders turn that paradigm on its head. You don't need to have all the answers, but you better be asking the right questions. And then you need to get your people thinking for themselves.

Polk's leaders recognized they had done a great job training their employees not to think. The more leaders jumped in to "save the day," the more they trained employees to check their brains at the door.

McCann concluded that rushing to rescue a colleague from failing limits that person's independent problem-solving ability and hijacks the ability to perform at a higher level. Making all the decisions also created bottlenecks. So many things needed to get done that Polk's leaders depended on their employees to be in the middle of things, thinking for themselves.

Although the leadership team wasn't always comfortable letting go of the reins, the leaders trusted that doing so would reverse the course and give employees permission to think—and if necessary, occasionally fail. It was a big shift, and a move that produced more hits than errors.

ACCOUNTABILITY IS AFFECTION, NOT PUNISHMENT

For Polk, safety is the number one priority. As a result of a worsening safety record, the company instituted a compliance-driven safety culture based on zero-tolerance protocols: "Break the rules and face disciplinary action or termination."

The company required a sense of urgency around these safety issues, and yet the harder they tried to enforce those protocols and the more disciplinary measures that were instituted, the worse their safety results got. After about a year with no improvement in results, the leaders recognized that punishing people doesn't help them learn what they're doing wrong, and it darn sure doesn't help them to do it better. In fact, it puts them on the defensive. Polk brought in a new safety leader and under his direction the company converted its enforcement mentality to a "Coaches, not Cops" approach to safety.

"There is no better way to show our employees that we care about them," says McCann, "than to have a robust safety program that ensures they go home every day the same way they came to work."

Under the new direction, instead of writing up an employee for an unsafe act—like standing on the top rung of a ladder, which didn't help the worker understand the risks associated with being on the top rung of the ladder—the company shifted to a coaching mode. Supervisors would call a worker down from the ladder and ask, "Are you aware of the risks associated with being on the top rung of the ladder?" And the worker would say, "Yeah, I could fall." Then the supervisor would ask, "So if you were to fall from a 10-foot ladder and hit the concrete, what do you think would happen to you?" And the worker would answer, "I could get a concussion, I could break a leg, I could snap my neck." And the supervisor would say, "That's not what we want. What do you think you could do to prevent yourself from falling?" and walk employees through that process. The employees understood what Polk was trying to accomplish and saw that the company really cared about their safety; as a result, the employees took ownership in the process.

Polk instituted a program called "Is it safe? Make it safe." It's simple and effective. Workers ask themselves, "Is what I'm about to do safe, and, if not, what do I have to do to make it safe?" The blame game shifted to an educational dialogue. "Now," says McCann, "it's not about filling file folders with written warnings. That doesn't do us any good. Over time, as our guys realized that we meant what we said and they saw us being coaches, that approach created an environment where it's okay to tell on yourself."

Polk also took a fresh look at its safety indicators. Most companies track the incident and the incident rate. But once an employee is injured there's nothing the company can do to get him uninjured. McCann concluded that they had to get ahead of the incident if they were going to make a real impact on safety and the incident rate.

The company determined the leading safety indicator that could prevent injuries: near misses. If an accident almost happened, employees would complete a "Near Miss" form and report it. Leaders studied the causes, visited job sites, and shared their observations as part of the company's "Toolbox Talks." Leaders used these near misses to develop the "Toolbox Talk" topics and increase awareness.

"The whole safety process became part of a dialogue with our employees," says McCann. "When employees realized they were not going to be punished, it was amazing what people would tell on themselves. In this case, there was a consequence but it was a positive consequence. They actually got recognized for coming forward and helping others learn from an 'almost' accident. Now reporting near misses makes someone a hero and not a tattletale."

Polk changed the way people were looking at it. They changed the behavior. Employees began thinking of themselves as heroes and having a sense of purpose about preventing an injury or saving a life.

"That's an act of accountability," says McCann, "but it doesn't feel like what most people think of when they think about accountability because it is born from affection. It's a true desire to keep employees safe."

MAKING GOALS ACHIEVABLE

This new approach to safety produced extraordinary results. Polk Mechanical Company's workers' compensation premiums dropped from a high of $1,359,091 in 2007 to $780,974 in 2013, a 43 percent reduction.

At its peak, Polk and its insurance provider incurred $1,188,734 in paid claims, and in 2013 paid claims dropped to $31,327, a reduction of almost 97 percent.

In 2012, the Associated Builders and Contractors (ABC), a national construction industry association, awarded Polk Mechanical Company its National Safety Excellence Award as one of the safest firms among its peers in the United States. In 2013, Polk Mechanical Company was awarded ABC's Pinnacle Award, recognizing the company as the safest mechanical contracting company in the United States.

"The trophies are a cool thing, and the national recognition is nice," says McCann, "but what's more important is that the awards recognize the safety revival that we put in place has done the job it was intended to do, which is to make safety a core part of our culture. We drove a behavior change and proved that we can create a positive environment where our people take the lead in operating in a safe way and looking out for each other." When Polk Mechanical started the safety revival process in 2006 the company was incurring more than one injury every month. In a safety meeting, McCann asked his 300-plus employees a question: "Who thinks we can go a year without an injury?" Not one person raised their hand. "Who thinks," asked McCann, "we can go a month without an injury?" A couple of people raised their hand. "Who thinks we can go one day without an injury?" All employees in the room raised their hands. "Our call to action," recalls McCann, "was easy: 'When we leave the safety meeting tonight, tomorrow will be the first day we go without having an injury.' And when we went that day without an injury, we challenged our team and said, 'Guys, we did it. We made it one day without an injury. Now let's see if we can make it two days.' And when we had two safe days we turned that into a week, and we said, 'Guys, we went a week without an injury. If we can do a week we can do two weeks. If we can do two weeks we can do a month, and if we can do a month we can do six months.' And here we are, years later, having achieved a record of more than four years and more than 2 million labor hours without a recordable injury."

Ebby Halliday called this step-by-step, day-by-day process "making first downs." Brian Lacey calls it lowering your golf score. Fran McCann and his team achieved their safety objective by breaking it down it to manageable chunks. Each leader instilled urgency, and each made the task for their teams achievable.

"If, at the outset," says McCann, "I had said our goal is, 'We're going to go a year without a reportable injury,' I would have had a roomful of nonbelievers, and nonbelievers cannot accomplish great things. But when there's a group of people who believe they can do it for a day, I'm just going to call on them to do it for that day. That is a victory. And they turned it into days and now all of a sudden we have got these rallying points and we have excuses to celebrate. In the big picture it gets our people to focus on the positive outcomes of their actions. It gets them focused on what they can do, not what they can't do. That's powerful psychology.

"The 'a-ha moment' for us was inviting the active participation of our employees in the process, as opposed to setting a policy and telling them what to do, which didn't work. Now, they are the ones doing near-miss reporting. They are the ones doing the observations. They are the ones participating. We employ more than 300 workers at our company. We work in high-risk environments every day, and we do all that just with two safety professionals on staff, one in Houston and one in Dallas. I now have more than 300 safety professionals looking out for at-risk behaviors every day. If I have 60 active jobs and 30 employees in service vans making service calls, there is no way two safety professionals can touch every employee over the course of the year. It's just too many people spread out. Now we have an army of folks who are looking out for each other. And they are not all accredited safety professionals, but it doesn't take an accredited safety professional to recognize at-risk behavior.

"What we're talking about is accountability," he says. "I think the big mistake that so many companies make is they think accountability is what you do to employees to hold them accountable. For us, accountability is really all about what we do for employees to show how much we care about their safety and what they do for themselves as well as holding each other accountable: 'I am my brother's keeper.'"

YOUR THOUGHTS ARE A TRAIN

"It's just a different way of looking at things, of thinking about things," says McCann. "Your thoughts are like a train. They're going to take you somewhere. So be careful what you're thinking."

ACCOUNTABILITY INSIGHT

- Processes beat craftsmen.
- Minimize "red tape;" emphasize focus, commitment, and immediacy.
- Remember: No decision is a decision to do nothing.

TAKE A FRESH LOOK

Reexamine your score from the Urgency Pillar of the assessment, and then consider these questions:

- How speedy is our decision making?
- How quickly do we convert decisions into action? Are we spending too much time planning, researching, and debating, or can we accelerate our implementation?
- Where am I in the way? Do we invite our best people to help us plan our future?
- Have we asked our people throughout our organization—not just at the top—to help us minimize waste, variations, and errors in order to increase speed, quality, and profits?
- How do we optimize value? How do we apply profit?
- What should our growth trajectory look like? What's the appropriate, most sustainable rate of growth?
- Which of our engines—our people, processes, or programs—is not delivering the results we expect? What tough decisions must we make now to improve our performance?
- We are the average of the people we spend time with. Are the people we're hiring and retaining delivering the character, competence, and chemistry we need to raise the average?
- How must we structure *ourselves* and the *company* to handle effectively the growth we want and expect?
- Do we have the mental toughness, financial wherewithal, and executional urgency to see our dream become reality?
- When will I make time to do what I say is important?

Albert E. N. Gray was an executive of Prudential Life Insurance Company of America. In a speech to executives at the 1940 National Association of Life Underwriters annual convention in Philadelphia, he spoke plainly about why some people are more successful than others. Here, in part, is what he said:

> The common denominator of success—the secret of every person who has ever been successful—lies in the fact that he or she formed the habit of doing things that failures don't like to do. It's just as true as it sounds, and it's just as simple as it seems.

Perhaps you have wondered why it is that your most successful peers seem to like to do the things that you don't like to do. They don't. And I think this is the most encouraging statement I have ever offered to anyone.

But if they don't like to do these things, then why do they do them? Because by doing the things they don't like to do, they can accomplish the things that they want to accomplish. Successful people are influenced by the desire for pleasing results. Failures are influenced by the desire for pleasing methods and are inclined to be satisfied with such results as can be obtained by doing things they like to do.

Why are successful people able to do the things they don't like to do while failures are not? Because successful people have a purpose strong enough to make them form the habit of doing things they don't like to do in order to accomplish the purpose they want to accomplish.

9

WALKING
THE TALK

Reputation

We watch results to reward achievement and address underperformance, earning us a reputation—internally and externally—as an organization whose behavior matches our values.

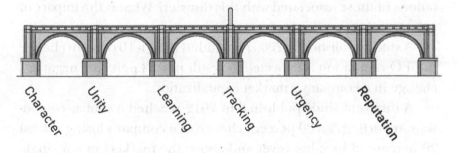

Character   Unity   Learning   Tracking   Urgency   Reputation

Many a man's reputation would
not know his character if they
met on the street.
—Elbert Hubbard

The April 10, 2010, explosion of the Macondo oil well off the coast of Louisiana gutted the Deepwater Horizon, resulted in the deaths of 11 workers, and caused the worst offshore oil spill in U.S. history.

Though British Petroleum has since settled the criminal lawsuit with the U.S. government for $4.5 billion, the Environmental Protection Agency temporarily blocked the company from obtaining new contracts with the federal government, citing a "lack of business integrity." When the suspension was announced, it was expected to be "short-lived . . . leaving no discernible effect on BP's drilling or development pipelines."[1]

Here's the rub: On one hand, a tragedy of epic proportions caused loss of life, widespread damage to a coastal ecosystem and its wildlife, and billions of dollars in damages. BP's chairman was ousted by his board within weeks of the explosion. On the other hand, the event is expected to have "no discernible effect" on BP's operations and future earnings.

Was BP's reputation damaged? What about the personal reputations of those associated with this disaster? What is the impact of a damaged reputation?

A study published in 2000 concluded that "a 10 percent change in CEO reputation is expected to result in a 24 percent [negative] change in a company's market capitalization."[2]

A different study published in 2012 reached a similar conclusion, reporting "an 80 percent chance of a company losing at least 20 percent of its value (over and above the market) in any single month, in a given five-year period," and "in each case, the value loss was sustained."[3]

Warren Buffett once said, "We can afford to lose money—even a lot of money. We cannot afford to lose reputation—even a shred of reputation."[4]

Reputation, the sixth pillar of the Pillars of Accountability, is at risk as your colleagues watch to see how you handle adversity, conflict, and character flaws.

The Character Pillar and Reputation Pillar are linked. Character is who you are. Reputation is how others see your character being lived out. If your character and reputation "met on the street" would they know each other?

REPUTATION
STARTS INSIDE

Of the executives I surveyed, 84 percent say, "We know that a favorable reputation is dependent on our behavior matching our values."

Just as most leaders answer "*customers*" when asked "*to whom does your organization make promises?*" most leaders' first thought when asked about "reputation" is to consider it as something that occurs outside the organization.

Although technically true, this assessment is only half the equation. Your reputation as a leader is also being formed by your ability or inability to live up to your promises inside your organization.

Are you living your values? Are you walking your talk?

Seventy-eight percent of the executives surveyed "strongly agree" or "agree" that "we recognize that failure to address underperformance costs us personal and institutional credibility that damages our reputation." And 60 percent of the executives surveyed "strongly agree" or "agree" that "we reward results, not activities."

Yet only 47 percent, about one in two leaders, "are not afraid of respectful conflict so we will initiate a tough conversation." Leaders of these companies are focused on getting results, but their responses indicate that holding people accountable is difficult.

The principles, practices, tools, and techniques in the preceding chapters help remove, or at least mitigate significantly, the subjectivity and emotion that constitute the reasons most leaders delay having straightforward conversations about poor performance, whether it's a missed deadline or delivering terrific results in a manner inconsistent with the organization's values.

A delay in addressing underperformance signals to your employees that you are either oblivious to the problem or afraid to confront the issue. Neither choice inspires confidence, and such behavior diminishes your credibility.

Leaders tell me that conversations about performance problems are delayed or altogether avoided for three primary reasons:

- **"I want to be liked."** The leader is concerned that having the conversation will harm their relationship with the under-performer and also anticipates that the conversation will be tougher on them as they initiate the conversation than on the underperformer. The opposite is generally true: The underperformer is often relieved the conversation is happening because they have enough self-awareness to know they're not meeting expectations. When a leader fails to confront underperformance, that leader's reputation within the organization takes a hit because it's disrespectful to top performers, plus those employees know who's performing and who isn't.

- **"Their poor performance is temporary."** Underperformers seldom improve without prompting. A leader who believes otherwise has entered the final phase of the three phases of employment: faith, hope, and charity. You have hired on faith, you hope the person performs the work they've been hired to do, and you keep them on charity (i.e., your payroll) long after they have shown they are unable or unwilling to meet their performance expectations.

- **"That's just how he is, but look at his results!"** Leaders can be held hostage by top-performing employees who are delivering great results at the expense of their peers, their supervisor, or perhaps even their company. Who's in charge, you or a renegade employee? What values really matter?

Addressing a performance issue is more difficult and more emotionally gut-wrenching if the up-front contract has not been established. Without that contract, the result is ambiguity instead of clarity around the performance expectations, tracking, and the if/then component that spells out rewards when expectations are met and penalties when they are not.

THE CULTURE CRASHERS

In Chapter 2, we said that some members of your team will be excited about the journey to Point B, but others—usually the vast majority—will take more of a wait-and-see approach. And a third group of employees may resent the changes you are asking of them and may try to undermine efforts to reach Point B.

Employees in this third category are culture crashers.

Party crashers aren't new. Every year, people make headlines by strolling uninvited into private parties.

The uncomfortable reality is that every business has its crashers. The irony, of course, is that unlike a party crasher, the people crashing your culture have been invited into your organization. These culture crashers survived a hiring process and managed to beat the system.

Now they're hanging around your organization wreaking havoc with the high-performance culture you're building and nurturing.

It's hard enough battling the world outside your organization without having to fight discourtesy, turf wars, and inefficiency on the inside. So if people in your office show behavior that does not match the values you say are important, your credibility as a leader is at risk and your organization's performance is suffering.

Are any of these characters crashing your culture? Do you recognize yourself?

- **The Sugar-Coater.** Willing to address 90 percent of what needs to be said but avoids, downplays, or glosses over the difficult 10 percent that can drive positive change. Unwilling or unable to talk about tough issues that must be addressed to improve organizational or individual performance.

- **The Control Freak.** Doesn't trust anyone or anything so she can't let go and, as a result, is always doing someone else's job . . . except her own. She erects barriers to her colleagues' initiative.
- **The Monday Morning Quarterback.** Armed with 20/20 hindsight, this second-guesser says little of substance before a decision is made, and then spouts off afterward about what he would have done differently.
- **The Gossip.** Spreads rumors and loves to dissect problems while rarely suggesting a solution. Avoids speaking directly to the people who are the subject of her rants as well as to the people who can fix things.
- **The Dictator (aka Emperor, no clothes).** Known to banish from plum assignments and key meetings those who answer hard questions truthfully. Also regularly shoots messengers who observe and report problems.
- **The Know-It-All.** As the unofficial expert on everything, he has rarely met an idea of his that wasn't the best solution. Tone deaf to other possibilities.
- **The Fire Fighter.** Rushes in to save the day but cannot or will not prevent the problem. Occasionally lights fires herself in order to play the hero.
- **The Cover-Up Artist.** Dodges responsibility by deflecting blame to others. First in line, however, to take credit, regardless of whether he was responsible for success.
- **The Joker.** Loves to poke fun at principles, policies, projects, and people. Everything's funny to this one, except herself, which she takes far too seriously. *The Joker*'s deadlier cousin is *The Assassin*, who's more vicious in his ruthless approach to dispatching anyone or anything not to his liking.
- **The Quitter.** Surrenders at the first sign of difficulty. Is tired of the fight, but not the paycheck.
- **The Sandbagger.** Protects budgets, goals, and deadlines with plenty of cushion to ensure underwhelming results. Has never seen a stretch goal she couldn't shorten.

- **The Empire-Builder.** More interested in how many people report to him than developing talent, fixing problems, and getting results.

As a leader, you get the behavior you tolerate. So like a lot of tough decisions, deciding how to handle a culture crasher in your organization may be a decision that falls to you.

You have two choices.

You live with the unwanted behavior. If so, what is the cost to your personal reputation as your colleagues see you let some people get away with behavior that's counter to your values? What are these culture crashers costing your firm's morale? What is the cost to your organization's performance as distractions multiply, deadlines pass, and productivity drops? It is hard for most culture crashers to change their behavior. It doesn't mean they can't, simply that it is more likely they won't.

Your second choice is asking them to leave. Doing so isn't always as easy as you might think. That's what Rob and Ed Grand-Lienard learned.

A COMMITMENT TO CULTURE

Bob Grand-Lienard started Special Products & Manufacturing out of his garage in 1963, and today his two sons and 240 employees deliver electromechanical assembly, precision metal fabrication, machining, welding, and powder coating to customers such as Alcatel-Lucent, Baker Hughes, Caterpillar, and GE from a 140,000 square-foot state-of-the-art facility 30 miles east of Dallas.

When Rob, CEO, and Ed, COO, joined the company in the early 1980s, getting things done was simple. "We did everything ourselves," Ed told me, "and we were in charge of the workflow, so you had ultimate accountability over yourself as well as all the people. With only three dozen employees, it was easy."

"We knew how to manage processes and people when we were that size," adds Rob. "Today, it's the classic difference between managing and leading. As we grew, we added people and our decisions became bigger. They weren't $50,000 decisions, they were $500,000 decisions."

By 2009, SPM's growth to 148 employees prompted the brothers' realization that the company was a boat without a rudder. "We were allowing the company to be blown around," says Rob, "and we realized we needed a vision. I heard some people define their vision by dollars or by size, and I thought about that and realized those things don't define a vision."

Yes, the brothers wanted to grow. It took 48 years for the company their father started to become a $20 million company, and Rob and Ed figured they could double that in five years, and then double it again. But when the brothers talked about where they wanted this company to be in 10 years the conversation turned to becoming the best contract manufacturing partner for Fortune 500–type customers.

"When Rob and I developed that vision," says Ed, "we thought we were committing to changing our processes, and we've certainly improved our processes. But what we were really committing to was changing our culture."

SPM had grown using a command-and-control approach typical for a manufacturing firm. The first big change occurred in 2009 when the brothers brought 30 shop floor employees into a room and asked, "Do we have any problems between the time a customer calls us and when the money's in the bank?" No one spoke. "They didn't trust that we really wanted to know," remembers Rob, "but we kept fishing and finally someone was brave enough to speak, and the first issue came out. And then the issues kept coming. After three hours we had sticky notes all over the wall, and we saw the excitement in their eyes. I turned to Ed and said, 'If we get everybody engaged like this and believing in themselves like this, we can accomplish great things.'"

But they encountered two culture crashers who didn't like what these changes meant for them.

THE DICTATOR

The Dictator was hired 38 years earlier by the brothers' father, and Rob and Ed had grown up with him as their mentor. The Dictator had flourished in the command-and-control environment because he was in command. He had risen to oversee all plant floor operations.

After the meeting with their 30 employees, Rob and Ed started walking the shop floor more regularly. They initiated a practice of inviting small groups of employees to monthly lunches in SPM's conference room to ask employees for their input and learn what barriers were making it difficult for them to perform their work.

"As people realized that we really did want to hear what they had to say," says Rob, "and as we listened to people who reported to [The Dictator], it became apparent he was one of the barriers. He was telling us he was changing and moving in the direction we had charted for the company, but his behavior didn't match his words. He wanted to be the big man. Talking with him didn't help. Coaching didn't work. We came to the realization that every job he had ever held had passed him by. We also concluded that we were giving every appearance of playing favorites, that we were talking out of both sides of our mouth when it came to accountability."

With The Dictator, the behind-the-scenes conversations were uncomfortable. The brothers were talking to a man who had raised them in the business. They spelled out the expectations and the consequences. And when the expectations were still not met, Rob and Ed Grand-Lienard were faced with a reputation-defining decision: all employees—even those they loved like a father—must be held to the same standards. Leadership is not doing what's easy or popular, it's doing what's right and necessary. It was time for The Dictator to go.

"We had to be sure," says Ed, "and we needed to be fair to a guy who had been here for nearly 40 years. So after 18 months of empty promises by him, I woke up one day and said, 'Today's the day.' He was holding his people back, and he was holding us back. He was costing Rob and me credibility. When we told him we were separating, he didn't want to leave but he wasn't surprised." A generous severance package was offered and accepted.

Despite the differences and disappointments, The Dictator's exit was handled with dignity. Rob and Ed held an all-employee luncheon in the plant to celebrate and honor The Dictator's many years of service, concluding the ceremony by handing him the keys to a new pickup truck.

THE COVER-UP ARTIST

The Cover-Up Artist, on the other hand, was a similar story with a different ending. For years she had been a key part of SPM's front office team. But as the company grew and performance expectations were raised, it became clear she didn't have the skill or the will to move forward with the changes under way at SPM.

After more than a year of coaching and being placed on two separate performance improvement plans for missing deadlines and being less than supportive of the changes that were occurring, The Cover-Up Artist was caught in what Rob Grand-Lienard calls "a blatant disregard for one of our core values. Her supervisor came to us with a recommendation to terminate her that very day, and we supported that decision."

"Some people just don't want to be part of what we're building," says Ed, "and some, when they finally realized that we would hold them accountable for their performance, decided to leave. But 80 percent of the employees who were here four years ago and who were watching our commitment to changing the culture now see that accountability is a good thing. Accountability creates a stable work environment where we trust each other and help each other improve. The big lesson to me in all of this is that I must hold myself accountable to clearly communicate expectations to my direct reports and then make sure they communicate their expectations to the people who work for them."

"All employees in the organization have to know what's expected of them," echoes Rob. "When they go home at night and sit at the dinner table and their spouse says, 'Honey, did you have a good day?' they must be able to say, 'I had a great day because I hit all the results I was asked to hit.' If we don't give them the specifics, then they can't be held accountable."

Lack of accountability, says Rob, "is the time you lose getting to your goal."

Rob and Ed Grand-Lienard have doubled their business in the last four years and along the way they have earned a reputation—internally and externally—of setting high standards, making tough choices, and changing the command-and-control culture to a workplace that walks the talk of one of SPM's core values: Teamwork.

ACCOUNTABILITY AT MARRIOTT

Leaders of successful organizations set the performance bar high and believe that doing so drives high performance.

Marriott is clear about the performance it expects from its associates. And its associates are clear about what they can expect from Marriott.

"Our company," says Bill Minnock, "constantly reinforces the values and principles of our founder, J. W. Marriott, Sr.: 'If you take great care of your employees, they'll take good care of the guests and the guests will return again and again.' Our number one value is 'Put people first.' And Bill Marriott says it all the time that treating each other well is central to creating a culture where we all treat guests well. We can all quote this stuff."

Those values translate into performance for Marriott, and may explain why half of the company's general managers were once hourly employees. The average length of tenure for Marriott GMs is 25 years.

At the property level, performance measurements are clearer, the increments are smaller, and timing is faster.

"If you're a desk clerk and you're upsetting the customers or you're a housekeeper and you're not cleaning your rooms, we go quickly to progressive discipline," says Minnock, formerly GM of Marriott's Bethesda, Maryland, hotel. "And progressive discipline can occur in 30, 60, or 90 days depending on the longevity with the company and the severity of your nonperformance."

Marriott is focused on a balanced scorecard: Satisfy the customer, satisfy the associate, drive revenues, make money, and be a good member of the community.

"The accountability model is a little more difficult in a headquarters environment," says Minnock, "because it's a little less clear about who is really driving something, and that's definitely one of the challenges that all businesses face.

"When you have a team of 20 or 30 people working on something that goes well, everybody's trying to take credit. If it doesn't go well, whose fault is it? Sometimes it's hard to really pinpoint, but we work at it."

No organization bats a thousand when it comes to achieving high performance, but successful companies are better than most at identifying underperformers, balancing "humanity and performance" as they coach these underperformers, and then moving them out if the employee can't or won't improve.

"Once an underperformance issue is identified," says Minnock, "you can generally put them into two buckets of folks. In one bucket, you have those people who have good self-actualization and, in the other bucket, you have those who don't. Those who do generally can see that they're in a job where they're not performing and they understand that they need to find another place. It's not fun to have those difficult conversations, but it's your job. You've got to say, 'This is not about you being a bad person. It's about this not being the right fit.' When you have that difficult conversation, it's often almost a relief to those people who know they're not performing well.

"For those who don't see how they're performing," says Minnock, "you've got to have clear conversations about how they are performing. Sometimes, no matter how many times you tell them, there's denial, and for those, it's a complete surprise. But you've still just got to do it, and we move them out of the organization."

BEST JOB THEY'VE EVER HAD

Rick Kimbrell has an entrepreneur's blood flowing through his veins.

He worked with his father, mother, and brother in a sanitation business they owned that was purchased in 2000 by DeLaval, Sweden's leading producer of dairy and farming machinery.

Kimbrell worked through his earn-out, cashed in his chips, and then joined another large sanitation company where he was the top sales producer. Delivering the performance he had sold his customers was an issue for this company. "Of the 30 people I was working with," Kimbrell told me, "12 of them needed to go, but I didn't have the authority to take that action."

When Kimbrell saw that nothing would change, he launched StartKleen in 2009.

StartKleen's work is dirty, smelly, and back-breaking. Kimbrell's company cleans meat production facilities to ensure these plants meet USDA and OSHA requirements. Most of the work is performed at night; Kimbrell's supervisors release the plant back to their customers around 5:30 a.m. after meeting strict quality assurance metrics.

"I knew when I started this company," says Kimbrell, "that I only wanted to work with great people who would pour themselves into their daily work and be passionate about it. From the front office to the employee on the plant floor, we all love working with each other and we respect each other."

In just four years, StartKleen has achieved an annual revenue run-rate of $24 million servicing blue chip customers such as Hormel, Kraft, Sysco, Bob Evans Foods, Ben E. Keith, and Tyson.

Kimbrell's team of 580 employees has earned a reputation as the best in the business for helping manufacturers reduce their labor costs, decrease water consumption, and avoid the red-tape and high cost of government-mandated shutdowns.

When you meet Rick Kimbrell, you know that his word is his bond. His customers know it. His employees know it. He expects great things of himself and those who work for him. He holds them accountable to those standards, and those who don't measure up exit the company quickly. Those who perform share the profits, praise, and pride in a job well done.

Even with his employees scattered across so many locations, the StartKleen culture is shaped by Rick Kimbrell's passion for his work, his commitment to deliver on what he promises, and his fairness in dealing with his employees.

"My job," says Kimbrell, "is to make this the best job my employees have ever had."

CHARACTER TESTED, REPUTATION SOLIDIFIED

Tough times, it's said, doesn't build character. It reveals it.

When the Great Recession was at its worst, Herman Miller was forced to furlough people because customers were not buying the office furniture and home furnishing products the Michigan-based company designs and manufactures.

"Leadership worked hard to minimize the impact on our employees where possible," says Tony Cortese. "We shut down all operations every other Friday. All employees worked and were paid for nine out of ten days every two weeks, which meant a 10 percent cut in pay. The executive leadership team took even larger cuts in pay, including the CEO, who took a 20 percent cut in pay. We did this for approximately one year before restoring everyone to their normal work schedule and pay at 100 percent."

During that year, Herman Miller developed a quarterly incentive plan that gave employees the opportunity to earn back dollars.

At the end of that year, employees earned back half of the 10 percent pay cut. "This plan," Cortese says, "was well received by our employees. They understood what we were doing and why. Communication was critical."

Two years later, the company reported net sales of $1.77 billion, a year-over-year increase of 2.9 percent, and noted the company "achieved quarterly sales, earnings, and cash flow generation at or near their highest levels in more than four years."[5]

Loyalty, like accountability, is a two-way street, so as the market recovered and the company's production increased, Herman Miller brought back "most all of the manufacturing-based employees," says Cortese.

As hiring resumed at Herman Miller, candidates brought tough questions for the manufacturer. "A common question for candidates to ask," says Cortese, "is, 'Herman Miller's been through a tough time here and I know you've done some downsizing. Talk to me about what's going on here and how you're handling that. How do employees feel about that? What are my future prospects given what the economy has done within this industry?' We get questions about diversity and the environment. People are asking questions today much differently than I would've asked years ago when I was interviewing," says Cortese. "People are checking us out and when they come in to explore a job possibility, it's becoming much more of a dialogue as opposed to just a one-sided panel or a gauntlet. And that means that employers need to be prepared with frank and candid answers on these issues."

When The Container Store cut benefits rather than lay off any of its 6,000 employees, the company's reputation as a straight-talking and empathetic employer helped it navigate the tough times.

"We're not going to act like we're not affected by this recession," says Casey Shilling, "so we told our employees what was going on. 'You see the sales every day, you know what's going on. This is why we're making these decisions.' We hire smart people who are invested in the business. People are not dumb. They can see right through anything that is less than the truth. So I would say to a leader who tries to sugarcoat difficult news, 'You can do that, but people will not follow you. They will not feel that you care about them.' They would rather hear the real scoop and understand how we're going to get through it together than to hear something that ends up not being the truth."

THE HEROIC EVENT REVISITED

Why do good projects go bad? Often because of a bad culture.

In toxic cultures, blaming colleagues is more likely to occur than accepting responsibility and supporting one another. The president of a family-owned and -operated business once told me, "We're a murder mystery waiting for the first act to begin." You can cut the tension in that office with a knife, and I'm confident the cynic's six phases of a project are alive and well in that company:

1. Enthusiasm
2. Disillusionment
3. Panic and hysteria
4. Search for the guilty
5. Punishment of the innocent
6. Praise for the nonparticipants

Let's return to the Heroic Event from Chapter 4. This event occurs when a promise to a customer has been broken or is about to be broken because one colleague failed to keep his or her commitment to another colleague. Someone—perhaps you—will step in and save the day. As the project is rescued, timing, workflow, and cost issues need to be addressed internally, and your people will wonder how much longer the underperformer will be allowed to get away with this disruptive behavior.

Externally, you have broken your commitment to your customer. Your reputation with your customer is tarnished from missing a deadline or delivering poor service or a shoddy product.

So you get on the phone with your customer and make another promise. *This time we'll get it right,* you say. Whether you get another chance depends on your reputation with your customer.

What happens next is another reputation-defining moment for you as a leader. As you "search for the guilty," you must decide what role you played in the event. Is the process broken? Were you unclear in setting expectations? Did you make it difficult for someone to come forward and warn you of the impending disaster?

If the problem lies with the individual, you must decide how you will address that person's performance.

"The hardest thing about accountability," says Ernst & Young's David Alexander, "is consistent performance evaluation. If you are inconsistent with how you're communicating expectations or you're inconsistent in evaluating performance, then it will tear down the fabric of your culture."

In other words, if you have accountability in four out of five instances—business units, departments, or employees—you have it in none.

CONFRONTING UNDERPERFORMANCE

Just as consequences have come to be viewed as unfavorable when in fact a consequence can be favorable or unfavorable, the idea of confronting an issue has taken on a negative meaning.

The origin of the word *confront* is two Latin words—*con* (originally *com*), meaning "together," and *frontem,* meaning "forehead." *Confront* is a neutral word meaning "to stand in front of."

So when you confront an issue, you are simply bringing that issue front and center to be addressed. You are attempting to get at the truth. Perhaps the negative connotation occurs because the longer we wait to confront a small problem, the bigger the problem can become. We tend to be mad at ourselves for not having set clear expectations and frustrated by our unwillingness to confront the issue, then we have these conversations in our head and not with the underperformer. One-person conversations aren't useful.

Neither is delaying the conversation. Bad news, unlike fine wine, does not get better with age.

For that reason, as soon as you see a problem developing, it's a good practice to say something about it. Doing so takes less energy than waiting. And, as we discussed in Chapter 7, you are more likely to have a range of options to address a budding mistake or fast-approaching deadline.

"First, if we don't confront substandard performance," says Nucor's Ray Napolitan, "then we are not being fair to the rest of our teammates in our division and in our corporation. So I'm not doing my job if I don't hold everyone accountable, including myself, and especially myself. Second, your people know who the performers are and who the performers aren't. If you as a leader do not address the substandard performance, your respect in their eyes will diminish. You'll lose credibility, you'll lose respect, and overall the top performers may decide that it's not worth giving that extra."

Brian Lacey of Clark Builders asked a simple question to confront underperformance he observed two levels below his position in the organization.

"I had a senior field guy who had to manage a personality issue on site," says Lacey, "and my take on it was that the individual was probably not best suited for the company. Yes, I can walk in there and dictate that this guy's got to go and potentially disrupt the friendship and maybe his respect for me.

"I struggled with how to approach this. And I went out there and said, 'You know, I have to allow you to be responsible. That's what I ask you to do, and you make decisions and you manage people. I'm going to ask—when you make the decision relative to this individual—would you write it down on a memo and say "To whom it may concern" and post it in the lunchroom for every one of the shareholders to read and say, "Yes, he's representing our interest well"?' And I said, 'I'll let you think about that.'

"The next day he called me back and said he terminated the guy. He realized that he was being called upon to make decisions that affect a lot of people's interests, and he said, 'I'm hoping that everybody else out there is looking after me as well.' It's interesting what happens when you empower people to make those decisions as opposed to dictate them."

SEVEN QUESTIONS ABOUT UNDERPERFORMANCE

When you see material changes in someone's performance, whether it's a top performer or an average performer, you will need to figure out what's happening in their life to account for the drop-off in their performance.

What signs have you missed along the way?

If you have been having one-to-one sessions where you regularly allocate a minimum of an hour of time each month to talk—not hallway conversations, not in staff meetings, and not even about the latest project they're leading—you may have picked up on these signs.

As an executive coach, I find that even the most successful leaders need someone to talk to, which is true inside your organization as well. Carving out time to meet with those who report to you will save you countless hours and dollars down the road. The form I use as a guideline for these discussions is in the Appendix, page 275.

Communication helps, but it cannot explain away poor performance. As you consider your next steps with an underperformer, answer seven questions:

1. How important is this person to the organization?
2. Is this person capable of doing what is required to get his or her performance back on track?
3. Is this person willing to do what is required to get his or her performance back on track?

4. How much of my time am I willing to invest in this person to help get his or her performance back on track?
5. How much of the organization's time can we invest as this person works to get his or her performance back on track?
6. What's my backup plan if this person is unable or unwilling to change and meet my performance expectations?
7. What's my commitment to executing the if/then contract?

Get clarity around these questions.

SKILL OR WILL?

"When a high-performing person stops being high-performing," says Southwest Airlines' Elizabeth Bryant, "I'm consistent every time. The first thing I do and that I expect all of our leaders to do is to sit down with that employee and find out what's going on with that person.

"Chances are there's something happening. So seek to understand what that is. If it's a work situation, can we remedy it? If it's a personal situation, do we need to take a little time off and give that back to you? You can manage that and then come back. Everything comes down to the ability to sit down and have an honest, thoughtful, transparent, no-agenda conversation."

It's up to the leader to have those conversations so the employee knows where he or she stands. Leaders must recognize that mistakes happen. Underperformance is a pattern. The conversation with an employee who's consistently not meeting expectations is different from one with an employee who's made a mistake.

"At Southwest Airlines," says Bryant, "we sit down and say, 'I understand why you made that decision'—especially if you leaned toward the customer or the employee, we're going to forgive almost anything—'but it's a mistake.' So I'm going to encourage the person to get back up and try again."

Leaders who fail to tell an employee where that person stands are doing the employee and their organization a tremendous disservice.

"If low performers are comfortable in their role," says Bryant, "they're never going to make a change. They're never going to improve. Typically, an employee doesn't want to be a low-performing employee. Something isn't working. Is it a will issue or is it a skill issue? If it's a skill issue, that's what you address. If it's a will issue, that's a pretty easy decision to make and most of the time it's moving them out of the organization."

Determining your course of action with an employee comes down to caring about the person and asking lots of questions.

THE ICEBERG CONVERSATION

Less than 20 percent of an iceberg is above the water's surface and visible.

To address underperformance, you must figure out what's happening below the surface, the part you may not be able to see. What is the underperformer thinking? Feeling? Has that person's beliefs changed? How aware is the person that his or her performance has gone south?

"If you care enough about your employees to really sit down and truly know them," says Bryant, "then there aren't too many mysteries. You can figure it out. It's not even about length of time in the relationship; it's about the quality of the relationship."

When Bryant first moved into her current position, she went from leading a team of a couple of dozen people to a team of about 200 people. During the first three months in this role she met one-on-one with every employee for 30 minutes to an hour to talk about that employee's history, hopes, and concerns. She immediately identified areas where employees were struggling.

Although it took Bryant about 90 days to meet with everyone, she considers it a great investment of time. "I can't lead a team," she says, "if I don't know who the team is."

Knowing your colleague (e.g., Do they prefer a direct approach? or Do they need to be loosened up before getting down to business?) is your responsibility and will determine the effectiveness of this conversation. When you sit down with an underperforming colleague, bring your curiosity to this conversation to understand what's causing the problem. Questions are less likely to put the person on the defensive, and questions help you avoid making incorrect assumptions about a person and a particular behavior. Find out what's going on beneath the surface.

To help determine your next course of action, ask the person who is underperforming to answer questions such as these:

- "How would you describe the situation?"
- "What am I—your supervisor—missing?"
- "Are the expectations clear?"
- "What does high performance look like?"
- "If you could do it again, what would you do differently?"
- "What's *your* plan for getting your performance back on track?"
- "What's the first step you plan to take?"
- "If you were me, what action would you take?"
- "What can I do to help you achieve the expected result?"

Asking the right question is essential. General questions (e.g., "How's it going?) yield general responses ("Fine.").

Avoid accepting the pat answer. They may be telling you what they think you want to hear.

Listen patiently without thinking about what you will say next. Drill down to locate the root of the problem. Consider not just the words you're hearing but the tone being used to convey them. Listen for what's not said. Watch body language.

Assess the gap between their reality and yours. Determine whether they are able and willing to improve. You cannot want success for them more than they want it for themselves.

Your assessment will help you answer the hardest question of all: How much more time will you invest in them to get their performance back on track?

CELEBRATE OR SEPARATE

High-performing companies are diligent about recruiting people who match the company's values. Their leaders articulate clear performance expectations and then provide tools, training, and development to help the employee succeed. Leaders take a genuine interest in the person's career, mentoring, and coaching along the way to let the employee know where he or she stands.

It's up to the employee to take advantage of the opportunities that are presented.

Performance is a choice. If you want to be treated differently, you must start acting differently. The employee who is unable or unwilling to perform has made a choice and must be prepared to accept the consequences of that decision.

"Performance is a high expectation at Southwest," says Elizabeth Bryant, "though we do have examples across the company where people aren't in the right seat. So the leader needs to determine (A) Are you a right fit for Southwest, which means do you follow the values of Southwest but you're not a fit for the job? or (B) Are you not a fit for Southwest?

"If it's option A, we have several different opportunities within the company. We have a career transitions group that you can work with to help you assess your skills for a better job opportunity at the company. We only make that option available to people who are a good Southwest fit, just not a good job fit. If you're not a Southwest fit, then we work on helping you find another opportunity outside Southwest."

Herman Miller provides the tools and coaching employees need to be successful.

"If they can't improve their performance, if moving them to a position that better suits their capabilities is not feasible . . . or if they choose for some reason not to address their performance, then we look at exiting them from the organization," says Tony Cortese. "When that is the decision, we make every attempt to do that with dignity and respect."

Each of the leaders I spoke with uses some variation of this approach to address underperformance and hold people accountable for improving:

1. Revisit expectations + consequences (the if/then contract).
2. Diagnose the problem + agree on corrective action and put the plan in writing.
3. Establish a timeframe for getting performance back on track.
4. Celebrate or separate.

With this level of clarity, the underperformer either improves, leaves on his or her own, or is terminated due an unwillingness or inability to perform. Once that happens, your colleagues often ask, *"What took you so long?"*

CHANGE BEHAVIOR TO CHANGE CULTURE

"In the short run," says Nucor's Ray Napolitan, "you might think it's the right thing to do by being nice to people [by not confronting the issue]. But in the long run, you're absolutely not taking care of your teammates and your obligations by letting substandard behavior continue. The key to changing any culture is changing behavior. If you don't change behavior, you will not change your culture."

If you can't change the people, change the people.

ACCOUNTABILITY INSIGHT

- Reward results, not activities.
- Address underperformance with a clearly defined process.
- Double-standards hurt everyone, starting with you.

TAKE A FRESH LOOK

Reexamine your score from the Reputation Pillar of the assessment, and then consider these questions:

- Who am I being that is causing people to perform the way they're performing?
- Do we reward results or activities?
- How do we celebrate milestones and victories?
- Does everyone know the difference between a mistake and underperformance? How do we respond to a mistake?
- Do our employees tell us the news and information we need to hear?
- Do our employees speak up when they observe underperformance? If not, is it because they believe underperformance is acceptable performance? Because they don't care? Because they figure it won't do any good? Or are they afraid of someone or something?
- What is our process for addressing underperformance? How do we address a high-performer who doesn't share our values?
- How consistent are we in addressing underperformance?
- Whose job am I doing—mine or someone else's? What's driving my behavior?
- How much of my time am I willing to invest in coaching an underperforming employee? What causes me to continue supporting an activity or person who is not delivering the results I expect?
- Have we earned the reputation of walking our talk?

When you avoid confronting underperformance, it costs you: time, money, opportunity, and reputation.

10

CHANGE PRACTICES, NOT PRINCIPLES

Evolving

We continuously adapt and change our practices
to grow our marketplace leadership position.

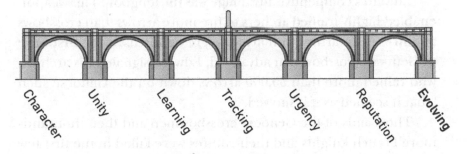

Character Unity Learning Tracking Urgency Reputation Evolving

Yesterday's home runs
don't win today's games.
—Babe Ruth

In 1346, in the early stages of the Hundred Years' War between England and France, England's Edward III had invaded France, sacking Caen before retreating to Crecy near the coast.

France's Philip VI pursued Edward, caught up with his forces, and readied his attack. Edward's army of 12,000–20,000 knights and archers prepared to meet a force of at least 40,000 French cavalry sheathed in armor and 6,000 Genoese mercenaries armed with crossbows.

What the English lacked in numbers they countered with superb organization and superior weaponry.

Until the Battle of Crecy, knights fought one another on horseback. But a new weapon—unleashed as never before on this day—would change the way future wars were waged.

Edward arrayed his troops in an open V toward the French in a 2,000-yard battle line, instructing his knights to dismount and his archers to move forward. Philip counseled patience but his generals, hot with emotion, refused to delay the attack. Philip's troops began to advance without any apparent order.

Edward's competitive advantage was the longbow. This weapon enabled highly trained archers to fire more arrows than crossbows and fire them farther with armor-piercing force. As the first wave of Genoese crossbowmen advanced, Edward signaled his archers, who rained more than 30,000 arrows down on the Genoese such "that it seemed as if it snowed."[1]

Thousands of the Genoese crossbowmen and then thousands more French knights and their squires were killed in the first few minutes of battle, disrupting what order existed and devastating morale.

At the conclusion of the eight-hour battle, the French had lost up to 10,000 men while the English just several hundred. The victory at Crecy went to Edward because his approach to an old problem had evolved.

SONY'S MODERN-DAY BATTLE IN WALES

The longbow helped the English win the Battle of Crecy and changed the way battles were fought for the next 50 years. Accountability can help you win your toughest modern-day battles.

Accountability is a set of beliefs as much as a set of actions, and it may be the deciding factor that drives you and your team to accomplish a task or achieve an objective despite heavy odds stacked against you.

Of the executives I surveyed, 75 percent agreed with the statement: "We regularly ask, 'Is there a better way?'"

For Steve Dalton of Sony, there was no other choice but to find one.

In 1973, Sony opened its first Western European plant in Bridgend, South Wales, to manufacture color TVs and later began producing its cathode ray tubes from the same facility. The superior quality and worldwide demand for these products earned Sony three Queen's Awards for export achievement. A second Welsh plant at nearby Pencoed was built, and in 1992 Queen Elizabeth officially opened the factory.

"I moved to the managing director position just as TV production was dying," Dalton told me. Sony closed the Bridgend factory that had been making cathode ray tubes on a 24/7 basis, and as the layoffs reduced headcount in Wales from 3,500 in 2005 to 250 people, it fell to Steve Dalton to sell the Bridgend factory and terminate people he'd worked with for a long time. "It wasn't a pleasant exercise," Dalton recalls with classic British understatement.

Dalton had four battles to fight, and he won all four: First, Dalton's peers at five other Sony manufacturing plants in Europe were each vying to continue their plant's operation; only Dalton's plant in Pencoed, Wales, remains. Second, Dalton transformed the business. Third, he transformed the employees. Fourth, he won the first three battles just in time to face a worldwide recession and come out ahead.

CHANGE IS DIFFICULT

"There is nothing more difficult to take in hand, more perilous to conduct, or more uncertain in its success," said Niccolo Machiavelli, "than to take the lead in the introduction of a new order of things."

Change is difficult for many because:

- We're giving up one thing for another. The more we have to lose—money, our job, prestige, power, a relationship—the more difficult we find change.
- It's often prompted by pain. We may see opportunities that require change, but usually it's a problem that forces us to take action.
- Things usually get worse before they get better.

Financial analysts call this type of change the "J curve."
Counselors call it the "Seven Stages of Grief."

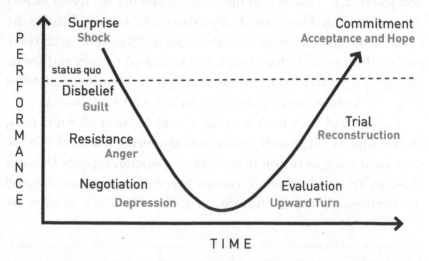

Figure 10.1 The Seven Stages of Change and the Seven Stages of Grief

As you and your team move through the type of change management program Steve Dalton implemented, remember the importance of addressing the emotions that accompany the logic of change.

"You must always keep asking yourself, 'What if, what if, what if? What if this doesn't come up? What if we don't get it? Do I have a plan B? Have I got a plan C? Do I know what I'm going to do when that happens?' Now some people call that pessimistic thinking," Dalton says, "but I believe you can be realistic with confidence and that is how you have to think now. Business is so unpredictable. You have to know with your eyes open what you're going into, otherwise you could be in a sticky position."

SONY'S BUSINESS MODEL EVOLVES

In Peter Drucker's 1964 landmark book *Managing for Results*, he repeated what he first wrote a decade earlier: "The purpose of the business is to create a customer."[2] Drucker also believed that "economic results are earned only by leadership, not by mere competence."[3]

A leader must accept that customers' needs are always changing, and so the company you're leading must be ever-evolving. Therefore, two of the most important questions a leader must ask and answer, said Drucker, are "Who is our customer?" and "What does the customer value?"[4]

An organization's top leader is responsible for getting answers to these questions and accountable for executing the changes that will enable the company to provide the products and services customers want. Of the executives I surveyed, 79 percent responded that "In the past 24 months, we have developed and introduced a new product or service based on customer feedback."

To obtain meaningful customer feedback, says Dalton, "you have got to get close to them; you have to have a relationship with them, because if you are not satisfying them, they'll go elsewhere.

"Take our broadcast camera, for example. We're not a pure manufacturer, so we don't design on the site. The designing is done by Japan, but our business development people work with the major broadcasters in the United States, in Japan, and in Europe. Maybe the customer doesn't always know what they want. Maybe they're asking Sony, 'What technology is next? How good is this picture going to get that I'm going to shoot with these cameras?' In those cases, it's our job to show them."

Dalton characterizes the Wales operations in 2005 as being in "quite a dangerous place," and he made three critical strategic decisions based on customer feedback that saved the business.

First, Dalton changed the products Sony was manufacturing at the Pencoed plant.

"We had been making broadcast cameras since 2000," says Dalton, "and one of our biggest export markets was the United States, so we'd seen the recession there two years before it reached the UK. We'd seen what was being reported in the U.S. and it was showing up in our sales data. We knew it would be a ripple effect in the UK so we started to think TV wouldn't be here forever. The end came very fast. The real urgency came in 2005, so for us it was, 'Okay, we better do something.' We had to reinvent ourselves."

Dalton transformed the Pencoed business from a manufacturer of low-value, high-volume products into a manufacturer of high-value, low-volume products. The plant is the only facility outside Japan to fully manufacture high-definition professional and broadcast camera equipment that includes the latest Blu-ray Disc technology, and this equipment can be found in sports stadiums, in studios, and outside broadcast units around the world.

Dalton's second critical decision was to change the business model by expanding significantly Sony's customer service business.

Dalton's team wasn't supporting the entire Sony portfolio, so it pursued new broadcast business from within while also pursuing third-party business more aggressively. They also moved from relying on just one product in only one market (i.e., selling to themselves) to diversifying customer service, expanding their repair business for Sony, expanding the camera business, and launching non-Sony third-party manufacturing contracts. Dalton's team began managing most of the bulk returns and postal returns of all consumer products on a seven-day repair turnaround as well as the high-end professional camera repair for all of Europe. "We're much more diverse, much more multiskilled," says Dalton, "and the things we're doing today are actually far more complicated than making TVs."

Dalton's third critical decision was to create a state-of-the-art business incubation center for start-up companies in the media, digital, gaming, and renewable sectors. Today, the Sony UK Tech Centre is home to 28 organizations.

"We have got to keep moving, keep evolving, raising the bar," says Dalton, "otherwise we will fall behind. Since completing the transformation of our business model in 2006, we have been profitable every single year.

"It's always been a challenge," he says. "That's without a doubt. I've found the last year one of the toughest, probably in my lifetime."

Changing a business model takes smarts and guts. Transforming people is even harder and takes leadership.

"ARE WE NEXT?"

Of the executives I surveyed, only half (50 percent) said they "strongly agree" or "agree" that "New approaches and initiatives are received enthusiastically versus being resisted."

For Sony's remaining employees at the Pencoed plant in Wales, everyone's future depended on whether employees would take ownership of the new plan Steve Dalton was proposing or resist it. Dalton says that of all the pieces of the turnaround plan, the "most difficult transformation was the change management program" he led with his employees.

"We'd gone from making TVs to saying, 'We're going to teach you how to talk to a customer when they walk through the door.'

'We're going to teach you how to service a customer's product.' 'We're now going to teach you how to negotiate a contract with a third-party company.' That was a whole new ball game for our people. For an engineer or technician, they just opened a whole new box of tricks."

The steps of a change management program, says Steve Dalton, are "not rocket science: casting a vision for the future, getting change agents on your side, getting some quick wins, communicating your vision without exception to everyone, achieving buy-in, and figuring out how to reward people. Yes," he says, "many people know those steps.

"The issue for me was this: You have got to believe in it yourself if you're a leader. And how you implement and execute your plan is the key.

"When we were left with 250 people, most of them were saying, 'Okay, when are we next, Steve?' One of the biggest obstacles to overcome was to get people to understand there is life after the TV business. The communication started with me. I stood up once in front of our senior team to talk about our turnaround plan at the time, and when I went home my wife asked me, 'How was your day?' and I said, 'I think I'm the only one who believes we can survive more than six months.' But I did believe and we achieved the vision we set for ourselves."

Dalton rallied his troops with honesty, hope, empathy, and accountability.

THE PARTHENON

"The soul," said Greek philosopher Aristotle, "never thinks without a picture."

Steve Dalton borrowed from the Greeks by depicting his plan for the future in a pictorial vision of the Parthenon.

"We called it the 'picture of perfection' vision, and that was our first midrange plan at that time," says Dalton.

The vision consisted of three major components that served as the Parthenon's base:

1. Financial competitiveness. "We had an index measure of our cost per square foot that we had to reach that would allow us to make quotations for new work and not be considered too expensive."
2. Differentiation. "We had to differentiate ourselves in our customer offering. We called it 'the obvious choice.'"
3. Heroes. "We needed heroes, people with good knowledge who were willing to learn new skills and put that new knowledge to work. We've got this thing about kaizan, or small improvements, so we have a requirement that everybody must participate in one kind of innovation activity at least once each year. We put it in their performance document. And we measure it and we hold people accountable."

The columns of the Parthenon represented lines of business (cameras, OEM equipment, service, etc.) that the plant would now focus on given its change in product mix.

Dalton stopped production for two days and brought all of the employees together in two different groups on consecutive days.

"You don't get trust without being honest," says Dalton, "so I opened it all up to them." Dalton reviewed the financials, described operating costs, examined sales forecasts, and shared profit targets. Dalton told them that these were the key financial indexes and explained that Sony would need to capture the high-definition broadcast system and also capture and service other products to survive and then grow. "No one who ever ran this plant in the previous 40 years ever showed financial information to our direct workforce," says Dalton.

He made it clear that he didn't have all the answers, so he organized the employees into small groups, encouraged their input, and then posted their ideas. "They felt they had given the answers to some of the problems," he says.

Toward the latter part of the employee meeting, Dalton did something so simple its impact on his team surprised even him. "I put at the top of 'Parthenon' a date of '2010,' and we were in 2006 so that was our four-year plan," says Dalton. "And that was the most significant thing that made people realize there's a future because I told them we were going to do all these things and we would still be here by 2010."

TREAT PEOPLE LIKE ADULTS

Highly skilled people were working on the shop floor at base wage, and Dalton remembers that when he had been in their shoes he believed he had the latitude to perform his job. So Dalton made a symbolic change that demonstrated his belief in his employees.

The plant had a claxon that would sound for each of the departments' breaks, and sound again when the break was over. All over the factory. All day until the end of the day. And again in the morning to start a new day.

Dalton switched it off.

"I told them. 'You don't need a beeper to tell you when to go to break or to come back. You know what the time allocated is. You know what job we have to do. I trust you will do it because you're adults.' So after 30-something years," he says, "I switched it off and cut the wires. That was one of the simplest things I did early on to say, 'I trust you, do your job.'"

COMMUNICATE, COMMUNICATE, COMMUNICATE

Dalton kept up a steady communications drumbeat.

"Lots of people tell me, 'Oh, yes, I'm communicating.' And I say, 'Hang on, I sit here with these employees and this poor fellow over here has never heard about that new product or new scheme.

How can it be that you're telling me you've done it?' And this manager or leader of this team might have only said it once and then thinks that is enough. So that sort of thing—communication—is not difficult to think about," says Dalton, "yet it's not easy for them to do when it comes to the actual implementation of your plan. You've got to ask and answer, 'Did the message get through?'"

To ensure that his message was getting through, Dalton developed digital signage that's displayed around the plant, created a weekly paper bulletin that's posted in the canteen, launched a blog on the plant's internal Internet for employees, and distributed a quarterly bulletin.

Making yourself visible to your employees and showing them that you care are smart steps for a leader to take under the best of times, and they are essential when the uncertainty of change causes anxiety among the workforce. Dalton formed a 12-person employee consultation committee that he meets with regularly to check morale, listen for new ideas, and determine whether any barriers are obstructing performance that he can remove. He also formed a breakfast club comprised of employees from all over the organization. "I sit for an hour and have breakfast with them in the middle of the canteen so everyone can see it and we talk about topics and they can ask me anything they want," he says. "That's a great way of sharing information and listening to what they say."

ACHIEVING THE
TURNAROUND OBJECTIVES

By the end of 2006, the plant had produced its first high-definition camera. "That was something fairly early that we set our minds on and we succeeded," says Dalton. The plant celebrated the success, and Dalton wrote, signed, and sent personal letters to people that said, "You did a great job. You did a job that aligned yourself with our values. 'Speed, teamwork, accountability, and focus.'"

He also put his money where his mouth was.

"I gave a performance-related bonus to this production site. I had said, 'When we achieve profits for this level of our budget, I will share some of that with you.' We made the profit and I shared it with them. I don't think they could believe that."

The plant turned around, and, as is always the case, it was the people who led the way. A time of adversity unleashed Steve Dalton's leadership and revealed his team's full potential.

"We're laughing today and having fun along the way," says Dalton, "but we've got to be realistic. People can never say, 'You didn't tell us this, Steve,' so I can say, 'Yes, I've been telling you this, so come on.' That's why people are up for the challenge."

Towers Watson conducts an anonymous survey every year across Sony's 160,000 employees with 13 indexes measuring areas such as leadership, communication, engagement, values, and performance against objectives. Dalton's employees have moved from turnaround mode to setting the bar globally.

"We have been improving bit by bit," says Dalton. "We have the highest scoring across all the Sony organizations. We smash the global company benchmark; we smash the European UK benchmark. We are now higher than the global manufacturing company benchmark. An ultimate goal is a high-performance global company of any kind and we're two or three indexes off hitting that, so I know we're getting it right."

In 2013, Sony's Pencoed, Wales, plant was recognized by Cranfield School of Management, one of Europe's leading university management schools, as the "Best Factory in Britain" as benchmarked against other companies. The Sony plant also was named "Best Electronics & Electrical Plant" and received the "Innovation" award. "Sony's facility in Pencoed is a high performance plant in every sense," says Dr. Marek Szwejczewski, director of the Best Factory Awards program, now in its twenty-second year. "It has a highly skilled workforce, state-of-the-art electronics manufacturing equipment and processes, and a visionary and proactive leadership team, who are ensuring continued growth. The factory's unique combination of skills meant that it recently started production of a range of professional camcorders, the only factory in Europe to do so for Sony. The fact that global production of the new Raspberry Pi minicomputer moved from China to Pencoed is testament to the factory's ability to manufacture high-quality products."[5]

GET ON THE SHIP

Dalton transformed the culture at Sony's Pencoed plant from one that had been linear and hierarchical to an environment where adaptability and accountability were valued and rewarded, and the employees shared a sense of ownership in achieving the "picture of perfection" depicted in Parthenon.

Yet as often happens in every organization, it seems that some are either happy with the ways things used to be or unable or unwilling to perform at the new levels required.

As the Pencoed turnaround moved into its third year and new customers were being acquired and profits were returning, Dalton faced his next toughest decision: addressing members of the leadership who hesitated in taking action aligned to the agreed-upon vision and values. "They were nodding 'yes' in meetings," says Dalton, "but implementing different things against our values inside the operation. I got wind of this behavior and I tested it out a few times. Now, I'm a patient person, and I worked with them, and I'd say, 'You know what has got to be done now,' and they would say, 'Yes, I understand,' and then when it gets down to it, they can't perform. After 12 months of this behavior, I met privately with each individual and said, 'I've given you enough time, this ship's got to go this way, you're not moving in the same direction so you're going to have to get off. I'm sorry.' And that was tough because I knew them personally for a long time. But it had to be done because they were slowing the progress for the rest of our 400 people." In his 30 years with Sony, Steve Dalton has seen his share of change and adversity. Just as his British ancestors responded to the French at the Battle of Crecy with new strategies and a new weapon, Steve Dalton responded to an upheaval in the market by changing his business's product mix, evolving the Pencoed business model, and reshaping the culture so that trust and accountability are now the bookends of high performance.

"What I've learned in the past 12 years," says Dalton, "is never think you are safe. Yes, celebrate success, and do it is much as you can, but the battle carries on."

EMBRACING CHANGE AT MARRIOTT

Most people resist change.

Bill Minnock drives changes every day for Marriott International.

William F. Minnock III is a 30-year Marriott veteran and senior vice president of Global Operations Services where he's responsible for program management and deployment of the company's product and service innovations for all 18 brands worldwide. In this position, Minnock also oversees the communication, training, and quality assurance aspects of performance improvement programs in the company's sizable portfolio, and these changes can range from implementing a new breakfast program systemwide and leading a new design and décor scheme modification to updating changes in technology.

Minnock has held senior vice president positions for the company's architecture and construction division where he oversaw finance, for its resort development for Marriott Vacation Club, and for the company's asset development management group. Like nearly half the company's managers, Minnock has also served as general manager of a Marriott hotel.

One of Marriott's values is "embrace change."

Since its founding by J. W. Marriott, Sr., in 1927, the company has evolved from a nine-stool A&W root beer stand to an international company of 18 brands with 3,700 properties in 73 countries and territories. Bill Minnock is in the middle of change at Marriott.

"We tell people that if you want to be part of our culture you have got to expect change," Minnock told me. "We're always trying to do things better, whether it's the check-in process, how we prepare food, how we serve guests, how we clean rooms. To continue to be excellent, which is another one of our values, you've got to evolve. There's truth to this statement and we use it all the time: 'Success is never final.'

"Each one of the disciplines is constantly trying to figure out how to evolve the business model given changes in the economic environment and changes in travel patterns and preferences," says Minnock. When ideas have potential, Marriott names a person to lead that initiative and gives them the appropriate level of resources to test the idea and develop a proof of concept to determine whether that new idea will work. "They're accountable," says Minnock, "for driving implementation of that new idea."

Marriott has a "bias for action," says Minnock, "and that means let's study it, but let's study it a little less longer than we used to do back in the 1980s."

Marriott has moved decision making closer to the customer to increase the odds of getting it right the first time. When a new idea is proposed, Marriott considers the desired outcome, gathers insight from consumers, studies the competition, and then relies on the team's expertise as it moves rapidly to test, observe, obtain feedback, evaluate, and enhance the concept. "When you're driving product and service innovation projects from start to finish," says Minnock, "you need stage gates along the way for decision points. You need to make sure you're doing good work, but at the end of the day you've got to get it done."

As you would expect from a multinational company with lots of stakeholders, ideas encounter more people who can say "no" than "yes."

"The way we push new ideas over the finish line," says Minnock, "is, first and foremost, by doing good work. We also do a lot of stakeholder assessment and communication to get feedback and buy-in along the way."

Marriott has been extremely successful for decades. "We are clearly the leading portfolio of brands with the baby boomers," says Minnock. "We need to understand the Gen X and Gen Y consumers as well as we understand the baby boomers, so the change we're driving now is all about the next-generation consumer. Let's use Courtyard 'Refreshing Business' as an example of how this brand continues to evolve."

EVOLUTION MEETS URGENCY

In 1983, Marriott responded to changes in business travel with a risky bet: its launch of its Courtyard by Marriott concept, a 150-room hotel concept that debuted in Atlanta. "We surprised everybody," says CEO Bill Marriott. "Competitors came out to take a look and said, 'It wouldn't work.' And it worked."[6]

"Courtyard by Marriott was a real home run when it was launched in 1983," says Minnock "but in the mid-2000s it had started to lose some of its preference."

Courtyard was losing ground to competitors as measured by guest satisfaction and revenue-per-available-room index.[7]

The next evolution of this storied concept—a repositioning program called "Courtyard Refreshing Business"—was a textbook case of Marriott's "bias for action."

"As we looked at the evolving customer base and did a lot of customer analysis and research," says Minnock, "we decided we needed to completely reposition the restaurant and the lobby area at Courtyard into a much more inviting all-day atmosphere. We redesigned the entire space and redeveloped the menu offering with the result that a more activated, more energetic lobby at night makes it much more comfortable for people to relax, for small meetings to occur, to spend time with your associates in an inviting space to shed the day. This move has really repositioned the brand.

"In order to get that Courtyard refresh decision approved, Janis Milham, the brand's VP and global manager, was the advocate," says Minnock, who estimates that up to 100 people at

Marriott worked with outside architects and Marriott's ad agency to push the refresh idea over the finish line. "We needed to get Marriott's operations organization aligned with the idea, and it was a big operating change. The franchise organization had to believe the idea made sense. And ultimately the senior executives of the entire corporation had to buy in on the idea, right on up to Bill Marriott, who definitely weighed in on the decision. Getting all of those stakeholders to agree that this was the right answer was a major, major challenge."

That's because the Courtyard refresh was another big bet by Marriott and its franchisees: $750,000 per property, about twice the investment of a typical renovation.

Minnock says implementation was "pretty darn quick." Marriott identified the issue, completed the analysis, achieved buy-in, and developed the first in-hotel mock-up in just nine months. Most of the 900-plus Courtyard hotels completed the upgrade within an astounding five years.

Minnock says the evolution of Courtyard by Marriott is "a great success story and the brand is realizing improving revenues and increasing market share."

SEVEN WORDS YOU CAN'T SAY

Comedian George Carlin was known for mixing observational humor with larger, social commentary.

His groundbreaking 1972 album *Class Clown* featured his most famous monologue, "Seven Words You Can Never Say on Television."

Regardless of what you think of Carlin's brand of humor, the point is that he spent a lifetime appreciating and poking fun at the power of words. Words, after all, give voice to our thoughts. A thought that's spoken, then acted out, produces a result. The result can be good. Or the result can be bad.

George Carlin had his seven words, and here are seven you shouldn't say:

"We have always done it this way."

If you are serious about getting better, you must be fully committed to considering new ways of running your business. Do not change your principles. You must, however, be willing to look critically at changing your practices—your business proposition, your programs, your processes, your people—to evolve and propel your organization to the next level of success.

The flip side of "always" is "never." Here are five other words that will kill your efforts to evolve, improve, and achieve your organization's performance potential:

"We've never done that before."

Ron Farmer doesn't use those words, though he has found himself in some tough spots.

You met Farmer in Chapter 2 and may recall that he founded US Signs, and then led his company through nine tough months the company's first year as well as through three recessions before selling his company for top dollar 31 years later. Farmer started a second company, US LED, and this company was an Ernst & Young Entrepreneur of the Year finalist.

Of the executives I surveyed, 77 percent said they "strongly agree" or "agree" that "We won't compromise our values, but we appreciate that mistakes can lead to breakthroughs."

Farmer would readily admit that he's made mistakes along the way, but he's made a lot more great decisions than poor ones, he's never compromised his principles, and he's had more than his share of breakthroughs.

STARTING US SIGNS WITH NOTHING BUT A PHONE

In 1979, Farmer accepted an out-of-state company's offer to start a new operation in Houston with a pay structure that would enable him to triple the $41,000 he'd made the previous year, and "that was big money in those days," he recalls. Farmer sold his home in Austin, moved his family to Houston, and then traveled to the company's headquarters in Wisconsin to sign the agreement. But the company owners reneged on their commitment. "They had me trapped because I had no cash," says Farmer, so he returned to Houston and went to work. During each of the first five months, he sold more product than the company could produce and was paid just $1,750 the month of his record-breaking sales effort. He realized these "were not nice people," so he made plans to start his own company.

Farmer rented a building and purchased equipment and office supplies. On his last day with his current employer, he cashed his most recent paycheck because he "didn't trust those guys." With high expectations and enthusiasm for his future he went to his new business and discovered that someone had broken in and stolen everything—all of the production equipment, supplies, pads, paper, pencils, the pictures on the wall, the chair behind the desk. Everything. The only things left were a desk and a telephone. That was the first day of US Signs.

"It was a scary moment," Farmer admits. "When I called my wife that Friday and told her what happened and she asked, 'What are you going to do?' I quickly realized my answer and replied, 'The only thing we still have is this red telephone in my hand. I've got 30 days before I get the phone bill and eight or nine days before I pay them, so I've got that much time to figure out how to make this phone make money. I'm going to call people I know in the sign business, find out what they need, and accumulate enough orders to buy quantities where I can make some spread.' I was temporarily in the sign supply business. I made enough money to buy equipment, and, little by little, I started my sign business, which, by the way, was a business I knew almost nothing about."

Farmer's new company grossed $186,000 its first year and grew to $2.2 million in five years. This performance landed US Signs at 196 on the Inc. 500 list. In between the start-up and the sale,

US Signs was profitable each of those 31 years except 1986, 1991, and 2001.

LOOKING FOR A BETTER WAY

In 2000, US Signs was looking for a better way to light signs.

Using LEDs (light-emitting diodes) was an appealing solution because LEDs use less energy than neon, won't short out, and last longer. Only eight companies manufactured LEDs for signs at that time and in just one color: red. Farmer bought samples from all eight companies, chose the best and started using them. He believed in LED lighting to such a degree that he proposed a $3 million retrofit of all his top client's signs. Realizing he needed a better product, he engaged Mike Wilkinson's firm Paragon Innovations to help develop his own product and launched US LED in 2001. In four months, US LED was in the market with its first product. Over time, US LED developed all colors, including white, which is now an industry standard.

"From the time I was little," says Farmer, "I was always the kid willing to work." Along the way, Farmer learned three important lessons as an entrepreneur.

First, his way of solving money problems—whether as a kid or as an adult—was often to start a company. "When I saw opportunities," says Farmer, "a new company was not far behind. I even helped my employees and others start companies when we changed to an outsourcing model."

Second, he realized that change is profitable and that he is an innovator. In 1986, when one-fourth of all sign companies in Houston were going out of business, Farmer changed his business model from a manufacturing operation to a sales operation, outsourcing all manufacturing. "That approach," says Farmer, "was denigrated by the industry, and for years our sales people were reluctant to reveal that we didn't manufacture what we sold." Today, this model is more accepted. About that same time, the use of aluminum extrusions was growing, but virtually no company made their own extrusions. Farmer developed two aluminum extrusions that gave his company a decided advantage. "Most inventions are not original," says Farmer, "and the things I did with our business were mostly evolutionary."

Farmer's third, and, he believes, most important lesson, was his ability to make decisions with imperfect information. "You're going to come to impasses where you can't see beyond the veil," says Farmer, "so if you're going to make it in business, you have to be willing to make decisions without all of the information and show by your deeds how much you really believe in yourself and your ideas. In every case where I've been willing to put the last dollar on the line, we've made it."

HOW MANY CHANCES AT ACCOUNTABILITY?

A lot of variables go into deciding how many chances to give someone.

"There's no bumper-sticker slogan, no one-size-fits-all answer," says Farmer. "We, like most people, probably keep underperforming employees too long. But you've got to give people time to show signs of development."

At Farmer's company, outside sales reps get 6 to 12 months to show their willingness and ability to grow or they are dismissed. For the inside team, Farmer considers several factors. "Sometimes we promote up and find out they can't do the job," he says. "We don't fire them just because we made that mistake. We'll find someplace else for them in the company if possible. We've created a lot of goodwill in the company doing that.

"If there's a mistake," says Farmer, "and someone says, 'I didn't think my way through that' or 'I didn't understand that,' those are a different class of mistakes. But when I've trained someone and everything is understood and the person performs several times correctly and then they do it wrong, I'm not very forgiving. Unless there's a really great explanation, they're probably not going to stay."

Farmer once caught an employee sleeping in the bathroom and that person was gone in 15 minutes. Other decisions aren't as straightforward.

"There was one instance where a really good employee was disrespectful to another employee" says Farmer, "and I asked the employee who had committed the infraction to do certain things—apologize, go through some training, the normal stuff—and he said he would do it and then he didn't follow through. Now keep in mind that this guy is really smart, really good, and I didn't want to lose him. But I had to let him go. If you are unwilling to keep your word, what are you doing with our clients and other employees?"

Some people are better interviewers than workers.

Farmer says that if he asks someone to do something they can't do, then it's his misjudgment. But when he asked someone to do something they said in the interview they could do and they are unable or unwilling to perform, they may not have a place in the company. "Accountability for us," says Farmer, "is tempered by giving people the benefit of the doubt. But when there is no doubt, I must act, because I'm accountable, too."

WESTERN GRAPHICS: ADULTS DON'T ARGUE WITH REALITY

Western Graphics is a commercial printer in St. Paul, Minnesota, founded in 1967. CEO Tim Keran purchased the business from his father, who purchased the business from his partner, who purchased the business from the founder.

The company's counterintuitive tagline reflects Keran's commitment to continuous improvement in order to deliver the most value: "Helping our clients print less."

"We're a pretty small company," Keran told me, "so when a big customer leaves or a key employee leaves it hits the bottom line and it hits the emotional line harder and faster."

Keran saw the worst recession in 80 years heading his way and told his employees in their monthly meetings that the approaching storm would either hit the company directly or move past them.

"I often say, 'Adults don't argue with reality,'" says Keran, "so we reviewed finances, shared team-by-team results, and recognized employees for their performance while we were providing monthly updates that showed the recession was moving from storm watch to storm warning."

GETTING BETTER AS THINGS GOT WORSE

The storm turned into a Category 5 hurricane.

"While we were going through the storm, it didn't make sense for us not to get stronger," says Keran. "We used those two years during the Great Recession to make improvements. While things were getting worse around us, we were getting better."

During the recession Western Graphics continued its streak as a six-time recipient of Printing Industries of America's Best Workplace in the Americas award, which is based on eight criteria, including management practices, training and development, financial security, and work-life balance. Keran earned national recognition from the same organization for his "success at creating a culture that has inspired Western Graphics employees to share their knowledge and creativity."[8]

By virtually any yardstick, Western Graphics got better while everything around was getting worse: sales per employee increased 22 percent, rework improved 74 percent, employee morale improved from 3.87 to 4.06 (out of 5.00), and the company's profitability allowed incentive bonuses to be paid for seven consecutive quarters as the recession ended.[9]

Keran says the company's values guided them through the tough times: team, trust, attitude, and results. "Because we had a healthy accountability culture," says Keran, "we were able to rely on teamwork, attitude, and trust to drive results. We continued to build trust with our communications going into the recession, and we were open about what was happening. We didn't let the economy be the excuse, and this allowed people to say, 'Okay, we're not going to be in fear mode, we'll pick up a shovel and get something done.'"

IDEAS DON'T COUNT

To survive an economic downturn while the printing industry moves through seismic change, Keran kept things simple, fun, and connected to his employees' day-to-day work. The company's definition of "Results" is "We continually get better," and it's mandatory to make improvements. "Half your job is making your numbers," says Keran, "and half is making your job better."

Here's how Keran and his team drive improvement:

"Ideas don't count," Keran says. "An improvement is an idea that's completed. It can't be regular work. It has to be something that makes your work better, your department better, or the company better."

Keran encouraged his team to view improvements as positive versus mistakes. "There's a saying that problems are gold," he says, "and finding gold makes you rich. So we were happy to see the mistakes because to us it's a way to get better. We celebrate mistakes in kind of a twisted way."

Employees drive improvement. "We built the system," says Keran, "so our people could lead their own improvements instead of us trying to manage them to make improvements."

Keran employed an annual theme to make the continuous improvement journey fun while getting better and accomplishing more.

Past themes include Real Estate Tycoons, Crime-Solving Detectives, Pirates, and Survivors. "The first year we felt a little weird," says Keran, "but I got people dressing up in '80s gear for the meeting. Fake long hair, tattoos, and bandanas. You think it would wear off on adults, but it's still a way of having fun while we're getting better. And then some employees created these medals for 'Best Improvement' winner for the month. I thought they were kind of cheesy, but people love the medals and love to keep score. People want to be part of something that just flat-out works. We've got to get better every day."

For many, change is stressful. "Business," says Keran, "is a game, so let's have some fun around that. And then let's go home and take care of the real-world stuff."

Keran encouraged small improvements, the smaller the better. "If you start asking for big, crazy $20,000 ideas, then a lot of people say, 'I can't play that game. I don't have an MBA. I don't have a project management degree.' So we stayed simple, saying, 'Is this going to make you, the department, or the company better?' If 'yes,' then it counts as an improvement."

Western Graphics developed a process called the "system bust," a one-page form on bright lavender paper that employees complete every time something doesn't work as intended, from parking lot lights, to equipment problems, to missing a deadline.

Keran also instituted a profit sharing plan that rewards employees for improving efficiency and driving customer satisfaction.

Western Graphics averaged 300 improvements per year before the recession. "In the middle of the recession," says Keran, "we got up to 650, so we doubled our improvements during one of the worst years we had."

APPLYING THE LEAN
PROCESS TO COACHING

Western Graphics' commitment to accountability was an outgrowth of the Lean manufacturing process developed by Toyota to eliminate waste.

"Lean really launched us into our accountability culture," says Keran. "Our attitude became 'We've got to get better. Let's find the better way.' You should do that every day."

Productive employees are happy employees, and Western Graphics discovered that as morale improved so did performance. Turnover and quality defects decreased. "We asked, 'Why wouldn't this approach work with performance reviews? Why wouldn't this work with coaching people instead of managing them?'"

Western Graphics scrapped its twice-a-year performance reviews and moved to coaching conversations every two weeks with quarterly reviews.

"It's great for the employees," says Keran, "because they hear about what they need to do to get better. It's easy on managers because they can get it off their chest right away instead of thinking about it for six months. If you're coaching people on poor performance, it's difficult if you're doing it once or twice a year. If you're nudging them every two weeks and every 12 weeks, you are really telling them the score on their performance, that's easier and less stressful for the manager and for the employee."

The process borrowed from Lean, says Keran, "is one of feeding forward versus feeding back because there's nothing we can do about the past. We're giving you information every two weeks so that you can perform better. With an annual review it's all feedback. Now, it's an opportunity to say, 'Let's not worry about the past, this will be an opportunity to get better.' You're building trust instead of fear."

YOU CAN'T QUIT AND STAY

Every leader I spoke with has a similar but slightly different take on addressing underperformance, but it all starts with clear expectations and then moving quickly to celebrate a coaching victory or separating the underperformer from the company.

"Tell people the score," says Keran. "They all want to know what the score is. And they want to know how the company is doing. They want to know how their department is doing, and they want to know how they are doing. Why is their performance rating in your head? They can't hear what you're thinking. You've got to share the score."

For underperformers, Keran says, "Don't allow people to quit and stay because that's not good for anybody. It's not good for you as a leader, it's not good for the people who are around them, and it's not good for them. So when someone won't perform and they quit and stay, we get rid of them immediately."

When things got tight during the Great Recession, Western Graphics laid off 10 percent of its workforce. "We did them on merit," says Keran, "not based on seniority. We terminated a great guy. People were emotional about it. I was emotional about it. But he just wasn't one of the people we were going to keep. How we handled that layoff built trust because we said, 'If you do your job and you help yourself get better, your job is safe.'"

Nice people who can't or won't do the work can be the toughest terminations, but, says Keran, "they just don't fit our core value of 'results.' They are the right person at the wrong company."

NUCOR'S MOUNTAIN WITH NO TOP

Nucor acquired Magnatrax in 2007, and Ray Napolitan was promoted to lead one of the four brands, American Buildings Company. When I visited Ray in Eufaula, Alabama, the Great Recession was in full swing.

Napolitan had already begun the evolution of transforming the company into a high-performing company, and the previous year the plant's production rose 14 percent with fewer workers.

Nucor's response to the recession, Napolitan told me, was "to train our folks, develop techniques, improve our processes, and get ready so that we will emerge stronger when the market turns," noting at the time that "many of our folks at American Buildings Company have said they've had more training in the past 12 months than they had their 20-year career with American Buildings."

Safety is at the top of every Nucor plant's list of priorities and each year the company raises the bar, looking for new ways to keep employees safe and healthy. "The target for the President's Safety Award used to be one-half the industry average for our business segment," says Napolitan, "and we changed that target to one-third the industry average."

Nucor also works with OSHA on a voluntary protection program, working side by side to identify improvement opportunities. "We don't wait for an audit," says Napolitan. "We reach out, bring OSHA in, and work with them proactively and collaboratively."

In order to evolve, 69 percent of the executives I surveyed said, "We look outside our industry for practices we can adapt to our business." Looking beyond your four walls is critical. How do you know what you don't know?

Nucor calls its approach to bringing in the best ideas to drive performance "bestmarking." "Bestmarking doesn't have to be within your corporation," says Napolitan. "We do bestmarking with outside companies—not as much as within our own company, but there's no reason you can't go down to your neighbors or some other manufacturing facility and bestmark."

Proprietary information is not shared, though occasional visits to competitors occurs to examine nonproprietary issues such as safety, environmental initiatives, and quality—even ways to improve manufacturing processes that aren't proprietary.

Improving, adapting, and evolving, says Napolitan, is like a game of King of the Mountain. "When you're at the top of the mountain there's only one place to go: down. So our executive chairman Dan Damico asks us to envision our business lives and personal lives as though we're climbing a mountain with no top, so that we're continually learning, continually improving, continually getting better, not just for ourselves, but for our entire team. When we do, we will continue to excel in the marketplace and in everything we do."

DAN EDELMAN'S THREE
SIMPLE QUESTIONS

Dan Edelman started his one-person business in 1952.

Today, Edelman Worldwide is the world's largest independent public relations firm with fees of more than $660 million and employing 4,600 in 63 offices in 26 countries.[10]

For four years, I led the Dallas office of Edelman Worldwide.

Dan was a taskmaster and held his senior leaders accountable for four things: providing great work to existing clients, winning new business, ensuring the team was up to the challenge of delivering what was promised, and staying ahead of the pack with new ideas.

Dan would travel to Dallas twice a year to meet with our biggest clients and best prospects. Our business grew and the Edelman empire evolved and expanded because of Dan's energy, curiosity, and focus on high performance, and today his son Richard continues to lead the firm to new heights.

In those face-to-face meetings with clients and prospects, Dan always asked three simple questions that strengthened relationships, uncovered valuable information, and created more opportunity for new assignments, often in ways that allowed the firm to move into new lines of work:

1. "How's your business?" A great icebreaker that gets people talking about their favorite subject: themselves.
2. "How are we doing for you?" An invitation to assess the firm's performance and occasionally vent frustrations to the firm's founder. You can't fix a problem unless you know about it.
3. "Is there anything you're working on or thinking about that we might be able to help you with?" When you're hired for a particular reason, clients can forget or overlook the range of other services you provide.

Asking a few simple questions can help you grow, adapt, and evolve along with your clients and customers.

EVOLVING AT EVERY TURN

Tastes change. Habits evolve. New expectations develop.

The headlines remind us that reading these shifting behavioral sands can be tricky: "Kodak determined to survive,"[11] "Newsweek Quits Print,"[12] "Ailing BlackBerry to Reduce Work Force and Post Big Loss,"[13] "Ron Johnson's Desperate Broadcasts to J.C. Penney Workers Fell Flat as Company Faltered."[14] The list goes on.

For those leaders, like those at The Container Store, Ernst & Young, Herman Miller, Marriott, Nucor, Sony, and Southwest Airlines, who can navigate change, they look for an opportunity to widen the gap between themselves and the competition.

"The travel habits of our customers have evolved," says Southwest Airlines CEO Gary Kelly. "That's why we've updated our fleet with newly refreshed cabins . . . and introduced the sleek, new Boeing 737-800 series aircraft into our fleet for longer flights. We've revamped our Rapid Rewards Frequent Flyer program, and we're equipping Southwest for international service."[15]

Smart leaders make big, smart bets and are held accountable for the results those bets produce.

Nucor's leaders weighed the risk of "the long-term uncertainty that currently exists on the carbon tax issues in Washington" against the opportunity to "achieve our long-term goal of increasing control over our raw materials supply" and built a $750 million 2.5 million tons-per-year iron making facility in St. James Parish, Louisiana. The facility is the proposed first phase of a $3.4 billion investment that will bring 1,250 jobs to Louisiana.[16]

The plant uses direct reduction technology to convert natural gas and iron ore pellets into high-quality direct reduced iron (DRI) used by Nucor's steel mills, along with recycled scrap, to produce a variety of high-quality steel products. Nucor said that the "DRI facility was chosen for the first phase of our project . . .

because it offers a carbon footprint that is one-third of that for the coke oven/blast furnace route for the same volume of product but at less than half the capital cost."[17]

Ernst & Young evolved to balance the demanding work it requires of its people to meet client expectations with the reality that hard-working people need time away from the firm to meet other obligations and to recharge their batteries.

Arthur Andersen's implosion after being indicted by the Justice Department related to its auditing of Enron sent shock waves throughout the business community.

"There was a real scramble in the profession," says Ernst & Young's David Alexander, "and the 60- and 70-hour weeks went to 70- and 80-hour weeks. We couldn't keep up with the volume of work and we started losing a lot of people. So we started a global survey and we started asking our people, 'What are you looking for?' and we learned that they wanted more flexibility with their time, they didn't want an 8-to-5 job. We had already made a commitment to being a 'people first' culture, so we developed some of the strongest technology that the profession had ever seen as a way to support our people."

Ernst & Young also made huge investments in its people, changing everything from maternity leave and working from home to establishing flex time and creating four-day weekends for holidays. The firm encouraged employees to take time off. "We later found that for every day that a person would take off," says Alexander, "their annual performance ratings improved. By working fewer hours, our employees were happier, their families were happier, and, overall, our employees were more effective."

Good ideas are copied quickly. Replicating a culture is more difficult. "In the 1980s there were more than 800 companies selling organization knockoffs to The Container Store," says CEO Kip Tindell. Big companies like Williams-Sonoma had their version; small companies had theirs. Not 800 stores, but 800 companies, some of which had many stores. Fewer than a handful remain.

Having survived those copycats, The Container Store is taking its organizational and storage skills into customers' homes. The company's concept of "we'll bring the store to you," which it calls ATHOME®, that it's testing has gotten top marks from customers, so the service is expected to be expanded to other markets.

In 2007, CEO Kip Tindell made a bigger, braver decision in The Container Store's evolution.

Some of the company's investors wanted to retire or cash in their chips. At the same time, other companies were looking to recruit The Container Store's key managers and were offering stock options. "I didn't have any stock or options [to offer]," Tindell says, "so I set out to find one extremely sophisticated investor, and by sophisticated I mean somebody who understands it's better to own 50 percent of the dollar than 100 percent of a nickel. That's hard to find."

"We interviewed more than 100 equity firms," says Tindell. "We were looking for somebody that would contractually agree to management retaining operational and strategic control. So these guys are buying the majority of the company but they don't control the company. That's unusual. They're giving away about three and a half times the average of the equity not just to a management team but to almost 200 employees.

"I felt this was to be the perfect stakeholder model of conscious capitalism," says Tindell. "What I was trying to do was keep the exiting shareholders happy, keep the employees happy, keep all of the stakeholders completely happy, and maintain the culture. The bravery was that nobody had ever done the private equity transaction like that before. I remember telling the JP Morgan people, several of whom I knew very well, 'We've got to do this, but I want your very top people involved. I want you to personally run our deal. It will be the smallest deal you've worked on in the last 5 or 10 years of your career, but it will be the most joyful.'"

Before it was joyful, it was frightening.

"I've never been so stressed out in my life," says Tindell. "I guess that's where the bravery came in. But I just thought the whole future of the company depended on getting this thing right, and I thought it could work. And we did it. We're still with equity firm Leonard Green. We love them, they love us. Things couldn't be better."

As you've seen before, Tindell is a "win-win-win" guy. That's what happened with this deal. "Everybody won," says Tindell. "The employees won because they got this equity. The shareholders won. The bankers won. They say, 'We're on the side of the angels.'

"And the employees retained control. We don't need the private equity firm telling our employees or our merchants what kind of Christmas wrap to buy. How we do things is part of our culture, it's part of the accountability of how we operate. But I was so unaccustomed to doing billion-dollar private equity transactions that I didn't know that all this stuff was impossible."

The relationship worked so well Tindell got his college roommate John Mackey of Whole Foods involved with Leonard Green. "That turned out to be the best investment in Leonard Green's history," says Tindell.

Big deals. Small improvements. Calculated risks. Follow-through. Your ability to leverage change, your willingness to evolve, and your conviction to execute your plans will drive your future performance.

ACCOUNTABILITY INSIGHT

- Dig for gold versus spotting mistakes.
- Eliminate the "We've never done that before" attitude.
- Look outside your industry to adapt.

TAKE A FRESH LOOK

Reexamine your score from the Evolving Pillar of the assessment, and then consider these questions:

- What if we took the steps in good times that we take in tough times? Would the tough times be as tough?
- What one thing will we change in the next 60 days that isn't delivering the expected results or that customers (or clients) no longer value? What's the impact of not changing?

- What was the best decision we made last year? What made it great? How do we plan to replicate it?
- What was the worst decision we made last year? What did we learn from it?
- How do we respond when we hit a barrier? How can we turn a setback into a breakthrough?
- What are we willing to give up or stop doing?
- What are the most significant changes our competitors have made recently? How do these changes affect us? How will we choose to respond?
- When was the last time we asked our customers about their priorities? About our performance? About the barriers to doing business with us? About their next big decision?
- In what areas are we not at our best? To what three to five priorities are we most committed? When we compare our priorities and our customers' priorities to our list where we're not at our best, what calls to action do these comparisons suggest for our organization?
- Are we playing to win or playing not to lose? What's the next great thing we will do together?

All organizations wrestle with accountability in much the same way. Although the scope and complexity may differ from organization to organization, the problems leaders encounter on their journey from Point A to Point B are the same.

High-performing organizations create and sustain a culture of purpose, accountability, and fulfillment that is guided by a set of principles and practices that are simple to say and hard to do.

The key to accountability is bringing together these principles and then acting on them with consistency to sustain a high-performance culture.

You now have a bridge, supported by the Seven Pillars of Accountability, to help you reach Point B.

Where will your bridge take you?

APPENDIX

HEAVEN & HELL (FOR INDIVIDUAL)

This exercise was inspired by my friend and fellow Vistage International Chair John Younker, though he calls his version "A walk on the beach."

Heaven

Year ....

Hell

On the horizontal line, create a timeline by listing years from past to present. Make the first year on the timeline the earliest pivotal milestone in your life.

Now think about times in your life (including your career) that were joyful, fulfilling and overwhelmingly positive. Mark those events above the line on the "Heaven" side.

Now think about times in your life (including your career) that were painful, disastrous, and overwhelmingly negative. Mark those events below the line on the "Hell" side.

Each entry above the line and below the line is a character-building event. These powerful experiences reveal your personal core values.

For the events noted in "Heaven," ask, *"What values were present that caused me to be fulfilled?"* Write down the word or words. For the events noted in "Hell," ask, *What values were absent that caused me to be unfulfilled?* Write down the word or words.

This quick exercise will tell you more about what matters to you than any contrived exercise that arrives at a predictable and, frankly, lame set of great-sounding but otherwise meaningless words. That you can recall so vividly long-ago events provides huge insight into who you are.

Assign a single word to each of these phrases you used to describe the events and the feelings they conjure up. Review your list of words. Reduce the total number of words to as few as three and no more than five. You want to remember them.

These three, four, or five words are your personal core values: what you stand for . . . and the principles and beliefs you will not compromise.

THE 7 FS

Goal-Setting to Enhance Your Life

What's a hugely ambitious future that I passionately want to achieve for myself or my organization that it's worth reinventing not just our organization but my entire self?

_____

_____

_____

_____

What will these seven significant life categories look like to you one year from today?

Family _____

_____

Friends _____

_____

Faith _____

_____

Fitness _____

_____

Financial _____

_____

Function (career) _____

_____

Fun _____

_____

Now select the single most important goal from one of the seven categories of goals.

Write down the category and goal:

_____

Write down how you will characterize your progress toward achieving your goal at each of these points in the coming year (What will have happened? What will you have accomplished? What will remain to be accomplished?):

March 31, (year): _____

June 30, (year): _____

September 30, (year): _____

December 31, (year): _____

Write down the impact of **NOT** achieving your goal:

_____

_____

Write down the impact of achieving your goal:

_____

_____

Write down how you will feel when you achieve your goal:

_____

_____

HEAVEN & HELL (FOR LEADERSHIP TEAM)

Heaven

Year _____

Hell

Assemble your team of leaders.

Give all leaders a blank piece of paper and ask them to draw a horizontal line to create a timeline. On the line, list years from past to present. Make the first year on the timeline the founding of the organization (on the left-hand side of the line) and list the current year on the right-hand side of the line. Ask the leaders to think about pivotal milestones in the life of the organization (including their career at the firm) that were joyful, fulfilling, and overwhelmingly positive and then mark those events above the line on the "Heaven" side.

Now ask your leaders to think about times in the life of the organization (including their career at the firm) that were painful, disastrous, and overwhelmingly negative and then mark those events below the line on the "Hell" side.

As was the case with your personal timeline, everything each person has listed above the line and below the line is a character-building event in the life of your organization. For the events noted in "Heaven," ask each person to write their response to the same question in Chapter 1: *"What values were present that caused me to be fulfilled?"* Likewise, for the events noted in "Hell," ask individuals to write his or her response to this question: *"What values were absent that caused me to be unfulfilled?"*

Now ask each of your leaders to write a single word for each of the events and the feelings they conjure up.

Ask each person to share his or her words. As the leader of leaders, you should start with your list of words. Write your words on a flip chart.

Then ask for volunteers to read their words, listing all of the words on the flip chart until all of the leaders have declared their words.

Group similar words together. Toss out phrases because people can remember words but they can't remember phrases. Discuss the words on the flip chart.

Delete any words that you and your leaders cannot all agree on that reflect the character of your organization until you're left with a handful of words.

Assign your leaders the task of repeating this exercise with their direct reports.

The words that emerge from this process are the words that resonate most completely with you, your top leaders, and their direct reports: three levels of leaders within your organization.

These words codify your organization's character.

If you think that exercise was difficult, get ready to start walking your talk.

MIGRATION CHART

Migration Element	Moving From . . . (Point A)	Moving To . . . (Point B)
Revenue ($$+%) **Profit** ($$+%)		
Strategic Focus		
Major Challenges		
Infrastructure Changes • Structure, Operating Environment, Processes, Financial Administration, etc.		
Personnel Changes • Values (Will), Skill, Experience, Policies, Staffing needs, etc.		
Sales and Marketing Changes • Channels, Markets, Customers, Value Proposition, Materials, etc.		
Measurement Changes • Leading Indicators, Lagging Indicators, Reports, Visibility, etc.		

Pledge of Accountability

I pledge that I will faithfully execute the [company name] [year] action plan developed [date of planning session].

I will abide by [company name]'s values that we have reconfirmed at this planning session.

I will be open to change and supportive of others. I will offer comments and constructive criticism to my colleagues in a helpful, respectful manner. And I will receive others' comments with the understanding that they offer me their comments with the intention of helping me improve my effectiveness.

I agree to accept the consequences of my performance good and bad.

I further pledge to increase my personal effectiveness and enjoyment in order to help [company name] achieve its vision of [insert vision statement].

Signed,

[each participant in the planning process]

BENEFITS OF PLANNING

Effective planning sessions should deliver these 10 benefits:

10. **Breaks down silos.** Most people in a company are focused on making things happen in their own world. Planning brings together all department leaders to look at things from each other's perspective and then develop a holistic plan to solve problems and improve performance.

9. **Provides a safe harbor for "possibility thinking."** Planning should create an environment where creativity is encouraged, new thinking is expected, and disbelief is temporarily suspended. There's plenty of time later for analysis, reason, and judgment to determine whether a possibility can become a reality. Make your planning session safe, fun, and easy for people to speak up and offer their perspective on what's possible. Don't ask *Why?* Ask *Why not?*

8. **Motivates your team and increases their value.** The future can be intimidating or it can be exciting. It's your choice. Good planning processes make thinking about the future exciting. Employees who know what's expected of them will perform more effectively and increase their value to the company. What's more, people will embrace plans they've helped develop. Warning: Nothing saps the energy of your team quicker than developing a plan and not holding people accountable starting with yourself to follow through.

7. **Exposes blind spots.** We all have blind spots. We're simply oblivious to certain people, situations, or even our own actions that others see all too clearly or in a completely different light. Planning provides a framework to ask questions and expose blind spots.

6. **Ensures you're *working on the right things* versus *doing things right*.** Don't confuse budgeting with planning. Budgeting is a form of planning, but it perpetuates silo thinking and brings a mindset that says *The people are in place, other costs are givens, the work's what it is, so here's the number for next year.* When approached from a clean-slate perspective, planning prompts you to confront realities, fix problems, and improve performance.

5. **Brings focus, order, and clarity to your business.** Planning brings clarity and focus to your business by taking a methodical approach to breaking down the components of your business. Be specific about what you want, how you will achieve it, and who will be accountable to the commitments that are made.

4. **Uncovers new or increased revenue streams and improved operating efficiencies.** Use the planning process to uncover new or more effective ways for giving your customers more of what they want. Use the planning process to dig into operating systems and processes to improve efficiencies and, ultimately, margins.

3. **Establishes accountability.** Plans don't fail because there aren't enough good ideas. Plans fail because there are too many good ideas and not enough follow-through and accountability. Your planning process should establish how performance will be tracked and how underperformance will be addressed.

2. **Builds trust and achieves alignment among your leadership team.** Short of the plan itself, the single greatest benefit of the planning process is building or strengthening trust among the leaders who will be held accountable for executing the plan. If trust is absent from the planning session, meaty issues will not be addressed and your time spent planning will have been wasted. Each leader must trust that his or her peers can be

counted on to keep the commitments made during the planning session.

1. **Determines specific objectives and action items to be implemented.** Your written plan affirms your values, your vision, and your strategy for getting from Point A to Point B. It's a contract entered into by the organization's leaders that sets expectation and establishes commitments. And it's a road map with mile markers to track performance, hold one another accountable, and celebrate successes.

SWAT TEAM GUIDELINES

SWAT Team Guidelines and Questions

The basic SWAT team concept is elegant in its simplicity.

Four executives from noncompeting companies visit a peer CEO's company, ask questions of employees and managers, and report back to the peer advisory group. Based on what they learn they make recommendations to the CEO whose company has been visited.

Although Strengths, Weaknesses, Opportunities, and Threats (SWOT) are confirmed or uncovered during the visit, the process is called a SWAT team visit, borrowing its name from police units made up of highly trained officers who are specially equipped to deal with unusual situations.

The benefits of the SWAT team process include:

- Increased depth of knowledge and group bonding
- Team learning
- Uncovering hidden issues
- Sharper focus on key issues
- Higher levels of accountability

The beauty of the process is that value is received by the CEO being SWATed as well as the members of the SWAT Team who are making the visit.

The CEO being SWATed learns a lot about problem areas he or she may not have been aware of, and in many cases gets a reaffirmation of things he or she is doing right.

The members on the SWAT team get as much or even more out of the process. They pick up new ideas and new ways of doing things that they can translate into their own companies. Plus, it opens their eyes to what employees really think and say about the boss. They wonder, "Is that what my people are saying about me?"

It encourages them to take a closer look at how they do things in their own companies and why.

The SWAT team process is outlined here:

Preliminary
Host of upcoming meeting is the SWATee.
Select four executives to serve on the SWAT team.
Set a time and date for the SWAT team visit.
Before the SWAT team visit, SWATee's action list is:

- Determine who is to be interviewed. Interviewing a cross section of employees (senior management, middle management, and front-line workers) is key because perspectives will vary. No need to send this list in advance. The interviews can take a half-day, though the length of time is a function of the complexity of the issue and how many people are interviewed.
- Provide current, simplified financials to be sent in advance. Detailed financials need to be available during the meeting.
- Key Performance indicators are sent in advance and show the organization's current situation versus its forecast. If financials are tracked graphically or in tabular form, provide graphs or tables.

Each member of the SWAT team must review the information and be ready to hit the ground running.

SWAT Team Visit
The SWAT team meets with the CEO either the day of the SWAT team visit or before to understand concerns, background information, and his or her expectations for the SWAT visit.

The SWAT Team interviews key people individually *without the CEO present.* Confidentiality *must* be guaranteed. Information collected must be presented as "coming from the group" and not from individuals.

Key questions are shown in the last section of this document.

Tour the facilities only if it's helpful to the process. SWAT team members will be observing overall energy (or the lack of it), employee interaction, organization of work spaces, cleanliness of facility and work spaces, and communications (info on walls, in break rooms, on TV monitors, etc.).

The SWAT team should focus on the root cause of the problem, which may be (and probably is) different from the problem indicated by the CEO who's being SWATed.

Diagnosis

Following the completion of the interviews, the SWAT team members meet immediately among themselves to share information and prepare detailed recommendations for the CEO whose company was SWATed.

Categorize the information into two basic categories: *What's working well and Opportunities for improvement.* Compile a brief (one-page) report that the SWAT team can use to focus its thinking and then present to the CEO.

The team debriefs with the CEO either on-site or off-site immediately, while the input is fresh, and presents a proposed action plan to the CEO.

Action and Accountability

Following the presentation of the What's working/Opportunities list, the CEO responds by committing to take action on the top one or two issues reported by the SWAT team.

At the next regularly scheduled group meeting, the SWAT team leader informs the entire group on the recommended actions. The member commits to reporting back on action taken and progress.

To ensure accountability, actions committed to by the member are recorded and reviewed at the next meeting.

The CEO who has been SWATed reports progress against these commitments at subsequent meetings until the issue(s) is resolved.

SWAT Team Questions

Context: Meetings are to be a firsthand look by peers at a CEO's operation.

Intent: To provide the CEO whose operation is being SWATed with constructive, nonthreatening feedback to help him or her improve performance.

Questions for employees:
- How would you describe your organization's mission? (What's your purpose? Why are you here?)
- How would you describe your organization's vision? (Where are you going?)
- Where are you going? Are your personal goals aligned with the overall organizational objectives and strategies? If not, what causes this lack of alignment?
- When you think about the organization, what's working?
- What's not working?
- If you were in charge, what decisions would you be making?
- What can the organization do to help you be more effective?

Note: Other questions will flow naturally from the discussion.

Feedback to CEO
Organize the report to the CEO as Strengths and Opportunities:

- Here are your five greatest strengths.
- Here are five opportunities to consider improving/changing.
- Are there any surprises?
- Based on the SWAT team's observations, what issue(s) are you most likely to act on immediately?

THE ORGANIZATION'S SOUL—
OVERLOOKED KPIs

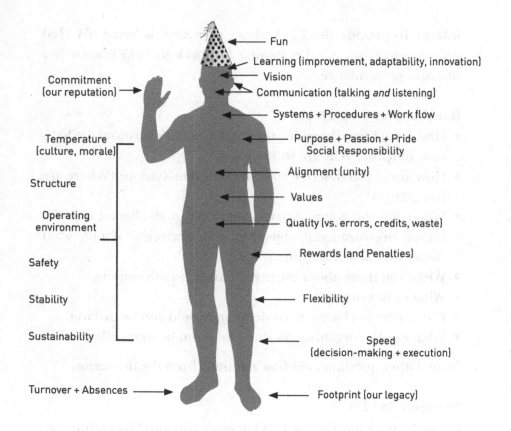

Fun

Learning (improvement, adaptability, innovation)

Vision

Communication (talking *and* listening)

Systems + Procedures + Work flow

Commitment
(our reputation)

Purpose + Passion + Pride
Social Responsibility

Alignment (unity)

Values

Quality (vs. errors, credits, waste)

Rewards (and Penalties)

Flexibility

Speed
(decision-making + execution)

Footprint (our legacy)

Temperature
(culture, morale)

Structure

Operating
environment

Safety

Stability

Sustainability

Turnover + Absences

PERSONAL ACCOUNTABILITY WORKSHEET

Various versions of this worksheet have been created over the years by many unknown Chairs of Vistage International. I have added my own tweaks to this form and today use it in coaching sessions with executives.

Name   Date

What projects are you currently working on? 1. 2. 3.		**What isn't working right in your organization?**
What's the largest long-term opportunity facing your company?		**What could you be doing about it this month?**
What's the most important decision you're facing?		**What's keeping you from making it?**
Who are your direct reports? 1. 2. 3. 4. 5. 6. 7.	**Effectiveness this month (1–5)** 1. 2. 3. 4. 5. 6. 7.	**How are you doing against your personal plan commitments for this year (the 7Fs)?** Financial: Friends: Fitness: Faith: Family: Function (career): Fun:
What commitments did you make at last month's session?		**What did you take away from last month's session?**
What single thing could you do this month to bring the most value to your company?		**What is the most important thing we should be discussing this month?**

NOTES

PREFACE

1. American Management Association, "The Clear Path to Strategy Execution" (February 7, 2007).
2. Janamitra Devan, Matthew B. Klusas, and Timothy W. Ruefli, "The Elusive Goal of Corporate Performance," *McKinsey Quarterly* (April 2007).
3. Vistage International brochure, Corporate Research Board study (2006).

1: ACCOUNTABILITY STARTS WITH PURPOSE

1. Viktor E. Frankl, *Man's Search for Meaning* (Beacon Press, 1959, 2006), p. 73.
2. Ibid.
3. Associated Press, "No Days Off from Work," *The Dallas Morning News* (August 7, 2010).
4. David Moore, "A Rush for Emmitt," *The Dallas Morning News* (August 8, 2010).

2: LEARNING FROM WINNERS

1. Rick Steves and Steve Smith, *Rick Steves' Provence & The French Riviera* (Avalon Travel, 2011), pp. 435–438.
2. "Past, Present and Future," *Spirit* (June 2013).

3: THE SEVEN PILLARS OF ACCOUNTABILITY

1. T. H. Nielsen and J. Roy, "Defining Ancient Arkadia," symposium April 1–4, 1998, Kgl. Danske Videnskabernes Selska (1998), p. 253.
2. Charles S. Whitney, *Bridges of the World: Their Design and Construction* (Courier Dover Publications, 2003), pp. 75–79.

4: CHARACTER COUNTS

1. David J. Collis and Michael G. Rukstead, "Can You Say What Your Strategy Is?" *Harvard Business Review* (April 2008).

2. Brent Schrotenboer, "Armstrong's Precipitous Fall," *USA Today* (October 18, 2012).

3. David Barstow, "Vast Mexico Bribery Case Hushed Up by Walmart After Top-Level Struggle," *The New York Times* (April 22, 2012).

4. Walmart website, timeline: "Sam Walton did the hula on Wall Street, making good on a promise to associates after the company achieved a pretax profit of 8% for the previous fiscal year."

5: GALVANIZING YOUR TEAM

1. John F. Kennedy, Memorandum for Vice President, John F. Kennedy Library, President's Office files (April 20, 1961).

2. Memorandum for the President from the Vice President, John F. Kennedy Library, President's Office files (April 28, 1961), pp. 1–2.

3. Peter Schutz, "Extraordinary Results with Ordinary People," Vistage All-City meeting (July 18, 2007).

4. Transcript of presidential meeting in the Cabinet Room of the White House, "Topic: Supplemental appropriations for the National Aeronautics and Space Administration, John F. Kennedy Library, President's Office files (November 21, 1962), pp. 14–15.

5. Ibid.

6. Ibid., p. 18.

7. Ibid., p. 19.

8. Ibid.

9. YouTube, "JFK—We choose to go to the moon," full length, 17:48.

10. "Culture on Purpose," Fellowship Technologies (October 2009).

11. Teresa Amabile and Steven Kramer, "Do Happier People Work Harder?" *The New York Times* (September 4, 2011).

12. John Waggoner, "Do Happy Workers Mean Higher Profit?" *USA Today* (February 20, 2013).

13. Terry Maxon, "Disgruntled Workers Cost AA," *The Dallas Morning News*, (December 22, 2012).

14. Richard Dickerson, "Values Focused Management," presentation to Vistage groups Key 9107, CE 3211, CE 3357 (November 5–7, 2009).

6: GREEN AND GROWING

1. Nikki Finke, "Walt Disney on 'How to Train an Animator,'" deadline.com (November 5, 2010).

2. Ibid.

3. Ibid.

4. U.S. Bureau of the Census, *Historical Statistics of the United States, Colonial Times to 1957* (Washington, DC, 1960).

5. Desmond Ryan, "Disney Animator Recalls Gamble That Was 'Snow White,'" Knight-Ridder Newspapers (July 24, 1987).

6. Nikki Finke, "Walt Disney on 'How to Train an Animator,'" deadline.com (November 5, 2010).

7. Eric Schlosser, *Fast Food Nation: The Dark Side of the All-American Meal* (Harper Collins Publishers, 2002).

8. McDonald's Corporation website.

9. Ibid.

10. Richard Alleyne, "Welcome to the Information Age," *The Telegraph* (February 11, 2011).

11. "Beverage Alcohol 50: *Beverage World* Ranks the 50 Largest Companies Based on Alcohol Revenue," *Beverage World* (October 2012).

12. "2012 Associate Engagement Survey: Management Review and Analysis" provided by RNDC, March 21, 2013.

13. Press release, MAKE website (November 28, 2012).

7: WHAT YOUR BEST EMPLOYEES WANT

1. Edward R. Tufte, *The Visual Display of Quantitative Information* (PR Graphics, 2001), p. 40.

2. R. G. Grant, *Battle: A Visual Journey Through 5,000 Years of Combat* (Dorling Kindersley), 2005.

3. Teresa Amabile and Steven Kramer, "Do Happier People Work Harder?" *The New York Times* (September 4, 2011).

8: INSTILLING A SENSE OF URGENCY

1. Alden Whitman, "J. Paul Getty Dead at 83; Amassed Billions from Oil," *The New York Times* (June 6, 1976).

2. J. Paul Getty, *How to Be Rich* (Playboy Press, 1965).

3. Michael Poss, *Ebby Halliday: The First Lady of Real Estate* (Brown Books, 2009), p. 2.

4. Provided by Ebby Halliday REALTORS, April 10, 2013.

5. Horatio Alger Association website.

6. Michael Poss, *Ebby Halliday: The First Lady of Real Estate* (Brown Books, 2009), p. 24.

7. Ibid., p. 33.

8. Ibid., p. 155

9. Ibid., p. 108.

10. Ibid., p. 151.

11. Ibid., p. 191.

12. Ibid., p. 214.

13. Ibid., p. 181–182.

14. Ibid., p. 155.

15. "Ranked Within Industries," *Fortune* (May 4, 2009).

16. Ibid.

17. "Ranked Within Industries," *Fortune* (May 3, 2010).

18. Marriott press release, "Marriott International Reports First Quarter Results" (April 23, 2009).

19. Nucor 2009 annual report.

20. Ibid.

21. Nucor 2012 annual report.

22. Aon Hewitt study, presented to Clark Builders, "Best Employers Employee Opinion Study Results" (November 2012).

9: WALKING THE TALK

1. Tom Fowler, "BP Blocked From Deals," *The Wall Street Journal* (November 28, 2012).

2. David F. Larcker, *Directorship*, vol. XXVI, no. 5 (Wharton School of Business at the University of Pennsylvania, May 2000).

3. 2012 Reputation Review, Aon and Oxford Metrica.

4. Anthony Bianco, "Talking to the Troops," *BusinessWeek* (July 5, 1999).

5. "Herman Miller Reports Strong Earnings Growth and Strategic Momentum in the Fourth Quarter of FY2013," press release (June 26, 2013).

10: CHANGE PRACTICES, NOT PRINCIPLES

1. Jean Froissart quoted by Winston Churchill, *History of the English Speaking Peoples* (Dorset Press, 1956).

2. Peter F. Drucker, *Managing for Results* (Harper Business, 1964), p. 91.

3. Ibid., p. 6.

4. Peter F. Drucker with Jim Collins, Philip Kotler, James Kouzes, Judith Rodin, V. Kasturi Rangan, and Frances Hesselbein, *The Five Most Important Questions You Will Ever Ask Your Organization* (Jossey-Bass, 2008), p. xii.

5. "Sony Plant in Wales Is Named Britain's Best Factory," Cranefield School of Management (September 27, 2013).

6. Patrick Maycock, "Marriott Courts Next Generation with Updates," *Hotel News Now* (June 4, 2013).

7. Ibid.

8. "Timothy Keran of Western Graphics Honored for Commitment to Continuous Improvement," press release (February 27, 2013).

9. Provided by Western Graphics, "Results from 2008 to 2012."

10. Greg Hazley and Jack O'Dwyer, "PR Giant Dan Edelman Dies at 92," *O'Dwyers* (February 2013).

11. Matthew Daneman, "Kodak Determined to Survive," *USA Today* (December 13, 2011).

12. Keach Hagey, "Newsweek Quits Print, *The Wall Street Journal* (October 19, 2012).

13. Ian Austen, "Ailing BlackBerry to Reduce Work Force and Post Big Loss," *The New York Times* (September 21, 2013).

14. Kim Bashin, "Ron Johnson's Desperate Broadcasts to J.C. Penney Workers Fell Flat as Company Faltered," *Huffington Post* (May 28, 2013).

15. "Past, Present, and Future," *Spirit* (June 2013).

16. "Nucor Selects St. James Parish, Louisiana, for Iron Making Facility," press release (September 15, 2010).

17. Ibid.

INDEX

ABOUT THE AUTHOR

Greg Bustin is a business and leadership consultant, an international speaker, and a Master Chair for Vistage International, the world's largest CEO membership organization. He writes a monthly bulletin sent to more than 5,000 executives globally and regularly speaks at events throughout the world. His perspective on leadership has appeared in the *Wall Street Journal*, *Barron's*, the *Dallas Morning News*, and other major publications. He and his wife, Janet, have one daughter, Jordan.